Praise for
Sustaining Executive Performance

"The best companies make the most of their most precious resource—human capital. *Sustaining Executive Performance* offers concrete guidance and a compelling rationale on how to achieve that. Critically, MacGregor shows that the responsibility for health and performance rests with ourselves and that this enhanced self-management enables us to exert a positive influence on those around us to create high-performing organizations."

—Bernardo Quinn, Global Chief Human Resources Officer, Telefonica

"Here at last is a book that hardwires sustainability to the individual and shows clearly the way in which we may all contribute to a future world that is about more and better, not less and compromised. MacGregor presents a vision of executive health that is immediately applicable, practical, and grounded in sound business rationale—thereby making a significant contribution to sustainable value creation for the self, enterprise, and society."

—Peter Lacy, Managing Director and Partner, Strategy & Sustainability Services, Asia Pacific Region, Accenture

"How you execute, and feel, as a leader changes throughout your career and is dependent upon many factors in your work and life. *Sustaining Executive Performance* brings together historic wisdom and modern research to set out the basis for sustained and effective leadership. MacGregor presents a compelling case for looking after one's self that will sit with other critical business requirements, for even the most skeptical of minds. This book provides sound advice and reasoning on how to tune your body and mind to provide improved performance throughout your career."

—Andrew Fenton, Vice President, Oracle UK, Ireland and Israel

"In our ever-complex world, organizations need to be thinking about all aspects of the health of their business. Steven MacGregor's book shines a light on the three most important: employees, customers, and the community. In *Sustaining Executive Performance*, MacGregor provides the tools to help leaders at all levels of a business achieve balance and lasting success.

—Nathan Waterhouse, Cofounder and Managing Director of IDEO's Collaborative Innovation Platform, OIEngine.com

"*Sustaining Executive Performance* offers today's leaders the foundations for developing a new model of lifelong, personal advancement. Grounded in MacGregor's personal experiences leading in the boardroom and on the trail, the SEP model can be integrated into one's daily routine immediately."

—William Cockayne, Ph.D., Lecturer at Stanford University and creator of the University's Foresight Engineering program

Sustaining Executive Performance

How the New Self-Management Drives
Innovation, Leadership,
and a More Resilient World

Steven P. MacGregor

Editor in Chief: Amy Neidlinger
Acquisitions Editor: Charlotte Maiorana
Operations Specialist: Jodi Kemper
Cover Designer: Alan Clements
Managing Editor: Kristy Hart
Project Editor: Elaine Wiley
Copy Editor: Barbara Hacha
Proofreader: Sarah Kearns
Indexer: Erika Millen
Senior Compositor: Gloria Schurick
Manufacturing Buyer: Dan Uhrig

For information about buying this title in bulk quantities, or for special sales opportunities (which may include electronic versions; custom cover designs; and content particular to your business, training goals, marketing focus, or branding interests), please contact our corporate sales department at corpsales@pearsoned.com or (800) 382-3419.

For government sales inquiries, please contact governmentsales@pearsoned.com.

For questions about sales outside the U.S., please contact international@pearsoned.com.

Company and product names mentioned herein are the trademarks or registered trademarks of their respective owners.

Printed in the United States of America

2   16

ISBN-10: 0-13-398700-0
ISBN-13: 978-0-13-398700-3

Pearson Education LTD.
Pearson Education Australia PTY, Limited.
Pearson Education Singapore, Pte. Ltd.
Pearson Education Asia, Ltd.
Pearson Education Canada, Ltd.
Pearson Educación de Mexico, S.A. de C.V.
Pearson Education—Japan
Pearson Education Malaysia, Pte. Ltd.

Library of Congress Control Number: 2014952345

To Pamela and Harry,
who provide the day-to-day joy and love that keep me moving.

Contents

Foreword

Executive health is an oxymoron. Or at least, it used to be. When I first started working in the field more than 28 years ago at Stanford University Medical Center, the incidence of worsening health in line with greater seniority was commonplace. Senior executives in key decision-making positions in all cultures were proactive at work and reactive about their personal health. Heart attacks, strokes, diabetes, and depression were accepted by the business leaders as "part of the territory," and people suffered and even died needlessly.

Thanks to tireless efforts and insights of the likes of Dr. Steven P. MacGregor, attitudes and health profiles of business leaders have changed. My own case study of the Mr. Timebomb scenario—which I have used in my teaching to raise an awareness of the need for change in professional business life at premier business schools, such as INSEAD, Cambridge, Skolkovo, IMD, and CEIBS—is starting to fade, slowly but surely.

In *Sustaining Executive Performance*, MacGregor makes a significant contribution to keeping us moving on the right road. He starts with a notion of physical health that extends to the mental level, ever more required in a world of 24-7 connectivity and distraction addiction. He connects ancient wisdom, some established medical science (noted over the years by myself and others), as well as the latest research, which shows why such timeless wisdom existed in the first place.

The key legitimizing process for the busy, skeptical executive is laid bare—so keeping us moving on the right road of executive health. But perhaps more importantly, MacGregor shows how this road connects with others on the map. By conceptualizing executive health as personal sustainability and then linking this to business and societal sustainability, we see the system in which the executive operates. Whether for the experienced manager or manager-in-training, here is a book that shows the connection points of self-leadership—to powerfully affect leadership of the many things that surround the self, for both the manager and leader of today, as well as for tomorrow.

We are all truly indebted to Dr. MacGregor for his seminal work.

Dr. Michael B. McGannon, M.D.

Medical Director, Leaders Health Challenge (LHC)

INSEAD, Cambridge, Skolkovo, CEIBS

www.mcgannon.fr

Acknowledgments

What looks neat and tidy in hindsight is anything of the sort. My life and work the past ten years has been a roller-coaster ride, during which I have shared part of that journey with a number of fantastic friends. Planning the journey is important, but it can take you only so far. Sticking to one's beliefs, values, and, dare I say, gut feeling takes you the rest of the way—as long as those fantastic friends are there to provide the fuel.

Sincere thanks to the "gatekeepers" during the journey: to Peppe Aurrichio, an innovator and risk taker, and the rest of my IESE friends and allies—particularly Idunn Jonsdottir and Josep Valor, who lead the best executive education team in the world. To Rory Simpson, a pioneering Scot who gave me the confidence to keep going on a different path, and who is developing Telefónica University into a place of transformation and inspiration for thousands around the world. On my first visit there, I remember remarking that it had "good air," and three years later I believe the same, with so much exciting potential ahead. To Katherine Semler and the rest of the talented team there, thank you for making my visits such a joy.

To Pablo Cardona and Juan Fernandez at CEIBS, and Mike Wade and Bill Fischer at IMD, it has been a privilege to work with you and see firsthand the powerful development you affect in leaders around the world. To Anne-Marie Hughes and Richard Cox, guiding me from my University sporting career through to the design of my first executive programs, you have both positively changed so many people in all walks of life and will continue to do so. To Simon Pickard and Nigel Roome, my good friends in the sustainability field who always guarantee excellent conversation. Thanks also to Ferran Bruguera and Daniel Solé, whose creative skills have made such a difference.

My thanks to chapter reviewers and interviewees Howard Stupp, Paul Mathieson, Lucy Kimbell, José María Álvarez-Pallete, Nuria Oliver, Elena Roura, Doug Gillon, Sergi Bayod, Brian Cookson, and Lydia Price. Your openness and generosity of time has made the book better. Thanks also to Michael McGannon for penning the Foreword. Your work provided inspiration when I was first looking for traction in a complicated market. To the Pearson team for their expertise, guidance, and hard work: Elaine Wiley, Barbara Hacha, Sarah Kearns, and Charlotte Maiorana, with whom I have the pleasure of working for a second time.

To Pamela, your creative confidence has transmitted to my own work and given it the best chance of success. To my brother Stuart, thanks for providing the emergency office and making great coffee, and the rest of my family and friends for providing energy, laughs, and inspiration during the "not so hot" Scottish summer of 2014. Six weeks I won't forget and an absolute privilege to be able to write this part of the ride.

—Barcelona, November 2014

About the Author

Steven P. MacGregor, PhD, is Founder of The LAB (Leadership Academy of Barcelona), which helps to develop talent from the world's top enterprises in the fields of executive health and performance, design thinking, and sustainable innovation. Since 2010, he has worked with more than 5,000 executives from around the globe, through talks, workshops, and coaching, and has taught more than 250 classes at the best-ranked business schools and universities, including IESE, IMD, CEIBS, and Pompeu Fabra. An international-level duathlete, he has trained with Olympic athletes, Tour de France cyclists, and Ironman champions. A native of Motherwell, Scotland, he lives in Barcelona with his wife, Pamela, and sheepdog, Harry, and can be found on a frequent basis running up and down the mountain overlooking the city.

1

Stronger, Faster, Smarter

In order for man to succeed in life, God provided him with two means, education and physical activity. Not separately, one for the soul and the other for the body, but for the two together. With these means, man can attain perfection.

—Plato

The Games of Olympiad V had just finished, and the star competitors were making their way around the stadium during the closing ceremony. The Stockholm crowd roared their appreciation and tried to pick out their heroes. Sixteen days of competition[1] had yielded dozens of gold-medal winning performances and new Olympic champions: the faster sprints, the higher and longer jumps, the amazing feats of strength. And of course, who could forget the following from Georges Hohrod and M. Eschbach:

> O Sport, you are Joy! At your behest, flesh dances and eyes smile; blood races abundantly through the arteries. Thoughts stretch out on a brighter, clearer horizon. To the sorrowful you can even bring salutary diversion from their distress, whilst the happy you enable fully to savour their joie de vivre.

The Olympic Gold Medal for Literature. The nine-verse "Ode to Sport" was highly praised by the judging panel: *"which without dispute appeared to us to carry away the literature contest, in our eyes has the great merit that it is of the exact type that we sought for the competitions in the matter of inspiration. It emanates as directly as possible from the idea of sport. It praises sport in a form that to the ear is very literary and very sporting."* They went on to say that it was *"full of merit everywhere"* and *"impeccable from the point of view of logic and from the point of view of harmony."* So who were these new Olympic champions? Hohrod and Eschbach were pseudonyms for Baron Pierre de Coubertin, the founder of the modern Olympic Games. A small man, athletically fit, always well dressed, with a strong moustache and lively, bright eyes, he was the president of the International Olympic Committee at the time and the driving force of those first Games. We do not know for sure if the judging panel was aware of the real identity of Hohrod and Eschbach, which were actually neighboring villages near the birthplace of de Coubertin's wife, Marie; neither do we know when or how de Coubertin was presented with his medal. Because these were the first Games of the Olympiad in which arts competitions composed of architecture, sculpture, painting, music, and literature would create new Olympic Champions in addition to the runners, jumpers, and throwers, perhaps de Coubertin was nervous about a low turnout from the arts community. Although the incorporation of the arts was part of his original intention since the first modern Games in 1896, the first two Olympics were merely a matter of survival. He was particularly embarrassed by the Paris Games, his "home" games of 1904, which were overshadowed by the Paris World Fair of the same year. The first major attempt at integrating the arts in the Rome Games of 1908 suffered a false start because of problems encountered by the Rome Committee in staging them, and further, because of the lack of time that their eventual late replacement, London, was afforded. And so to 1912, and 16 years into a still vulnerable Olympic Movement, de Coubertin was not to be denied, not by a deeply reticent Stockholm Committee who believed that art could not be judged in the same way as a running race or jump, nor by the Greek delegation of the day who wanted Athens to be the permanent base of the Games every four years. Perhaps when receiving the news of the medal, yet surely when writing "An Ode to Sport," de Coubertin would have reflected on the famous Greek artists who won titles in the Ancient Games, through long years of physical training, intellectual debate, and reflection, which marked the gymnasia of the day. Dotted in and around the public libraries and business *Agora* of Athens and elsewhere, men of all ages would go to train their bodies and their minds. Lectures on philosophy and art would take place in addition to the physical training and competition.

And so he wanted his modern conception of Olympism,[2] like the Ancient Greeks who awarded Olympic Champion Laurels for sculpture, music, and literature in addition to feats of strength and physical prowess, to promote a holistic form of human development. His struggle to integrate the arts within the Games was symptomatic of the struggle that de Coubertin had experienced the past 30 years of his life in establishing the modern movement. Like any athlete, his was a long journey of focus, sacrifice, and the quest for progress and achievement. The starting pistol could be viewed as his lecture at the Sorbonne in 1892, in which he made the first public call to reestablish the Olympic Games, a lecture which, on the whole, was received badly, but would only temporarily derail a then-despondent de Coubertin.

In that lecture, Stockholm was presented as a world capital of sport, with the Swedish school of gymnastics together with the German and English models presented as best practices for improving the educational system. Believing sport to be a mechanism by which the world could unite, de Coubertin's principal aims were peace and education. His strong belief in the power of sport to achieve these and more are reflected in the nine verses of "An Ode to Sport," in which sport is characterized as "pleasure of the Gods, beauty, justice, audacity, honour, joy, fecundity, progress and peace." In his writings before and after establishment of the modern movement, de Coubertin's aim was for Olympism to be "a doctrine of the fraternity of the body and the mind." His expectation was that sport could reestablish this balance in the younger generation that had been missing for so long, with an educational system he saw plagued by barriers and a complete lack of free thinking. In 1887, when Coubertin was formulating his plans, the word *overwork* was on everyone's lips. He believed that permanent and excessive fatigue derived essentially from "physical weakness, intellectual dullness, and moral degradation" and believed that the body, rather than being perceived as inferior to the mind, was actually the means by which the mind could function better. Tracing the loss of this ancient wisdom, he wrote the following:

Olympia did not disappear merely from the face of the earth. It disappeared in peoples' minds. A belief took root, this belief was that the body is the enemy of the spirit, that the struggle between them is an inevitable and normal thing, and that no understanding should be sought out that would allow them to join together in governing the individual.

Athletics was viewed as the means by which this individual "governance" could work—and excel. Defined by de Coubertin as "the voluntary and habitual practice of intense muscular exercise based on a desire for progress and extending as far as will," it contained at its core five key attributes: initiative, perseverance, intensity, search for perfection, and scorn for potential danger. Coubertin also wrote about the importance of maintaining body-mind balance into adulthood, bemoaning the lack of modern gymnasia and questioning where adults would go to keep themselves in good athletic condition "in the few fleeting moments they might carve out for it in their busy professional schedules."

Yet although Coubertin was merely reconceptualizing the Ancient Greek virtue of whole person development, where going to the gymnasium was considered a civic duty, such ideas were not readily accepted. Even after the establishment of the International Olympic Committee and several editions of the Games, de Coubertin's energy was devoted to reenforcing his message. Between 1918 and 1919, he published 21 "Olympic Letters" in *La Gazette*, the Lausanne newspaper, to try to rouse the sympathies of the readers in support of the Olympics and the work done in Lausanne. One of those letters concerned one of the primary objectives of de Coubertin, that of education, which, in the broader context of lifelong education or human development, is also the core concern of *Sustaining Executive Performance*. It is reproduced below.

Olympic Letter III: Olympism and Education

Somewhere, Montaigne wrote that one should imagine the body and the soul as two horses yoked to the same shaft. He hitches them up two at a time. I prefer to hitch them up four at a time, and to distinguish not only the body and the mind, which is too simplistic, but rather the muscles, the understanding, the character, and the conscience. This corresponds to the four-fold duty of the educator. But both cases involve hitching things up, and the major flaw in modern education is that it is no longer conversant with the art of hitching-up, i.e. of associating the action of divergent forces into a harmonious convergence. It has allowed itself to be carried away by extreme compartmentalization, by which it was then swept away. Each strength works in isolation, without any link or contact with its neighbour. If the topic is muscles, the only thing they want to see is animal function. The brain is furnished as though it were made up of tiny, air-tight compartments. Conscience is the exclusive territory of religious training. As for character— no one wants to take responsibility for that. In a short time, the educated man will end up looking like those primitive mosaics in which little pieces formed larger, crude and stiff pictures. What a decline in comparison to Greek education, which was so lucid, its outline so clear!

Let us not try to hide the fact that Olympism is a reaction against those unfortunate tendencies. Olympism refuses to make physical education a purely physiological thing, and to make each type of sport an independent, separate exercise. It refuses to catalogue the knowledge of the mind, and to classify it into mutually isolated categories. Olympism refuses to accept the existence of a deluxe education reserved for the wealthy classes, no shred of which should be handed out to the working classes. It refuses to condense art into pills that everyone will take at set hours and to establish timetables of thought along the lines of railway schedules. Olympism is a destroyer of dividing walls. It calls for air and light for all. It advocates a broad-based athletic education accessible to all, trimmed with manly courage and the spirit of chivalry, blended with aesthetic and literary demonstrations, and serving as an engine for national life and as a basis for civic life. That's its ideal program. Now can it be achieved?

La Gazette de Lausanne, no. 294, October 26, 1918, p1.

The Ancient Greek Virtue of the Scholar-Athlete

That "clear" and "lucid" Greek education system was driven by the purpose of producing good citizens,[3] based on the training of the body through physical exercise, and of the mind (primarily, though not solely) through music. The Olympic Games were the arena in which these virtues were displayed, with such arenas playing witness to the peak of this dialogue between mind and body. Participation rather than victory was the main aim. The Greeks believed that the formation of a strong character demanded the cultivation of the body, and that by cultivating the body in athletic meetings, they broadened and strengthened the mind, thereby creating a complete person. It was such a vision that Coubertin wanted to re-create, primarily for the youth of the modern era. If the Games were the public expression of this whole person, the progress toward it was honed through daily attendance in the Gymnasia of the day. Regarded as civic duty, the great and good of Ancient Greece—writers, politicians, and philosophers, from Socrates to Sophocles, Aristotle, and Pericles—would all have spent regular time doing physical training. The main Gymnasia of the day, the Lyceum and the Academy, were managed by Plato and Aristotle. Plato's *Lysis* describes an encounter that Socrates had when making his way from the Lyceum to the Academy, describing his main activity there, not as wrestling but "words, mostly words." Indeed, the Gymnasia offered respite from the frenzied business of the day that would take place in the Agora or Forum, and where the more important issues of life were addressed, at least for people such as Plato and Aristotle. How can we be good? What makes us fall in love? How do we know what we know?

Plato was also, according to ancient texts, a champion wrestler, gaining honors at the Isthmian Games. This is where his name came from. Called Aristocles after his grandfather, his wrestling coach is said to have called him Plato on account of his broad shoulders—*Platon* meaning broad in Greek. For Plato, lectures at the Academy on the virtues of physical education were commonplace, and balance between the body and the mind was a critical factor; the goal was to "bring the two elements into tune with one another by adjusting the tension of each to the right pitch."[4] Just as much a danger as neglecting the body, focusing only on the body to the detriment of this balance would result in athletes becoming unadaptable and sluggish, "needing too much sleep."

So what of today? How is the "pitch" between body and mind achieved, particularly for adults in business with those "busy professional schedules" as noted by de Coubertin in the late nineteenth century? The word *overwork* remains on everyone's lips with a modern business environment often characterized by poor physical condition and excessive stress.

Why should we care? How may we legitimize the Ancient Greek virtue beyond health and well-being to executive performance? A key inspiration for integrating a more physical approach to management education and development comes from considering Maslow's hierarchy of human needs[5] and realizing that mental performance is often dependent on physical states in the same way that Maslow details the satisfaction of such basic human needs as food, water, and sleep before more advanced functions, such as creativity and problem solving, can be satisfied. Although Maslow's hierarchy lacks any significant level of scientific support, it was subsequently adapted and empirically supported by Alderfer[6] through his ERG (Existence, Relatedness, Growth) model. A critical mass of research to fully legitimize the body-mind link for performance has emerged over the past 10 years, in specialized fields including psychophysiology, which looks closely at the body's physiological bases and its link with psychological processes, cognitive neuroscience, and biochemistry. Several studies enlighten the real and actionable link between body and mind, particularly as it relates to the modern day executive or knowledge worker, and range from functional needs to performance enhancement.

On a functional level, *The New York Times*[7] reports on varied research that shows the need to periodically "unplug" from digital devices, whereas Sparrow et al.[8] show that Google is beginning to change the way we think and act on a fundamental basis. Such mental health issues are complemented by physical health research. In the performance domain, Colcombe and Kramer[9] found fitness training to increase cognitive performance, regardless of the type of task, the training method, or the participants' characteristics. Further, findings in neuroscience[10] show a 48-hour oxygen advantage being provided to the brain through exercise that specifically aids executive function—those tasks that include complex decision making and strategic analysis that managers are engaged in regularly. Other research[11] shows that exercise increases the size of the hippocampus, critical for memory, effectively reversing aging and further debunking the long-held belief that cognitive decline was irreversible. A groundswell of research is emerging in this area, not for management development specifically, but in the battle against cognitive disease, including Alzheimer's and Parkinson's, which shows the acute link between body and brain. Linking to innovation, Fields[12] discusses the significance of studies that show aerobic exercise contributing to the creative process, because the cognitive effects specifically lower fear and anxiety associated with the unknown. Finally, research has focused on the energy requirements of the brain, considering decision fatigue and "ego depletion"—where one is not consciously aware of being tired as with physical fatigue, but where glucose is required for self-control and good decision making.[13,14]

A critical mass of scientific evidence is therefore beginning to emerge that supports the performance imperative of the ancient Greek virtue that de Coubertin aimed to reintroduce. Behavior is indeed changing in different areas. If Plato, Aristotle, and Socrates could be viewed as the rock stars of the day, looking at the modern equivalent allows us to consider some of the basics.

Rock Stars Don't Trash Hotel Rooms Anymore

They don't. Think about it; in the 1960s, 70s, and 80s, there was frequent destruction of hotel rooms, and wild parties and televisions thrown out of windows were part of the de rigueur of rock star success and excess. But those days are gone. This very question was picked up by the *Guardian* newspaper in 2011[15] in which requests for a quiet place in the hotel, a comfortable bed, and late check-out were shown to be the new norm. So to help us answer the question, let's look at the day-to-day routine of a well-known rock star, Mick Jagger:

> "I train five or six days a week but I don't go crazy. I alternate between gym work and dancing, then I do sprints, things like that. I'm training for stamina. (I get to) bed early the night before. I give myself two hours to get ready for a show, to tune up the voice and get myself in the right frame of mind mentally and physically."

As you may expect, Jagger has a personal trainer and also frequently trains by running, swimming, kickboxing, and cycling. Yet he also spends a lot of time practicing ballet, yoga, and Pilates—activities that develop a key aspect of fitness: core strength, which is essential for athletes and businesspeople alike. He also places great focus on his diet and looks at consuming a large carbohydrate intake as well as lean protein for those high-energy and movement concerts.

How many miles do you think he moves in one concert? Quite a lot, actually: 12. So this changing rock star behavior perhaps owes much to the fact that the rock stars are simply too tired! Twelve miles every other night, in between media duties and sustaining the highest standards of performance. It's hard work being a rock star, and it's getting harder. The multimillion dollar business that is a world tour no longer leaves space for those heady days of excess, and this raising of standards and demands is reflected in many spheres of society.

Professional sports, home to another type of modern-day rock star, offer an additional example. The *Wall Street Journal* included a simulation in January 2014 during the Sochi Winter Olympics that placed all previous gold medal winners in speed skating in the same race. As you would expect, the first gold medal winner in 1924 was last in this simulated race of champions, but even the difference in the past 10 to 20 years, not just from gold to silver, but likely gold and nowhere, was quite staggering.

This pattern is good news for society in general. We are evolving as a human race, and standards are continually increasing. We are pushing the boundaries not just in sport, but in business and science. Yet at what price? Those raising standards in business mean that demands are also placed on you as a business professional. It's no doubt harder now to survive and thrive in the global competitive business landscape than it was 10 to 20 years ago, and that bar rises ever higher.

So, just like a rock star, how can you find that extra advantage, starting from your physical self, that ensures you attain and sustain a high level of executive performance?

Sporting performance of course requires a physical focus, and Jagger, in his 70s, perhaps needs to dedicate more time in this respect, yet the performance habits of another modern-day rock star shows the universality of the approach. Magnus Carlesen is the World Chess Champion and is 21 years old. Chess, from a distance, has nothing whatsoever to do with athletics and the physical self, yet Carlesen, in between modeling for clothing labels and his marathon chess matches, places a massive focus on his physical preparedness and fitness. In the 2013 world chess championships, he took his personal chef to the tournament. His older opponent had shed about 13 pounds (6kg) of weight in the 6 months prior to the championships. Yet Carlesen is only following the example of the greatest chess player of them all, Gary Kasparov. Kasparov would prepare for his chess matches like a boxer, putting himself through a punishing regime of strength training for another type of endurance event. A personal record of 102 push-ups isn't bad for a chess grandmaster, and he acknowledges that it played a role in his longevity, allowing him to sustain his grandmaster-level performance for more than 20 years.

Developing the Whole Person

So why does management development focus, almost solely, on the neck up, when the demands placed on you as a manager, as an executive, touch every facet of your life? My work is focused on whole person development where health and well-being are linked to executive performance. Since 2007, I have delivered an executive training program in which I aim to *remind busy professionals that they have a body*. As we advance through a career, we tend to increasingly live our lives on a purely mental level, with all of our emails and strategies and meetings and metrics, forgetting we have a body until something goes wrong with it! *Sustaining Executive Performance*—the pursuit of longevity at the highest level in an ever-demanding society—may be achieved through paying a little more attention to long-held wisdom and simple practices.

For the Ancient Greek philosopher and citizen, self-governance was achieved through a harmonious balance between body and mind. For the twenty-first century business leader, a new conception of Peter Drucker's *self-management*, as we develop in this book, offers refuge from an increasingly complex, connected, and out-of-balance life. Whether the focus is on personal productivity, work-life integration, the quantified self, or executive health, a myriad of pop-tech gurus offer endless management sound bites that pique the interest of the busy professional but fail to satisfy the deeper questions that accompany their daily craft and graft.

Sustaining Executive Performance will take a bottom-up approach, deconstructing the essence of basic human needs within the enterprise and society to show that such needs are universal at the individual, enterprise, and societal level, and also timeless in their fit with established philosophy—a powerful reminder in an age where only the "new" is held up as being of consumable value. What results is a reflection on leading a sustainable, happy, and productive life that starts with the individual but can apply to organizational and societal innovation, leadership, and resilience.

If such a claim sounds ambitious (it is, but I hope not overly so!), it is merely attempted through a work of synthesis. I attempt to join the dots of the patterns I have observed during my experiences and the teaching, coaching, and academic and field research that has characterized the past 15 years of my life, from around the time I started my PhD in Glasgow after rediscovering my own athletic journey. I therefore aim to make this text personal and *human*. Reading dull academic texts during my PhD studies actually put me off the reading process for several years! So I will present studies and experiences from real people, both from today and through history—those who have something to say and those who have had interesting experiences. It is also personal in that I recount many of my own experiences, including some of the major milestones through university, professional career, and sport. Key topics include design, innovation management, and corporate social responsibility, developed as I lived and worked in Scotland, Spain, and the United States, traveling worldwide and teaching thousands of amazing people.

I draw content from a broad range of fields, including management science, neurology, medicine, elite sport, and business ethics, and my overriding aim is to appeal to a broad audience and make the link between previously disparate issues. I attempt to join science to popular management to philosophy for a highly pragmatic resource and guide that nevertheless legitimizes action for the most skeptical minds and provides the base for continual action and lasting change. I will switch frequently between sources, such as the *Journal of Psychological Science* and the

Bulletproof Executive, from *Harvard Business Review* to Fast Company, and from Brain Pickings to the *Proceedings of the National Association of Science*. All are leaders in the themes I cover in this text, and those with less academic heritage are especially able to disrupt conventional wisdom and lead us to deeper insight.

The book aims to be a reference for life reengineering for the experienced manager, and a reflection on practice for management students. By life reengineering, I mean the adoption of new habits and practices that drive health and performance, and for the management student, a reflection on the practices that will drive their career as they begin to "design their life." This, I hope, will satisfy the increasing need of the executive education market at a time when enterprises worldwide recognize the key need for lifelong learning and development of their most precious resource, and at the MBA level where the new generation of leaders are under increasing pressure to perform and mend a broken system, yet where opportunities abound. The book may also serve as an introductory text or accompaniment for classes on leadership, design and innovation, and corporate social responsibility.

There are three main parts of the book. The first five chapters establish the foundations of the text, developing the driving rationale of the *Sustaining Executive Performance* as well as the levers that make it work. Baron de Coubertin's reconceptualization of the Ancient Greek virtue of body and mind, presented here, is followed in Chapter 2, "The New Lanark Mills," by a first examination of the *Triple Lens of Sustainability*, looking at several historical and contemporary business cases to link the individual, organizational, and societal levels. In Chapter 3, "Design Your Life," and Chapter 4, "Day-to-Day Reengineering," the field of design is then shown as the lever by which we may bring a more human-based approach to workplace performance, and make that actionable on the individual routine level. The Sustaining Executive Performance (SEP) model, a design-based framework, is presented in Chapter 5, "The New Self-Management," as a guide for the twenty-first century professional to better manage themselves (see Figure 1.1).

Figure 1.1 The SEP model

Parts 2 and 3 of the book are interlinked and attempt to show the Triple Lens of Sustainability in action. Each of the five elements of the SEP framework—MOVE, RECOVER, FOCUS, FUEL, and TRAIN—has a dedicated chapter showing how individuals may improve their own awareness of the key factors necessary for health, well-being, and performance—and think about change. These five chapters make up Part 2. Each is followed by a broader treatment of the concepts on an organizational and/or societal level—a further five chapters which make up Part 3. We therefore switch among the individual, organizational, and societal, each of the three levels of the Triple Lens of Sustainability—a concept that we develop throughout the book.

Pierre de Coubertin was an incredible visionary, and like many with vision, he perhaps suffered for being ahead of his time. The arts competitions were not sustainable without his drive and doggedness. They would continue until Zatopek's Helsinki Games of 1952 before disappearing altogether.[16] Having poured so much energy, not to mention financial resources, into the Olympic movement over the greater part of his life, he would suffer from financial difficulties, ill health, and to some extent, disenfranchisement with the IOC before his death in 1938. One may only imagine his despair in observing his final Games. In 1936, Berlin was used as a political pawn, contrary to his founding aim as a vehicle of peace between nations. Then again, perhaps a flicker of optimism would have burned bright after watching how sporting performance, and in particular that of a certain Mr. Owens, would show the way—the simplicity of a sporting event showing the complexity of sport, and also the value for a better governance of oneself, to become, just like the Ancient Greeks, stronger, faster, and smarter.

2

The New Lanark Mills

A company's responsibility does not end at the door to the factory or the office. The jobs it provides shape whole lives.

—Antoine Riboud

Around 60 years before Pierre de Coubertin was born, in the year 1800, Robert Owen was busy making his own vision a reality in Central Scotland. The small village of New Lanark, located on the only waterfall of the River Clyde, provided an ideal location for cotton mills, part of the key textile manufacturing industry of the time. Lanark, the neighboring large town, was the previous stopping point for economist Adam Smith on his frequent journeys from Glasgow, where he taught at the University, to Edinburgh, where he met Scottish Enlightenment friends for dinner and discussion. The work of Robert Owen and the case of the New Lanark Mills was to impact greatly on the accelerating Industrial Revolution that was fundamentally changing the shape of the world at that time, a world moving rapidly along the lines detailed by Smith in The Wealth of Nations, published just 10 years before the construction of the mills in 1776.

Owen, a Welshman and son-in-law of the mill owner, David Dale, was one of the founders of utopian socialism and the cooperative movement—the supermarket chain of cooperative stores being one of his legacies. He transformed the lives of the 2,000 people who lived in the mills, including 500 children, at the same time as delivering commercial success.[1] Although the cotton mills at New Lanark were not the worst in terms of worker conditions at that time, he improved them through a series of social and welfare programs, including special attention to the education and care of children, the means by which workers purchased goods with their money earned, and even the role of incentives in the workplace to improve performance.

New Lanark became celebrated throughout Europe, and many leading royals, statesmen, and reformers visited the mills. In contrast with the normal working conditions of the day, they found a clean and healthy environment with a happy workforce that did not compromise a prosperous business. Owen's philosophy was contrary to contemporary thinking of the time, but he was able to demonstrate that it was not necessary for an industrial enterprise to treat its workers badly to be profitable. The excellent housing and amenities, including the first infant school in Britain—and the accounts showing the profitability of the business—provided the tangible evidence to visitors and shareholders alike. Owen would later submit a paper to the UK parliament on the wider lessons of the New Lanark Mills. Although it would be dismissed as too idealistic, it would eventually be one of the factors in producing the 1833 Factory Act, which aimed to improve conditions for children working in factories, including placing limits on working age, hours worked, and the right to daily education.

The work of Owen highlighted the human factor at a time when the Industrial Revolution, built on technological innovations such as James Watt's steam engine, was in real danger of forgetting the human factor and treating people like machines. Growth was, and is, seductive. Rapid industrial progress resulted in the widespread adoption of a "sun up to sun down" work day, with many children foregoing their education to satisfy the demand for resource. Owen first implemented a 10-hour day at the New Lanark Mills and would later advocate an 8-hour workday as part of a balanced daily life that would include "8 hours labour, 8 hours recreation, and 8 hours rest" and which would form the focus of the International Worker's Day or Labour Day holiday of May 1st.

One of the first businesses in the United States to implement Owen's 8-hour day was the Ford Motor Company. In 1914, it not only cut the standard workday to eight hours, but it also doubled its workers' pay in the process. To the shock of many at the time, this resulted in a significant increase in productivity, and Ford's profit margins doubled within two years of implementation. This encouraged other companies to adopt the shorter 8-hour workday as a standard for their employees.

Progress, as discussed later in this book (particularly in Chapter 5, "The New Self-Management," and Chapter 16, "Leading Change in the Triple Lens of Sustainability"), is a positive and highly attractive phenomena for us as human beings. Yet the current capitalist system presents us with ample areas of potential conflict about what progress actually means. How do we measure it? Is it the same as growth? Even though Owen ensured the commercial success of the mills, he had to withstand pressure from shareholders who objected to his investment in the welfare programs. Yet Owen understood that growth in one dimension—at all costs, and to the detriment of growth in other areas—is not progress.

The Triple Lens of Sustainability

For me, the case of Owen's New Lanark Mills is an example of the *Triple Lens of Sustainability*. Organizational success is driven by individual care that combines to create a healthy and well-functioning business and society. Was Owen's paternalistic approach to the management of the New Lanark Mills purely driven by his socialist principles? Or was there also some understanding of the sustainable value creation of the mills on an economic level through a more holistic approach? Although the mills didn't exactly become a template for what was to follow in the Industrial Revolution, it would still heavily influence many areas, including urban design, community development, and education, as well as other business cases covered later in the chapter.

Aside from Owen's ultimate aim of creating a socialist utopia—his New Harmony community in the United States, established in 1825, although influential in the long term, would be a failure—I think he was a visionary in understanding the key role that work played in wider life: that business was changing in line with society, but that it shouldn't compromise life, which is the very fabric of society. Business has continued to play an integral role in society in the 200 or so years since the New Lanark Mills, with companies such as Danone, led by Antoine Riboud in 1972, recognizing that in addition to the company's responsibility "not ending at the factory door and shaping whole lives," that "it consumes energy and raw materials, and in doing so alters the face of our planet.

The public will remind us of our responsibilities in this industrial society." We may detect the three necessary elements of people, profit, and planet in this dialogue, well established in the domain of sustainable development, yet also the notion that responsibility lies not only with the enterprise but with us all. I return to this notion of sustainable leadership later in the chapter.

I was born a little further west on the River Clyde from the New Lanark Mills, in a town called Motherwell. Steel, rather than textile production, was the key industry when I was growing up in the 1980s, with the Ravenscraig steelworks becoming one of the largest producers of steel in the world. Motherwell had a long tradition of steel manufacture beginning in the 1870s when David Colville turned Dalzell Steel into a worldwide mark of quality for the shipbuilding industry. The Ravenscraig works were the focal point of the surrounding community, employing thousands—at its peak more than 13,000, including several members of my own family. Yet the industry was not sustainable. Steel production became much more cost efficient in other countries, and the plant would limp along for a few years before eventually closing in 1992, devastating the surrounding area over reliant on one main source of wealth creation. More than 10,000 jobs would be lost indirectly in addition to the 770 still employed directly at the time of closure.

So the role that business plays in society is clear, yet how close should business and society be? Motherwell was also home to the very first socialist community based on the ideals of Owen in 1825.[2] The Orbiston Community integrated much of the thinking developed in Owen's UK parliamentary paper. It was the first case of housing in Britain specifically designed for working class habitation, and the most comprehensive provision to that date for communal living, working, and leisure, in an attempt to emancipate the working classes of the time through a transformation of the economic system. Agriculture and industrial production was planned on the assumption it would attract investment from capitalists seeking a dividend until communal assets were eventually taken over by the tenants from expected profits. Unlike the New Lanark Mills where one industry was the focus of work, the Orbiston Community invited people of all trades, from watchmaking and tailoring to steam engine manufacture and printing, with goods to be sold in the larger markets of Glasgow, Edinburgh, and beyond. Just like Owen's

New Harmony community, the intention was eventually for trades to learn from each other, in a fashion of multidisciplinarity and cross-fertilization that drives innovation today. The communal living, working, and leisure—Owen's 8-8-8 model on a community level—was never to run smoothly, and Orbiston lasted only until 1827, with the death of co-founder and driving force Abram Combe a large factor. With such grand ambition and a complex range of issues from the beginning, no one factor could be identified as being key to its short-lived existence, yet commentary was passed on Combe's benevolent spirit and his admittance of anyone to the community with a pressing need. The resultant disparity of work contribution resulted in fractures of the community spirit that prevented cohesion and true progress.

A Modern, Broader Understanding of Sustainability

No ideal model of business in society exists today, 190 years after the failure of Orbiston. Yet I believe that a wider understanding of what sustainability means will help us along the road. Environmentalists held sway over the term in the 1980s, yet it has truly gone mainstream through a greater public awareness of our fragile Earth in the past 10 years, not to mention the economic crises of recent years that lead us to reflect on the durability of any success we may enjoy. Sustainability is therefore most often viewed in terms of sustainable development and the environment, connecting also to notions of responsibility. Yet it can also refer to the enduring competitive position or value of a firm—in other words, its ability to innovate on a continual basis[3] especially for established firms and/or incumbent leaders, which may include elements of disruption, organizational change, and culture.[4,5] I see a logical link between both perspectives because innovation and the long-term success of a company should not be swayed by actions focused on short-term gain, which often leads to irresponsible practices that destroy value for stakeholders. In short, the values-value interplay cited by many corporate leaders, but perhaps not as present in practice as we are led to believe. Another common viewpoint that links innovation to environmental and responsible-centric sustainability is the opportunities for new creative solutions.[6] Increasing awareness of these opportunities for social change and improvement gives even greater credibility to the term *corporate social opportunity*, which emphasized the positive nature of Corporate Social Responsibility (CSR),[7] a concept referred to in Michael Porter's 2011 thesis on how to fix the capitalist system.[8]

My own interest in sustainability began around the same time as the subprime mortgage crisis. I was especially interested in CSR, which I linked to innovation so as to be considered a value-adding mechanism within the enterprise, and led one of the first research projects to do so.[9] It was then that I started realizing that responsibility and value generation, or simply doing well and doing good, were not mutually exclusive. I therefore consider sustainability from the value perspective—the enduring competitive position of an organization and its ability to innovate on a continual basis as shown by its market results—as well as the values perspective in which the society-wide context of sustainable development has been complemented by the role of business within society through the CSR movement.

Competitive Through Responsibility

Value and values have rarely been comfortable bedfellows, at times due to problems regarding the nuances of language and resulting misconceptions, yet there is much common ground to be exploited in this increasingly collaborative era. Both take note of a broad church of stakeholders, whether they are end users, suppliers, employees, or other actors in an innovation ecosystem. CSR is traditionally conceived as action in five areas: *employees, suppliers, society, customer,* and *environment*. What mature innovation system, in an era of open innovation, would not look at the same areas? Indeed, I have examined in previous work[10] the overlapping action areas of CSR and good strategic management.

Stakeholder analysis, for example, is one of the fundamental tools in the CSR movement. Yet an awareness of, and dialogue with, company stakeholders can not only provide the basis for a more responsible approach to business but a better understanding of that business and value generation. Many enterprises will conduct a thorough stakeholder analysis, starting internally with their employees before moving to their key customers, as a means of uncovering the key strengths of the company and possible new strategic directions. Such an approach may have no specific targeted rationale toward CSR, yet the key remains to uncover a sustainable new means of value generation that can complement the core business in the short term and possibly supersede it in the longer term.

Short- and long-term competitiveness, as discussed in greater depth in Chapter 11, "On Building a Systematic, Continuous Innovation Capability," often depends on the interplay between an operations-based view and an innovation view. Economic crisis, austerity policy, and increasing resource scarcity have resulted in a range of cost-cutting measures, from the government level to that of the private firm and individual. A view of environmental CSR—for example, saving on energy bills—may provide a suitable template for analyzing costs and the means by which business processes and operations may be made more efficient. Within many engineering-based organizations, the implementation of lean philosophy looks at minimizing waste in a similar fashion, providing the basis for continuous improvement, which is first necessary before a company, especially a small enterprise, can innovate. Yet an operations-based view will not provide value in the long term. Enterprises need to be brave enough to leave behind the optimization and efficiency of the current way of doing things to find new ways of doing things. The innovations of today, therefore, are the operations of tomorrow. As touched on earlier, the conventional sustainability domain, driven by a need to take better care of the planet and address social problems, is crying out for innovative solutions, whether that is providing clean water for developing countries or saving water in developed ones. Finding solutions to such pressing problems can be profitable in addition to contributing to social responsibility, as evidenced by big businesses' approach to the bottom of the pyramid—the 3 billion of the world's population who live on less than $2.50/day.

Let me present two examples of the interplay between responsibility and competitiveness that demonstrate a wider understanding of sustainability. Both cases are also from my present residence, Spain, a country that has suffered more than most the past few years due to economic crises.

For ACTIU, a Valencia-based office furniture manufacturer, sustainability is at the core of everything it does. As well as mature CSR policies directed toward its workforce, it designs and manufactures furniture that adheres to the strictest codes of sustainable design and environmental management—an approach to design it believes will give them leadership in a competitive market. The company has further engaged its employees with the recent construction of a company headquarters that reflects its ethos—it was one of the first European businesses to attain the gold standard LEED certification, fully leveraging solar energy in the area and recycling nearly 100% of all rain water that falls on and around the company buildings.

A second company, Metalquimia, is a world leader in the design and manufacture of meat-processing machinery and technology for cooked and cured meats, such as ham and sausage. A family run business, it employs 110 people in its design and research plant in Girona and production plant in nearby Banyoles. Responsibility driven business is often an even more natural proposition for small and medium enterprises, often driven by the owner manager who feels a strong affinity with the local community. Metalquimia is active in community-based CSR, supporting several local initiatives in a philanthropic sense, yet it is the company's CSR activities related to workforce and across the value chain that help to drive economic value. Supply chain CSR drives an open innovation strategy within the strong pork cluster in Girona, and company creativity is driven by employee satisfaction and engagement. Each employee is made to feel part of the family—new staff are encouraged to think it could be a job for life. They are also rewarded financially more than most private enterprises, with 20% of the annual profits being distributed among the workforce. Productivity has remained the same with fewer hours worked. More free and flexible time has improved satisfaction, as well as providing the space for creativity and innovation, and fewer hours worked means lower overhead for the company as well as less environmental impact. The strong innovation culture that has developed over the years with such policies has resulted in a business where more than 50% of sales comes from products released in the past 5 years.

So the message is important and simple: it's sustainability, and it's both responsible and competitive. And for me, this is the new sustainable economy—one that will increasingly become the only way of doing business in a competitive world. It's not about being responsible because that's the right thing to do, but because it is in the best interests of long-term value creation. Some of the recent cases I've been involved in, at companies including Telefónica and Mango, no longer have annual CSR reports; instead, they have a more holistic sustainability strategy that looks closely at links with the business strategy. Nike, one of the leaders of sustainability today after having made massive changes in its supply chain in response to the well-publicized "sweatshop" controversies of the 1990s, changed the name of its Chief Sustainability Officer to VP of Sustainable Business and Innovation. If the tipping point for sustainability has now been achieved,[11] resulting in it being present on top managers' agendas and believed as being critical for competitiveness, it is just as important that a broad understanding of what that means is also present.

Examining the Sustainability Case for Business

For me, rather than the business case always being evaluated for sustainability-driven actions, for a wider conception of sustainability to take place, *the sustainability case for business* should be examined.

And this necessarily includes the human factor at the individual level. In *Sustaining Executive Performance*, beyond business and society, the principal focus is on sustainability at a third level, that of the individual and the development of sustainable leaders. We consider the sustainability of people as key to the sustainability of an organization, considering both enduring competitiveness and responsibility as inseparable and necessary. A strong culture should result that supports innovation, where both people and businesses take a longer-term view of value generation, and people become an integral part of the living, breathing organism that is the responsible enterprise. In the same way that a company is not a machine that outsources, for instance, innovation as a commodity, people are not machines who have an incomplete view of their whole self. A new type of leadership is critical to the sustainable competitiveness of a firm, which further permeates throughout the enterprise. This new sustainable leadership is built on a holistic view of self-management.

There are signs of movement toward this Triple Lens of Sustainability. A modern-day champion of a broader view of sustainability is Unilever, the Anglo-Dutch consumer goods giant. I conducted one of my Doctoral case studies in Unilever, at Port Sunlight's European packaging design center, in 2001. The village of Port Sunlight is a case that followed the example of the New Lanark Mills. William Lever, the founder of Lever Brothers, which merged in 1930 with the Dutch company Margarine Unie to form Unilever, built his success on the manufacture of soap. He began construction of the village in 1888 to house the workers of his rapidly growing soap factory and personally supervised the planning of the village, building 800 unique, high-standard of living houses for a population of 3,500. There was an art gallery, hospital, concert hall, schools, open-air swimming pool, and a church. As with Owen in New Lanark, Lever introduced welfare schemes and provided for the education and entertainment of his workforce, encouraging recreation and organizations that promoted art, literature, science, or music. He claimed Port Sunlight was an exercise in profit sharing and invested the profits in the village instead of sharing them directly. Although Lever did court controversy at times regarding the supply of oil, he still built a tradition of sustainability at the individual, enterprise, and society levels.

Today's CEO, Paul Polman, has attempted to build on those traditions with a new approach to big business. He believes that "capitalism needs to evolve, and that requires different types of leaders from what we've had before."[12] That new leadership, according to Polman, needs to recognize the social role of the world enterprise and be able to focus on the long-term, be purpose driven, think systematically, and work more transparently and effectively in partnerships.

Unilever is certainly being recognized for those traits within the traditional sustainability community. For the fourth year in a row, it is regarded as the number-one corporate sustainability leader by the Globescan/SustainAbility survey, and in 2014 by a huge margin (Patagonia, Interface, Marks & Spencer, and Nestlé round out the top five). Of course, sustainability surveys on their own count for little. The poster child only a few years ago in the same survey was BP, ever present in the top ten between 1998 and 2010, and in the top two until 2006. By listening to its CEO, Tony Hayward, in the aftermath of the 2010 Deepwater Horizon disaster, could anyone feasibly say that BP was characterized by executive leadership with sustainability values, or by positive transparency and communication? These were just some of the evaluation criteria used in the survey.

Yet Unilever's sustainability strategy is supported by concrete actions. At the core of the strategy is the Sustainable Living Plan, which attempts to double sales turnover, reduce absolute environmental impact, and increase positive social impact, keeping both the business and society happy. Driven by an appreciation of increasing resource scarcity and the need to reconfigure supply chains, the Sustainable Living Plan also places responsibility on the consumer and attempts to change the actions and habits of society at large, such as taking shorter showers or washing clothes at a lower temperature. Supporting a more long-term view, Polman has also stopped full quarterly reporting so that progress isn't measured on just the next set of numbers. Thinking in the long-term, according to Polman, has relieved the pressure on the organization and resulted in greater drive and engagement from employees. He believes this extra organizational energy to be the key factor in converting good companies to great ones.

Tangible progress has been made with large investments in small farmer training worldwide, industry-wide leadership to tackle the problems of palm-oil sourcing and its effects on deforestation, and irrigation innovation to decrease water usage in tomato growing. At the same time, the shareholder base has shifted to one that may support Unilever's strategy in the long term, with the share price rising in the period 2009–2013 (Polman took over in 2009). Yet the most recent annual results in 2014 disappointed the markets, and the share price has regressed for the first time since Polman took over. Unilever is therefore at a critical juncture. Can Polman and his team retain their nerve if markets start increasing the pressure? For their plan to fully succeed, they require change from society at large, and changing habits, discussed later in the book, is not an easy thing to do.

Sustainable leadership is therefore required at the consumer level, and for movement toward a critical mass of more enlightened capitalism in line with Polman's thinking, we need future CEOs and shareholders to take a similar view. This is where management education plays a key role. Although the MBA industry worldwide can be hindered by a pressurized ranking system that leaves little room for innovation, there have been signs in recent years of a more holistic approach. I will discuss my own and others' attempts to integrate design thinking in Chapter 3, "Design Your Life." Several leading schools have found success in a different form of instruction that may support the drive and direction shown by Polman and other sustainability champions.

New Management Education from the Old World

As reported by the *Wall Street Journal*,[13] leading business schools are increasingly integrating courses that force students to think on a deeper level, and where a philosophical approach based on the teachings of Plato and others is not out of place. London Business School has developed a course called Nobel Thinking, which explores the origins and influence of various theories developed by Nobel Prize winners. The aim is that students reflect on world-changing thought and the impact that new knowledge can have on society.

Generally however, dealing with the ambiguity and abstract ideas required for true transformation is proving difficult. Management students are often characterized by a focus on rational thought and concreteness in all aspects of their lives. Professor Michael Puett is trying to challenge that focus at Harvard University. Teaching one of the most popular courses there on Classical Chinese Ethical and Political Theory,[14] Puett shows that many of the characteristics of the "modern world"—challenging human relationships, increasing narcissism and self-centeredness, and disagreement on the best way for people to live in harmony—are the same as those of China 2,500 years ago. Using translations of original Chinese texts, he teaches his students to be less calculating and to pay attention to the small actions that comprise their daily lives. In line with the teaching of Confucius and other Ancient Chinese philosophers, he shows that the smallest actions can have the most profound ramifications, that decisions are less about rationality than we'd like to think, and of the importance of the body in affecting the behavior of the mind. All these concepts are key elements in the SEP program and are covered in detail as we proceed through the book. My own teaching success at China Europe International Business School (CEIBS) in Shanghai has surprised some of the faculty there who expected content around the physical self, positive practice, and habit change to be at odds with conventional business education topics, such as finance and strategy. Yet I believe that success is due to the fact that much of the content of SEP resonates with a Chinese society still acutely aware of much of the teachings of ancient philosophy and

Confucianism. At its core is humanism and the role that the individual plays in building a healthy community. In line with much of Ancient Greek thought, an ethical philosophy is applied to oneself to improve the health of individuals, recognizing the effect this has on the health of society at large.

From Ancient Chinese philosophy to their Greek counterparts and other more recent historic cases in business, such as the New Lanark Mills, I believe that many patterns exist. There is much to be said for revisiting such ancient wisdom and reflecting on it within the prism of modern life and business.

Leading the Sustainable Self

We work in a global, networked, knowledge age[15] where creativity, collaboration, complexity, and innovation are ever-present challenges. However, many companies still view their human capital in terms of machines, where the number of hours worked produces a quantity over quality paradox that does nothing to support sustainable competitiveness. Perhaps this is a legacy of the industrial age, which considered productivity in terms of time and resulted in a work culture that extolled the virtues of long hours in the company, and where seniority was demonstrated by being first to arrive in the morning and the last to leave.

Without necessarily moving toward socialist utopias, what simple changes can we aim for in a busy professional life in which we strive for health, happiness, and success? One of the main changes is that we have a responsibility to look after ourselves and reflect on our own behavior, not only in how we lead and manage others, but how we lead and manage ourselves. From a purely paternalistic model, such as Owen's Mills'—where the responsibility for worker well-being rests with the employer—to a model today where the source of ill health or disengagement could come from employees themselves, we are empowered to make our own choices. Of course, companies still have a duty of care to their workers and we may play a role in leading a positive culture.

Working and living are intertwined. Work is a key part of a healthy life, and yet work does not equal life. In the same way that life without work—without a purpose or contribution can result in dissatisfaction—so work without life, in the case that work becomes all consuming, also results in dissatisfaction. Although the work-life balance concept has been challenged of late, given the shifting nature of society and the deep integration of both, balance is still a key term. Balance does not mean that each are separated and that we finish work after leaving the office. Owen's 8-8-8 model has long ceased to be such a clean reality, if it ever was. Balance simply means getting the right amount of each. Too much of one and too little of the other inevitably causes problems. The challenge becomes how to be aware of this balance in a modern world where constant integration means there are no safe boundaries that give us the surety of being in one camp or the other. I hope to provide some simple ideas to achieving the requisite balance as we move through the elements of the SEP model.

I have come to understand through researching sustainability at the three levels of individual, organization, and society that *sustainable enterprises need sustainable leaders.* For me, sustainable leadership includes aspects of Polman's beliefs on a long-term view, being purpose driven and working collaboratively, yet I believe a second critical dimension is looking inward, and that the internal reflection of the sustainable self can drive the new leadership attributes that Polman advocates. The sustainable self considers the whole person as espoused by the Ancient Greeks—a mind-body balance that affects a change in mind-set to a more holistic, long-term view, based on personal health and well-being that drives performance. On a simple and practical level, how may basic human needs, in areas including mobility, recovery, the food we eat, the way we approach work, and the time we take to train our bodies and minds, be better catered for in the world of work—and legitimized as true performance drivers? Is it any coincidence that some sectors or enterprises that are notoriously low on ethics and societal care are also characterized by workers who regularly total 100+ hours a week and burn out before they're 40? A simple example shows how workload affects decision making. Research has shown that people are less likely to make ethical decisions, and more likely to lie, later in the day.[16] Basic human needs in the physical domain affect many business factors yet are often squeezed out. We need not divorce the needs of a worker with the needs of a human being.

I am not advocating, or rather preaching, for a highly disciplined monastic life that forgoes all earthly pleasures! I hope you find a highly pragmatic, flexible, and common-sense approach to a more sustainable self in the remainder of the book. The key is simply paying a little more attention and increasing self-awareness of the small actions that drive health, well-being, and performance, and that can drive the Triple Lens of Sustainability forward.

Robert Owen showed that a more holistic view of value creation was not detrimental to business success. Polman is trying to change the mind-set of people across the Triple Lens, from a new generation of sustainable leaders, to other businesses and society as a whole. When Ancient Greek and Chinese philosophy make small inroads into modern management education, it shows us the great potential and feasibility of incorporating ancient wisdom into the modern world. Ambitious visions of work-life harmony may have failed throughout history, yet scope for a greater balance between business and society is rooted in a wider conception of sustainability, one which recognizes the individual actions of us all as a new generation of sustainable leaders.

3

Design Your Life

The designer constructs the world within which he sets the dimensions of the problem space, and invents the moves by which he attempts to find solutions.

—Donald Schön

Just 20 miles from the site of Owen's Lanark mills, I stood nervously on the start line at the side of Haggenfield Loch in Glasgow. It was the 1998 Freshers Race at Strathclyde University. In between National Schools Champions and more seasoned-looking exchange students, I stood there in borrowed shorts in a first return to athletics since high school several years before. This was the day my true academic career started, in my fifth year at University. Graduation was around the corner for my engineering master's degree but I had never been fully engaged, only fleetingly applying myself fully given the naturally interesting field of design in between the many distractions (and joys!) of student life in Glasgow. The possibility of continuing to do a PhD gave me a second chance to see what real thinking my brain could manage. Given that my friends were leaving to start their careers, I made the jump across the road to the sports center for social reasons as much as sporting.

The daily routine of thinking and running and writing sustained me through a successful doctoral research project, finishing in under three years and traveling around the world. My best thinking and answers to tough problems would come during my running, and I would often write most prolifically, scribbling furiously by hand while on various modes of public transportation as I traveled to and from my training sessions. Such a routine was repeated at Stanford, where I spent part of my second year, training with the track team, visiting Bay Area start-ups, and doing hill repeats to the satellite dish overlooking campus. Although I never gave it much thought at the time—various forms of mobility giving energy to creativity, productivity, and clarity—I just knew that it worked for me.

So does it work for everybody? I think it can, and I've seen it happen countless times with the executives who have attended my SEP program. Seeing some of the world's best-ranked executive education classes at close quarters, several years after my own athletic epiphany, led me to question how deep insight and learning could be achieved by sitting in one's chair for several days running. The simplicity of the MOVE element of the SEP model was conceived right there, but how could it be delivered within the rarefied elite MBA and business world where physical matters can be perceived as "nonprofessional"? The answer lay in my engineering education and the field of design. From a Master of Engineering Design degree to the PhD in Engineering Design Management researching the work of virtual design teams, I came to examine design from a variety of perspectives, contexts, and locations.

From the simple, yet insightful—research has found the design of a chair to affect creative methods, as we discuss in Chapter 6, "MOVE"—to the complex approach to society's "wicked problems," including clean water use in third-world countries, design is the lever by which we make the Triple Lens of Sustainability function. So what is design?

What Is Design?

On a simple level, design is the process whereby something is created. This creative process is followed by some manufacture or elaboration so that the design becomes reality. Design thinking has gained great interest in the management community the past several years, with much of that through the work of IDEO and its founder, David Kelley. Kelley was one of the first interviews I carried out in 2001 during my Stanford stay, later meeting some of his earliest collaborators with whom he founded David Kelley Design in the late 1970s. The defining characteristics of design as espoused by Kelley complemented my own engineering-centric Scottish education. I came to understand design as a process where rigor was balanced with the space and freedom for creativity. Strathclyde was (and still is) at the forefront of engineering design education worldwide, building on the rich design traditions of Glasgow (such as the work of Charles Rennie Mcintosh) to establish a design chair under the direction of Professor Stuart Pugh whose methods on Total Design,[1] principally concept design selection, would be exported to classrooms around the world, including Stanford.

Although we may argue that design has been part of human activity for millennia in terms of the world that we have created, design as a field of science is only about 60 years old. The birth of design as a research field can be traced back to the 1960s with the creation of the first design models, and the publication of *Design Methods,* by J. C. Jones in 1970[2] marked a milestone in moving design understanding to the masses. Basic design methods, such as brainstorming and morphological analysis, were formalized and related to an understanding of the process of design. In 2001, I worked with Larry Leifer at the Center for Design Research (CDR), which conceived several innovative research tools, including the Design Observatory, which allowed detailed observation studies to be conducted into the design process. CDR, still thriving today, was one of the key elements at Stanford from which the Hasso Plattner Institute of Design, or D-school, was formed in 2003 under the direction of Kelley.

Since then, the power of design has begun to be recognized on a global level, in different industries as well as education, where the creative thinking skills of a designer are appreciated for students of all types. Recognizing the success of Kelley and colleagues at IDEO, *Business Week* ran a cover on "The Power of Design" in 2007, the same year in which a call was made to change MBA-based education from the current B (business) school reality to the D (design) school. *Harvard Business Review* then published several design-driven articles that recognized this shift, with IDEO CEO Tim Brown's *Design Thinking*[3] improving global awareness yet nevertheless showing that design is no panacea; the main case study presented by Brown, the Shimano coasting system, was an unmitigated disaster. In spite of growing awareness and practice, the quality of that design practice has at times suffered, through an association with overly simple methods and a plethora of management consultancies worldwide who began to sell design expertise, armed with nothing more than a basic understanding of these methods and a collection of brightly colored Post-It notes. In general, however, the rapid growth of design in the public consciousness, and leadership of design-driven companies has been positive, with much potential for value in different areas of our modern world still to be realized. *What is Design?* is further answered by the following six defining characteristics.

Design Is Human

Design is, above all things, human. It looks to create a world that satisfies the needs we have as human beings. These could be the products we use, from a simple toothbrush to a car. Such products need to perform their job or function for which they are created (clean teeth, transport people) and so involve the necessary technical and ergonomic factors, fulfilling that function in as enjoyable a manner as possible. For the context of health, well-being, and performance, we may consider the design of our work environments, on both a physical level, such as building design and office furniture, to the wider systems that operate in our designed environment, such as city design and transport.

The human needs that design aims to satisfy involve some form of dynamic nature—during a day or, indeed, life. Although the ultimate need or function of a toothbrush will remain the same, the means of satisfying that need in the design of the toothbrush for a 3-year-old compared to an adult will be very different. In many cases, assumptions need to be challenged. IDEO challenged the assumption that young children brushed their teeth in the same way as adults—the "fisting" type process employed by children, whereby they wrap their whole fist around the handle rather than hold it with their fingers, meant that a larger, not smaller, toothbrush was required. The design of drug packaging for elderly users who suffer from dementia has to satisfy very specific needs for it to fulfill its function.

Empathy is a key term related to the human nature of design. How may we fully understand the needs of another human being if we have not walked in their shoes? The MIT transportation lab considered such a question for elderly users and developed the AGNES suit (Age Gain Now Empathy System), which allowed them to physically experience the effects of aging through, for example, reduced mobility and blurred vision. Such experiences help with a better grasp of those human needs that may then be satisfied through a better-designed environment. Empathy may also be driven in the workplace. A television program in the UK centers on a company CEO, incognito, spending a week working at some introductory level of the organization. The insights derived help them to fully appreciate the different daily reality of people in the organization, and therefore better understand the business.

Design Satisfies Needs

Design produces some solution that subsequently becomes reality, either as a manufactured product, a new service, or a solution of another type. These solutions satisfy some requirement or need. More than simply solving problems, needs may not even be articulated by the user, because the user doesn't know the solution is needed. Needs may also exist on an "extreme" level, of particular interest in design because these extreme needs are often characteristic of *lead* users, a part of the population who may offer insight into the future because they experience such needs ahead of the general population. Satisfying the needs of lead users also tests the boundaries of design solutions to such an extent that the needs of the general population may be more easily met. Needs in the developing world represent a powerful context in which design thinking may be applied in extreme conditions where, for example, the infrastructure or resources of the first world cannot be assumed. In the SEP model, extreme users include the CEO who has her focus at a premium daily, with multiple demands on her time, and the "road warrior" who needs to be able to sleep better on a plane.

Design Is Hidden

Human needs may be very difficult to articulate, and designers question aspects of our human life that are often difficult to see or appreciate as being necessary to improve. Donald Schön said that "we know more than we can say" and the subconscious part of our brains often drive our actions. Gerald Zaltman, a Harvard professor, has stated that conscious activity represents only 5% of cognition.[4] The hidden 95% is therefore the target of design if we want to satisfy human needs. Design, primarily through borrowing tools from sociology and anthropology, uses different methods to uncover those hidden needs.

Design Concerns Process

Although it can be conceived as a noun, a better way to understand design is as a verb. Design is about *doing*, and although there is freedom within a necessarily creative endeavor, structure and process are required for design to work, and to produce the desired end result. Design begins with a brief and follows a creative process, whereby potential solutions or *concepts* are generated and then evaluated, before the necessary details are elaborated to move that design toward reality. As part of my design education at Strathclyde, and following Pugh's Total Design methodology, I came to understand design as a process that followed the steps of product design specification, concept generation, concept evaluation, embodiment design, detail design, and manufacture. Irrespective of the exact stages, which may differ between organizations, such a process tends to follow a similar flow, whereby the solution space expands and then contracts, following a principal of divergence and convergence. Iteration is also a key factor whereby some element of testing allows us to more rapidly move toward a more robust solution. IDEO's process, the subject of a Harvard case study,[5] includes these notions within the conceptualization of the Three Rs (rough, ready, right) where physical prototyping plays a key role in developing insight early in the process.

Design Is Enabled Through Methods

Design is equipped through various tools or methods and is employed at different stages of the process to progress toward an optimum solution. Much of the design-thinking movement is based on a set of tools or methods that are used to understand the user, challenge assumptions, generate concepts, and essentially connect the need, user, and designer. Many of these methods have been taken from other fields, such as the shadowing method we discuss in the next chapter, which has its roots in anthropology. Others include the simple engineering-based method, root cause analysis. Prototyping is a specific method that allows the process to be both explorative and iterative and accelerates progress toward a solution.

Design Is Holistic

In addressing human needs, which are often hidden, design has a necessary broad base of coverage and is holistic and exploratory in its approach. Part of the iterative process of design is necessary as a means of exploring wide solution spaces and discovering new ways of doing things. It is also holistic in terms of the disciplines or expertise that it includes. Design teams are almost always multidisciplinary and may contain engineers, MBAs, lawyers, and doctors, who integrate their knowledge and experience to move toward the best design solution.

Design to Disrupt Education

Design, with these six defining characteristics, is the lever with which we may connect the individual to the organization and also society. It therefore acts as the key driver for innovation, leadership, and resilience, which are the true results of a holistic treatment of sustainability. What are the human, hidden needs required by the twenty-first century business professional to improve performance? How may we better design processes, cultures, environments, buildings, and even furniture to satisfy those aims? The SEP model and wider discussion in this book aims to address these questions.

Given that *Business Week* made the call for the B-school to become a D-school in 2007, how has design been taught within the leading MBAs of the world? The answer: it hasn't. With some notable exceptions, it remains the same model as before. Even at Stanford, the D-school and the Graduate School of Business have collaborated only relatively recently.

As well as design being a topic in education, it may be used as a tool to rethink the educational system. Higher education in particular is expecting a wave of disruption from the technological revolution and growing prevalence of Massive Open Online Communities (MOOC). However, MOOC usage seems to have stalled, perhaps only temporarily, and one of the reasons could be that the focus has been overly technological. Some of my own research on virtual teams argued for the balance to be redressed from what seems to be purely technical or technological issues to a more human-based focus—something that design shows us. And

Stanford D-school professors, such as George Kembel, have looked at how the learning experience may be redesigned to better reflect the needs of today, arguing in 2010[6] that "we're still running an educational model developed for the industrial revolution, designed to prepare workers for factory jobs." He says that the classroom of 2020 will be characterized by the lone professor being replaced by a team of coaches, and tidy lectures supplanted by messy real-world challenges, adding that students will "work in collaborative spaces, where future doctors, lawyers, business leaders, engineers, journalists, and artists learn to integrate their different approaches to problem solving and innovate together."

Such a vision is a reality in many design schools and courses worldwide, such as the D school, yet implementing such a vision in non-design schools is still a challenge. I have attempted to implement design education within one of the world's best-ranked MBA courses, at IESE Business School in Barcelona. The highly specialized structure of the MBA can make it difficult, while also conditioning the students to perceive the flexibility and freedom of design thinking as time off from their usual pressured yet still more "tidy" lectures and cases. The line between freedom and fun, yet maintaining diligence and learning, can be a difficult one to manage for those used to more rational thought and defined structure.

For greater insight into these issues and the means of integrating a design vision into the MBA world, I talked to a designer with several years' experience "in the field."

Design for Management Education

Lucy Kimbell has been teaching design to MBA students at Oxford since 2005. A designer, researcher, and educator, Lucy's Oxford-design elective covers areas including service design, social innovation, entrepreneurship, and scenario planning. Collaborating principally with the Operations Management department at Oxford, she entered design academia with a desire to find more sophisticated answers to design issues that she encountered in her consultancy work. These design issues concerned the adaptability and responsiveness of an organization to a deep understanding of customer needs and experiences. Having previously taught at the Royal College of Art, she is now establishing a design-driven MBA at Central Saint Martins and also forms part of the UK government think tank on applying design thinking to policy issues.

What Is Design? Can Anyone Be a Designer or Practice Design?

Different fields have their own view on design, such as the engineering school that was her own starting point to design, or more styling or communication-based approaches—yet all have some common features where design has a broad and divergent view of the subject matter and where ideas are made more tangible. Kimbell says that design, at its best, "brings things into view" and so can be potentially disruptive, both in the solutions it can offer as well as the differing mind-set required by those who practice it in an organization. The advantage and disadvantage of design, according to Kimbell, is that design has potentially no boundaries, which is good from the point of view that anyone can tackle, and contribute, to a problem, but that they may not always be qualified to do so. As the world has become more complex, with the necessity to link previously disparate areas to find a solution, so design has offered the potential to do so—promoting a culture of enquiry and curiosity, which nevertheless contrasts with the operational, routine base view of many company managers.

Why Is Design Useful?

As well as the previously mentioned potential for tackling complex problems and engendering a change in the culture of a company, Kimbell says that design has specific advantages to offer in the early stages of a project where there may be a poor understanding of a solution, or where people have a tendency to jump to the solution. Although fields such as anthropology and sociology offer a more sophisticated means of understanding the user (and issue), design offers a more accessible means of achieving the same aim. Many design features are reflected in modern concepts such as lean start-up methodology, including agility, iteration, and experimentation. Yet unlike design, Kimbell believes that such approaches don't always make it easy to scale up such an approach as the enterprise grows.

How May Design Be Successfully Delivered in the MBA World?

Having taught several hundred MBA students since 2005, Kimbell has come to understand what is required for this to work. From a core group of 225 students, each year around 50 to 60 choose Kimbell's elective, these days with a clear objective of learning about design thinking given the increased visibility of design-led companies and consultancies like IDEO, Apple, Frog, and AirB&B. Rather than talking about design, Kimbell focuses on practice and allows her students to *do* design, partnering with MA design students to follow the process of exploration, insight generation, and idea creation. She shows her students that ideas don't simply exist in one's head to be made tangible, but it is through the process of designing—sketching, prototyping, and role-playing—that ideas emerge. She finds it difficult to enable students to engage with real stakeholders in the field within the total 24-hour confines of the elective, but facilitates this through third-party research and user profiles.

Her students either love or hate the class, but all encounter an experience they are unlikely to forget. Much depends on the thinking style. Highly rational, ordered thinkers often encounter a deeply uncomfortable experience that they don't enjoy, whereas more disordered, messy, explorative thinkers are more at ease with the ambiguity that characterizes the class. Kimbell says that the class offers them an opportunity to put into practice some of the techniques and knowledge gained in other parts of the MBA and "offers an encounter with making the world." She believes that some of the barriers to accepting her different learning experience may even be traced back to primary education, which does not offer enough space for playing and creative thought.

Should We Rethink Design Thinking?

Although the great attention paid to design, and particularly design thinking, over the past few years has its advantages, there are also problems through some of the confusion it has caused. IDEO has been highly skilled at articulating and packing the product of design thinking, also progressed in a slightly different fashion by authors such as Roger Martin,[7] who offers a way of framing problems and asking "*What if?*" However, neither are based in deep academic research, and for many in the "design as a science" community, none of the recent discussion has been anything new. Design, in some ways, has become known as a toolkit, which misses the complexity and nuance of what design is and how it can have an impact.

Designing a Better World

In having a focus on social design methods and designing better futures, Dr. Kimbell's approach to design is therefore one that fits with notions of responsibility that we have discussed in the previous chapter. Greater attention is now being placed on how design, more than just helping, for instance, in the design of a new consumer product or first-world service experience, can make a difference in creating a better world. IDEO published the HCD (Human Centered Design) toolkit in 2009 with the specific intention of overcoming challenges in the nonprofit world through a deep understanding of human needs. Partly funded by the Bill and Melinda Gates Foundation, the toolkit is a free innovation guide designed specifically for NGOs and social enterprises that work with impoverished communities in Africa, Asia, and Latin America. Innovations have resulted in the areas of clean drinking water, blood donation, and heart defibrillation. Much of the ethos of the HCD toolkit is reflected in OpenIDEO.com, an online platform where anyone can form part of the community where people come together to design for social good.

Design, therefore, has the power of creating a better world because it looks at solving problems in unconventional ways, or in non-optimum conditions. Given that it is process based, method driven, human, hidden, and holistic, it can tackle complex "wicked" problems as well as drive common-sense solutions on a simple level, such as how we approach the world of work and it's fit within life to improve health, well-being, and performance.

Design reframes problems as opportunities. Nike looked at the problem of recycling massive amounts of plastic bottles and used them to manufacture football kits. It takes 18 plastic bottles to produce each full kit, with 100% recycled PET shorts, 96% recycled PET shirts, and 78% recycled PET socks—sustainable solutions designed for the developed world. Sustainable solutions designed for the developing world include the Lifestraw, which enables the consumption of clean water from almost any dirty water source given the ability to filter out harmful bacteria. One of the most impactful organizations in this space to date is Krista Donaldson's D-Rev. Donaldson, who was a colleague of mine at the Center for Design Research in 2001 when she was finishing her Stanford PhD, founded D-Rev in 2007 and has gone on to develop not only products, but the necessary systems—financial models, licensing deals, consulting services, and manufacturing arrangements—necessary for those products to work.[8] The original assumption, that market conditions would allow well-designed products to flourish, didn't work, because most developing communities don't have efficient markets. Cronyism, corruption, or just a simple lack of basic infrastructure or understanding of the value of a simple innovation meant that adoption wasn't straightforward. With a fuller understanding of the key adoption criteria and the necessary collaborations, D-Rev is helping thousands in the developing world with products including low-cost prosthetics and an LED machine that treats infant jaundice.

Design Your Life

Design has made a lasting impact on my life. Some of the attributes that have marked my career (and that have sometimes got me into trouble!), including an exploratory, curious nature seeking out new collaborations and a breadth first versus depth approach to tackling a problem, have come from my training in design. In a complex, shifting world where an appreciation of different fields is required to enable change on the system level, I believe this to be the greatest advantage of being a design thinker. Design also has the potential to impact powerfully on the lives of others and make them better. From an understanding of specific needs in extreme environments, the simple solutions are often the best. Being comfortable with possibility and ambiguity, when allied to a rigorous education in the business of business, has much to offer the leaders and managers of tomorrow. How may we better understand and empathize with the day-to-day reality of human beings around the world? What is your own day-to-day reality? And could we redesign that for better health, well-being, and performance?

And so, to the Freshers Race. I won, accelerating through one of the deep, omnipresent Glasgow puddles that lay around the loch as my rivals slowed, and opening a gap that would remain until the end. The prize, rather fittingly for a Scottish student, was six cans of beer in addition to the Fresher's Shield. It kick-started my athletic career, and I would go on to captain the University cross-country team as well as the Scottish Universities' select, later becoming national Duathlon (think triathlon for bad swimmers!) Champion. I graduated from the University of Strathclyde with a Double Blue in Athletics and Duathlon as well as my academic degrees. Racing later around the world against some incredibly tough full-time and part-time athletes, it increased my belief in the metaphorical and practical value of sport for business, but one in which an understanding of design, in all its depth, yet its simplicity, is necessary to make that transfer work.

4

Day-to-Day Reengineering

I get up, I drink coffee, I read the paper, I have breakfast, I go out on my bike and train. I come home, I have lunch with the kids, then I spend the rest of the day in meetings, playing golf, or in the park with the kids. And about 5pm, I open a nice cold beer and I think.

—Lance Armstrong

"They love to fight, they've got loads of character for such small dogs. It's one of the reasons I love them so much." The biggest man I had ever seen was seated on what I imagine was a stool in the middle of a large room surrounded by more than 50 out-of-control Chihuahuas. The surreal and chaotic experience was heightened by a radio in the corner playing loud Latin dance music. My eyes locked on a particular pair of dogs who were entwined in a joint movement to the music—and they certainly weren't fighting. It was January 2008, and I was in the Coyoacán neighborhood of Distrito Federale, Mexico City, interviewing a local dog breeder as part of a four-week ethnographic field study throughout Mexico for the dog food company Pedigree, part of the Mars group.

I remember the trip as an exhausting yet exhilarating first real experience of design fieldwork. The days were long, spent between traveling to the homes of the "target," followed by analysis and coding of the video footage at night, for days on end, and then interspersed by intense group sessions and workshops in the project "war room" on the 20th floor of the client building overlooking Mexico City.

I also found the journey very humbling, switching between a target in an expansive property within a gated compound in Chapultepec to one within a ramshackle hut using corrugated iron boards to re-enforce the roof and front door in Neza. Everyone was incredibly welcoming, and it was a privilege to spend time with them during the focus of the ethnographic work—the intimate experience of meal preparation with the family.

The specific method I was using and training my Mexican colleagues in was *shadowing*. It is a product and service innovation technique for uncovering in-depth human needs related to an experience. Researchers observe and interact with people in their real environment to identify these needs. Derived principally from the field of ethnography, other related fields include psychology, cinematography, and market research. Identified needs may be of any kind—current or future, conscious or subconscious—depending on the innovation objective. Shadowing is generally used for ambitious innovation projects because it tends to require a significant investment, as well as a leap of faith given that a culture of surveys and large data sets are usurped (or at least complemented and challenged) by a handful of "deep dive" shadowing sessions. Next generation projects are more suited than line extensions. Even though shadowing aims to discover all kinds of needs, its strengths lie in anticipating people's subconscious and future needs. It therefore benefits innovation through boosting the quality of generated solutions, and thereby enhances the probability of producing products or services with a high degree of newness.

From my education in engineering and product design, it was interesting to start becoming more aware of the universality of design and the possibility of applying the same principles to services and experiences. For Pedigree, the company found that its sales were being eroded from both sides of the market—from the premium brands as well as the cheaper supermarket brands. Therefore, Pedigree wanted to engage more deeply with the customer through an innovative marketing campaign that would be rolled out throughout Mexico. And so I traveled from Mexico City to Monterrey to Guadalajara and Puebla for 12 shadowing sessions to gain rich insights into the consumer, on which the campaign would be based.

That target consumer, specified by the client, was a housewife (ama de casa) with a young family and a dog, and the experience that we decided to shadow, based on a workshop and pre-field analysis in that 20th floor war room, was meal preparation with the family, which could also include picking the kids up from school.

Because shadowing is complex and costly, it is important to apply a well-structured and consistent process. Based on a shadowing guide, innovators observe and interact with a number of people in the real environment of the experience, which is the subject of the innovation project. People data is first captured in video, audio, and annotations. The resulting data is then analyzed for needs, which are leveraged for solution generation in subsequent innovation stages. The final output of shadowing is a multimedia document containing both textual-graphic and audio-video descriptions of needs. The following success criteria are critical to realizing the full power of shadowing:

- **Conduct shadowing in-project:** The overall shadowing process should be conducted by the core project team and not be outsourced or delegated to a separate research team. This is to avoid loss of tacit data, improve the data interpretation, and boost inspiration for solution generation.

- **Shadow the right people:** This is a basic condition for success. The objective is to find people who are advanced in their needs compared to the general market—lead or extreme users. It is recommended not to apply the same screener used for other research techniques, such as focus groups.

- **Complement shadowing with other techniques:** Even though shadowing provides important data, it will not uncover all the insights required for solution generation. Shadowing should form part of a mix of techniques—for example, in conjunction with experience diaries and structured surveys.

- **Make shadowing a key element of innovation strategy, process, and culture:** Shadowing generates crucial data for new product decisions, which in turn drive multimillion dollar investments in new product projects. If shadowing is not consolidated within the overall company, and highly regarded by top executives, it will not receive the resources required to conduct it properly, and results will lack credibility for strategic decision making.

Table 4.1   Design-Driven Methods Are Different

	Design Methods	Traditional Methods
Time Dedicated to Study One Person?	4+ hours	1–120 min
Where Is People Research Conducted?	Real context	Laboratory
Who Conducts People Research?	The core innovation team (internal or external)	Research team separated from core innovation team
What Is the Primary Data Type?	Audio, video	Numbers, text

So how about applying some of this logic on a personal level? From understanding the role that design played in my own life on a career level, to appreciating the opportunity to actually *design* (or, rather, redesign) my life, I've long been convinced of the value of tracking, experimenting, reflecting on performance, and planning. As discussed in the next chapter, Clayton Christensen asks how you will measure your life, and we often focus on the big goals and objectives—the five-year plans. Yet what of the small, tiny habits that make up your day-to-day activities? These are the equivalent of the insights we looked for in the Mexican mealtime experience. These are often the things that have the biggest impact on your health, well-being, and performance. Let's look at a couple of cases that show the great impact of the small changes.

Sweat the Small Stuff

Details make all the difference. I appreciated these on the marketing and manufacturing levels while conducting part of my PhD research at Unilever in Port Sunlight, England. The Fast Moving Consumer Goods (FMCG) market is in constant need for these deep insights as they launch new products into burgeoning portfolios. The type of insights they look for could best be demonstrated by considering a case from Unilever's main rival, Procter & Gamble (P&G), as reported by Duhigg.[1]

Febreze is a well-known star product in the huge P&G portfolio, yet its path to market success, after the potentially gold mine discovery of the technical formula, was far from straightforward. The value of the chemical substance at the core of Febreze, HPBCD (hydroxypropyl beta cyclodextrin), was discovered accidentally when a P&G chemist, and smoker, found his clothes to stop smelling so bad after working with it in the lab. The science behind the spray was so advanced that NASA would eventually use it to clean the interior of shuttles after they returned from space. P&G executives were obviously ecstatic, yet the team charged with marketing the product failed in its initial efforts—focusing on understanding users or targets who suffered particularly from bad smells—smokers, pet owners, park rangers, and sweaty athletes. Yet who would want to admit they had such a problem? Indeed, those who did buy the product didn't use it regularly, because we generally become desensitized to the smells around us. The turnaround came after noticing a small, yet significant, part of the *ritual* of household cleaning. After finishing making up a room, the targets would give a little smile at the result of their handiwork. Febreze was then tweaked to add a pleasant smell rather than just neutralize odors. And in the ritual of cleaning, it was used at the end of the cleaning process as a reward or celebration, in contrast to using it at the start. A deep insight on a seemingly innocuous level provided the about-face in a multimillion dollar business.

Details make all the difference in customer service, too. While staying in hotels the past couple of years, I have been acutely aware of the different actions that a room cleaner follows. I remember talking once to a fellow business traveler in China while staying at one of the new Marriott hotels. He was pleasantly delighted by the fact that the shower lever was repositioned to the default position each time he went for a shower, even if he had finished his previous shower experience by a blast of hot or cold water. Do Marriott cleaning staff therefore have an exhaustive checklist of such tiny actions? It may often be the case that guests are not fully aware of every single action, yet these small, seemingly innocuous, details can often add up to a delightful experience, even if a guest can't quite put a finger on where that delight is coming from.

Such details often mark the difference between success and failure in many other fields. In sport, there is the lauded Cumulative Effect of Marginal Gains, implemented so successfully by British Olympic Track

Cycling, which we cover in depth in Chapter 15, "On Learning and Development for Organizational Transformation." The strategy has been copied by other sports, including English Premiership Football. Former Southampton Director of Football Nicola Cortese refused to accept their poor performance away from home as a result of further travel compared to other teams. He asked all the players to offer insight into their daily routine and habits. What time did they wake up at home? Did their children wake them up or did the dog? Changes were made, and when the team traveled for an away match, the hotel was booked for two nights instead of one. On the first, club staff would arrive and clean the already serviced rooms. Specially made mattresses and pillows would be placed on each bed, tailored to each player, and all bed linen would be washed and ironed by the club. Wherever the players are, the beds smell and feel the same.

I remember my own football team's (Glasgow Celtic!) injury concerns a couple of years ago during a Champions League campaign. Their goalkeeper was injured for several weeks, simply by tweaking his neck on an unfamiliar pillow while traveling for an away game. Potentially millions of dollars were at stake over such a minor incident!

So what lessons can be gained from these cases for the busy professional? One direct takeaway might be to consider the use of pillows while traveling. Some of my clients have led a road warrior type lifestyle, and we have worked together to specifically improve their ability to sleep on a plane, so as to maximize their recovery during a busy time on the road. One of the things that has made the biggest difference is the simple action of taking their normal home pillow with them onto the plane, or make the necessary adjustments at home by using a smaller pillow on a normal basis that is more easily transported.

Given such examples, why don't we pay more attention to our own daily routine to get the best performance? In all areas of our life and work, we can focus on small actions in health, well-being, and performance instead of always focusing on the long-range goals and objectives and big strategies, and then feeling despondent when those aren't attained. The big objectives are important and give us a vision and reason for striving, but the daily focus gives us the quick wins and achievable action that builds momentum to these grander goals.

Since my Mexican sojourn in 2008, I have been engaged in several deep dives to gain customer insight. What struck me as I developed the SEP program was that the same insights from seemingly innocuous or hidden places, sometimes the insignificant actions that drive our day, could also hold the key to reengineering the daily habits of the modern professional. If such design thinking was so expertly leveraged by global champions such as Apple, BMW, and IDEO, why don't we turn this deep dive methodology inward? Ironically, this may leverage the sustainable performance of the very executives who approve these hefty budgets for the insights to be gained in the first place.

I remember painstakingly constructing the location, transport, and action map to gain a foothold into the lives of those Mexican housewives. A commonly used figure in design methods workshops is that shown in Figure 4.1, which illustrates the focus on human needs within a dynamic setting.

Figure 4.1 Design methods template for analyzing target reality

What if we put the busy professional at the center of such a study instead, as represented in Figure 4.2? Think about how you spend your own day. What are the choices you make that drive your executive performance? Let's look first at the modern "successful" executive.

Figure 4.2 Design methods template for analyzing the sustainable leader

The Modern, "Successful" Executive and the Self-Fulfilling Prophecy of Busyness

I believe there to be an erroneous perception of what working in business means, or even more dangerous, what being successful is. As we touch on in several areas of the book, being successful does not automatically mean being busy. Of course, successful people often have large demands placed on their time, but business has increasingly become *busyness* and many of us are uncomfortable when we are not busy, believing that to be a symptom of failure. We therefore create much of the chaos ourselves and transmit an image of urgency and busyness to those around us. And the self-fulfilling prophecy of busyness is highly contagious!

Two recent experiences illustrate some of this commonly held perception. During a recent writing visit to Mitchell Library in Glasgow, I observed at close quarters a typical business professional. With dozens of papers strewn across two desks, and surrounded by several electronic gadgets, he constantly switched among several tasks. Even the ringtone on his mobile phone, which sounded every few minutes, illustrated the general chaos and alarm of the work situation—that of an air-raid siren! Maybe he's always expecting bad news! In any case, this is a typically depressing approach to modern executive work—chaotic, addicted to multitasking, physically sedentary, yet mentally hyperactive and lacking true focus. I didn't want to think about his blood pressure and cortisone levels, although I did get an idea from the color of his face and tone of his voice.

I also took the high-speed train recently from Barcelona to Madrid. In the bar car was some new advertising for a technology company in which they added photos of typical food and drink products on the table surfaces around the perimeter of the carriage. What caught my eye was a photo of a sample agenda, notebook open, and pen, together with the following itinerary:

0900: Meeting with Pedro in Madrid.

1200: Colloquium and lunch with Sandy.

1630: Train Madrid—Barcelona.

1830: Airport pick-up.

2000: Project presentation.

2130: Business dinner.

Putting aside the question of whether your day should be like this—spanning more than 12 hours—we ought to consider the strategies for not just surviving, but thriving. Realistically, such days will occur and are often necessary for results; later we discuss in depth how such days may be met head-on with success. Yet I don't believe they should represent the norm or, even worse, an aspiration, both being suggested by their inclusion on the advertising.

So we must challenge the perception that busy equals success. The world of sport that has taught me so much about how to work is characterized by performance being attained where off time, whether for recovery, leisure, or reflection, is just as important if not more so than the actual "on" of performance. Yet we often grind through a long day, as we may appreciate through the following scenario of Brian, the "modern successful executive":

> Brian hears the familiar vibration of his smartphone at 6 a.m. and with a groan hits the snooze button before enjoying a fitful extra 20 minutes of sleep. On the third vibration, he clambers out of bed, wondering how he can feel more sleepy as compared to the first sounds of the alarm, and checks his email on the way to the bathroom. As he stands in the shower, his mind is taken with the updates of the U.S. project that have arrived during the night. Dressing while formulating his reply to the latest crisis in the U.S., he decides to skip breakfast to arrive at the office earlier to get more done. Traffic is particularly bad that morning. It seems others have the same idea, as well as drivers deciding to cut him off on a repeated basis! He arrives harassed at his reserved space in the parking lot; at least that's one thing he doesn't have to worry about! He decides to kill a few more emails on his elevator ride to the tenth floor, and arrives at the welcome sight of his familiar chair before confronting the carousel of calls and meetings and requests and mails. He's getting things done! He asks his secretary to bring him lunch at his desk, and the next thing he knows, he's heading out the door before taking that critical conference call on the drive home.

He arrives home to a large dinner, starving! A few glasses of wine help him unwind from a busy day. The kids decide to eat in their rooms, but at least he can message them from his tablet. He falls asleep on the couch after dinner and awakens late with a slight headache. Thinking he may feel better by getting ahead of the next day, he checks his email again. The U.S. will be moving toward lunchtime about now, and he goes to bed after his wife, again checking his email at the same time as setting his alarm half an hour earlier. He was busy today, and he feels like he's been through the mill, yet that's the life of busy executive after all. If he feels sleepy in the morning, he can always hit the snooze button after all.

I think we'd all agree this doesn't sound so attractive but is perhaps more reflective of our lives than we'd like to admit. There are about two-dozen areas in that scenario that we can improve on through the five SEP elements that are covered in the forthcoming chapters. I will not be so glib as to offer a "perfect" day. Many of us will encounter elements of the preceding scenario. Flexibility is key. Yet challenging such a scenario as the norm is what is required. Much of my teaching to younger managers around the world centers on trying to convince them that running around with an ear glued to a mobile phone, checking emails at breakfast, and constantly complaining about how many things you need to do is not the route to success.

So consider your own life for a second. Ask yourself a couple of questions. How do you start your day? When do you first check your email? What did you have for lunch? Was this a conscious choice or were you eating before you knew what it was? What time did you get to bed last night? What about your commute to work? On a more general level, when was the last time you changed any of these things? Was this change conscious and proactive, or was it forced?

Day-to-Day Reengineering

Rather than always looking at the big picture, what are the small areas of your life—your habits, routines, and rituals—that you can change, *reengineer*, to improve your own performance? I am not advocating stringent time plans for each day. The days of clocking 9 to 5 and then forgetting about work until the next day are long gone for most of us, and so Robert Owen's model of the 8-8-8 day, although still providing us with a template for balance in the long-term, is much more integrated and chaotic than it was in the years following the New Lanark Mills. Flexibility is important, and distractions will frequently arise that may actually represent huge opportunities.

Yet I strongly believe that there is still a key role for structure. As we have seen in our discussion on design in Chapter 3, "Design Your Life," the best processes are often a combination of control and chaos. The rhythm and the balance of a particular phenomenon, whether it be natural or industrial, is what makes it soar. What at first may seem like the unstructured chaos of a gifted artist, for example, may yield some key underlying patterns or rituals that make the art special. On a biological level, we all have the same underlying patterns as human beings. We all need to sleep, with that rest coming at night (usually!) after the sun has set. Our body temperature will rise and fall at certain times of the day, and certain hormones that aid alertness, activity, or sleep will wax and wane. Such biological factors, as well as their consequences for work performance and health, are covered as we move through Part 2 of the book.

Yet understanding our own secrets, those nuances within the general pattern, is the deep insight in the way that P&G found the way to make Febreze a market success and in the way we found Mexican mothers to care in a different way for their pets. Next, we'll look at some examples from others before moving toward the means of discovering those secrets. Who do you think this is?[2]

> The first, and best, of his work periods began at 8:00 a.m., after he had taken a short walk and had a solitary breakfast. Following ninety minutes of focused work in his study—disrupted only by occasional trips to the snuff jar that he kept on a table in the hallway—he met his wife, Emma, in the drawing room to receive the day's post. He read his letters, then lay on the sofa to hear Emma read the family letters aloud. When the letters were done, Emma would continue reading aloud, switching to whatever novel she and her husband were currently working their way through. At 10:30, he returned to his study and did

more work until noon or a quarter after. He considered this the end of his workday, and would often remark in a satisfied voice, "I've done a good day's work."

He made a point of replying to every letter he received, even those from obvious fools or cranks. If he failed to reply to a single letter, it weighed on his conscience and could even keep him up at night. The letter writing took him until about 3:00 in the afternoon, after which he went upstairs to his bedroom to rest, lying on the sofa with a cigarette while Emma continued to read from the novel-in-progress.

At 5:30, a half-hour of idleness in the drawing room preceded another period of rest and novel reading, and another cigarette, upstairs. Then he joined the family for dinner, although he did not join them in eating the meal; instead, he would have tea with an egg or a small piece of meat.

After two games of backgammon, he would read a scientific book and, just before bed, lie on the sofa and listen to Emma play the piano. He left the drawing room at about 10:00 and was in bed within a half-hour, although he generally had trouble getting to sleep and would often lie awake for hours, his mind working at some problem that he had failed to solve during the day.

This is Charles Darwin. Perhaps not an easy one to figure out, but certain clues were there. I think we may gain insight into the man and his life work through certain elements of his daily routine. Much of his daily activity is of course confined to a previous age, yet much of his approach is timeless. For example, many modern productivity experts continue to talk of the importance of scheduling your most important work for first thing in the morning (rather than checking email, for example). And we see that although Darwin was highly driven and produced an incredible canon of work throughout his life, there were periods of idleness and leisure designed into the day with his core work day finishing at 12 p.m. Time to think and reflect is critical to producing quality work.

Quality work is often creative work, and a creative writer whom I have followed for several years is Haruki Murakami. The award-winning Japanese novelist writes fiction that on its own would make him notable, yet the means by which he produces that work is also fascinating. Known to the world as a successful writer, Murakami is also a committed marathon runner and triathlete. His days are marked by a solid routine, writing for several hours in the morning before training for a few hours in the early afternoon. Much of his running and triathlon exploits are covered in the book *What I Talk About When I Talk About Running*, and he was interviewed in 2012[3] after the release of a major recent work, *IQ84*. Highlighting the value of his daily practice, he said:

> It's physical. If you keep on writing for three years, every day, you should be strong. Of course, you have to be strong mentally, also. But in the first place you have to be strong physically.

Anyone who has read IQ84 will know you have to be strong physically just to lift it! It is a major piece of work about 1,000 pages long. In the interview, he went on to describe how he starts his day:

> Every day I go to my study and sit at my desk and put the computer on. At that moment, I have to open the door. It's a big, heavy door.

Any writer or creative artist will recognize the metaphor of the "big, heavy door" in having to face a blank canvas or page each time, and the interviewer then asks him if there is an element of fear to overcome in those actions every morning. Murakami answers:

> It's just routine. It's kind of boring. It's a routine. But the routine is so important.

I think there are several reasons why the routine is so important. As touched on earlier, performance in any field is often gained through a balance of opposing concepts. Creativity on its own is not enough without control. Too much control, and creativity will be suffocated; too much freedom will mean that nothing is delivered. I also think that the routine means that the "big, heavy door" is opened with far greater ease. We look in depth at habit formation later in the book, and automation often takes the mental load from doing things that are difficult. Murakami's mental processing power is saved for the content of the creative writing ahead rather than the *process* of the creative writing. This has practical takeaways for many areas covered in the SEP model, from decision making to behavioral change and weight management.

Reflecting on Behavior Change

So routine is important, and so are rituals. And rituals ought to serve a purpose. Let us look at another creative person, dancer and choreographer, Twyla Tharp. Author of *The Creative Habit*,[4] Tharp has led a long distinguished career in dance, a field that I know well given that my wife trained as a dancer and choreographer. As we cover in Chapter 6, "MOVE," we can learn much from dancers in terms of their physical strength, and it is also a field characterized by the balance of opposing concepts—between discipline, technique, and structure on one hand, and creative expression on the other. Tharp's creative success is built on such discipline and, of course, daily rituals:

> I begin each day of my life with a ritual: I wake up at 0530, put on my workout clothes, go outside, hail a taxi, and tell the driver to take me to the Pumping Iron gym on 91st Street where I work out for 2 hours.

> The ritual is not the stretching and weight training I put my body through each morning; the ritual is the cab. The moment I tell the driver where to go, I have completed the ritual.

So again, we see the means by which hard things may be made easier. Tharp is looking for the "low bar" by which she may follow through on a tough, daily routine. The ritual empowers the routine, and vice versa. Research into behavior change around exercise has found a similar phenomenon. By placing workout clothes next to the bed at night, people were more likely to follow through on going for that early morning run.

So what are the means by which you can make your hard day easier? Maybe it involves your breakfast routine, or perhaps your commute to work. How can you simplify and automate? Productivity blogs over the years have commented on how to make your life *frictionless*—essentially cutting away non-necessary commotion in your life that uses up precious energy. How much time do you spend queuing, for example? One of the major sources of frustration I experienced on first moving to live in Spain after leaving Scotland was the far inferior customer service in public service institutions. Going to the post office, for example, was a traumatic experience! I then started to analyze how such killers of precious energy could be *designed out* of my life. Online banking and shopping are simple examples of how we may design out or even delegate parts of our life that some people take even further—for example, outsourcing different parts of their jobs to online providers in other countries.

I think rituals are also key because it gives us consistency when things change. The modern-day professional has a life characterized by change. Such a dynamic existence, reacting to crisis and opportunity, often means that each day may be very different from the previous one. Yet just like our biological selves, underlying patterns exist. This is the difference between routine, which can change, and a ritual. Different challenges will often require the same application, energy, and insight, and those specific secrets, the requisite rituals, are the coping mechanisms by which we may attain that consistent high performance in different scenarios.

A final point relates to the importance of change within the habits, routines, and rituals that drive performance. Another successful author, Anne Rice, commenting on the importance of routine, said: *"I certainly have a routine, but the most important thing, when I look back over my career, has been the ability to change routines."* Just like the ambidextrous organization,[5] we ought to know when to operationalize the good things for value maximization yet keep seeking the change and improvement in order to move forward. How do we innovate on a continual basis, adapt to our environment, and ensure that a powerful routine doesn't become a rut? I hope to provide some insight in the following chapters, but for now, reflect on some of the following questions:

- When was the last time you did something for the first time?

- When was the last time you did something, voluntarily, that filled you with fear?

- When was the last time that you changed, proactively and positively?

- When was the last time that you did nothing?

So what became of my Mexican Chihuahuas? There were two key insights that drove the design of the Mexican dog food marketing campaign. First, the target's relationship with the dog, and therefore the product, was indirect. This differed from previous campaigns that focused on the special, and direct, relationship between the dog and the target. In the case of this target, the attitude toward the dog was still loving, but at times, it presented added complexity to an already busy life as a full-time mother. The target's focus was on the joy that the children experienced from owning a dog, as well as what they learned in terms of responsibility. So the emotional trigger for purchase was related to their children and their growth and development. Allied to a very simple piece of information through interviews with veterinary workers regarding the extreme level of dog abandonments throughout Mexico, the resultant campaign was focused on dog "adoption"—sponsoring the company's care of abandoned dogs through product purchase—thereby fitting perfectly with the motherly instincts of the target without adding to her already complex life.

So what are the insights that may improve your own health, well-being, and performance? Or indeed that of your team? The following chapters that comprise the SEP model will give you the practical takeaways as well as the conceptual underpinnings to successfully reengineer your day-to-day activities. But first we'll look a little closer at the new self-management within which day-to-day reengineering resides.

5

The New Self-Management

The unexamined life is not worth living.

—Socrates

In the 1950s, when multinational corporations were experiencing rapid growth and becoming huge profit-making machines, Peter Drucker reminded everyone that, in fact, they were human communities—built on trust and respect for the worker. "The man who invented management"1 took a meandering role to his eventual U.S. home and work as a writer, teacher, and consultant. From his upbringing in Vienna (where at an early age he met Sigmund Freud) to Hamburg and London, where he worked as a journalist and trader, he was later influenced by Joseph Schumpeter, who said, "it is not enough to be remembered for books and theories. One does not make a difference unless it is a difference in people's lives."

After making a difference to thousands of lives around the world and pioneering ideas on decentralization, company culture, and the criticality of the customer—generally how a company manages people—he would later focus on how people manage themselves. He believed that companies were not sufficiently cultivating the careers of their "knowledge workers," and so it was up to them to each "be their own CEOs."2 Believing that the path to true and lasting excellence required deep self-knowledge, which is also necessary for a productive and rewarding career that may last 50 years or more, such self-knowledge was based on several key questions:

- **What are my strengths?** Feedback analysis over a period of at least several months, gained by writing down expected outcomes of a decision with the actual results, is the main method that Drucker advises to identify strengths. Such an approach will also result in the identification of bad habits, and Drucker also highlights the importance of manners, "the lubricating oil of an organization." Incidentally, furthering an awareness of Ancient Chinese philosophy first raised in Chapter 2, "The New Lanark Mills," both habits, as rituals, and manners in the form of etiquette, are at the core of the *Li* part of Confucian thought.

- **How do I work?** Drucker aims to distinguish between those who are readers and listeners in the way they assimilate information and communicate with others. The way we learn, which can be through writing or talking, whether we work well with others or work best alone, and in what type of organization, are all covered. In essence, this concerns the ways in which we perform at our best and so leverages our strengths in the right environment.

- **What are my values?** As well as identifying your own values, an important step is to check alignment of those values with the context in which you operate. Misalignment will result in frustration and poor performance.

- **Where do I belong?** Considering these three questions of values and their alignment, strengths, and the way in which you perform best leads to identifying fit. Achieving the perfect fit within a particular work environment will transform performance according to Drucker.

- **What can I contribute?** This final element recognizes the freedom we have in today's work environment to identify what value we can deliver—project, initiative, or change—as a result of our strengths, method of working, and values. If we advance our self-knowledge to an extent that no one else has the same level of knowledge, then why should we wait on others to tell us what value we can contribute?

Such development of one's self-knowledge allows the fulfillment of Drucker's concept of the twenty-first century knowledge worker.

Indeed, content on belonging, contribution, and values echoes some of Polman's thoughts on the new type of leader, as discussed in Chapter 2. I believe this can be used as a basis to move toward the new self-management necessary for a new generation of sustainable leaders.

What other factors are necessary to consider? We have developed several of these points in the preceding chapters and revisit them in summary form here.

Managing the Physical Self

As previously discussed, de Coubertin developed the Ancient Greek virtue of the whole person, and specifically the role of athletics as a neglected facet of modern society to improve self-governance. As Drucker states, it is commonplace for a career to last more than 50 years, and Drucker himself enjoyed a long and fruitful career. So issues of health and the physical self are absolutely necessary to sustain performance and give the best chances of longevity. An attention to health is not only for health's sake. An attention to causality, as we discuss later, attempts to develop insight into the relationship between health, well-being, and, ultimately, performance. Whole-person learning is required for today's leaders, who are often experts in their field yet can be novices in other key areas, including their health and fitness, which are critical to their sustainable performance. Without sufficient personal mastery in physiological areas as well as the physiological-psychological link, often outside the scope of conventional management development programs, performance is, I believe, unsustainable in the long term.

Although "business athletes" have far longer careers than professional sporting athletes do, we can learn and transfer many elements from the world of sport, both on a basic practical level as well as a deeper conceptual level.

Gaining an Outside-In View

Defining factors of the new self-management as we discuss here can lead us to a deep level of reflection, which on its own can be detrimental if not balanced with someone looking in from the outside. One of the things we can apply from sport is the value of coaching. No matter the skill or experience level of the individual athlete, there is always the need for the coach to offer a dispassionate view on performance and training, providing perspective to what can easily become bias around data or performance in general. Business coaching has gained great momentum in the past several years, and although compromised at times by opportunists with little of the necessary skill set, it is a positive contribution to business performance. Yet the level of coaches who may combine an understanding of sports coaching and, by extension, elements of the physical self into the business domain is lacking. Other areas, such as mentoring, have improved the retention rates and talent development in companies worldwide.

Taking Responsibility for the Self and Society

As discussed in Chapter 2, we are empowered more than ever before. We have the free choice and opportunity to look after our health, decide how we work, and build a new career. Of course, some people may be constrained in their options because of a combination of unfortunate factors, yet I believe society today is one where blaming others for our ills is wide of the mark. We must each act ourselves to address the ills of society. As we established in Chapter 2, and as I hope to develop in the remaining chapters, taking responsibility for the self and changing in small ways may drive a wider level of responsibility to society that affects system level change.

In his *Harvard Business Review* article, "How Will You Measure Your Life?"[3]—his own contribution to the self-management domain—Clayton Christensen states that management is the most noble of professions if practiced well, because "it offers many ways to help others learn and grow, take responsibility and be recognized for achievement, and contribute to the success of a team." Yet many students neglect the human factor in business, of others as well as themselves, through a lack of identifying or at least reflecting on purpose. This talks to us of empathy, a design skill that allows deep connection across the Triple Lens of Sustainability. The willingness to learn from everyone and every experience also helps to build that empathy as well as humility.

Applying Good Thinking Across the Triple Lens

Christensen also urged not to "reserve your best business thinking for your career." The same good practice that we apply so diligently in our careers could form the basis of a better self-management. Christensen talks of applying the right strategy to one's life, yet, as we discussed in Chapter 2 with the efforts of Professor Puett at Harvard and others, the focus of good thinking should not always rest on the analytical, rational, and calculating side. The opportunities afforded by more sophisticated measurement does not mean we increase such a focus. Rather, the data should allow us to experiment and iterate in the same way that designers do. Establishing the cause and effect of small actions in our daily lives, such as a glass of wine with dinner and our resulting sleep quality that night, can be established in a matter of days. Quick iteration and proto-typing is therefore afforded to us all to reengineer our day-to-day lives in a way that has not been possible until now. Essentially, this is *hacking*, which we discuss next.

Good thinking, therefore, combines the abstract curious nature of design thinking with the scientific rigor of causality. However, the danger is that the level of rigor is compromised, both in the quality of data collected as well as the conclusions drawn by the individual in an attempt to identify patterns. We are surrounded by a world of infographics where the presentation of data trumps deeper questions related to research methodology. Yet as business leaders we may be able to apply the knowledge we do have in research and business, as Christensen advocates, to ensure that quality of thought is applied to the self. He believes that theories of causation, extrapolated in business problems, could be applied to happiness, believing the causal mechanism to be the same although recognizing that how it manifests itself can be different.

Hacking Habits

When combined with the data we collect through more sophisticated tracking, as discussed later, this balanced thinking allows us to change, reengineer, or "hack" our habits. Hacking is a term that came from the world of computer programming and is still used primarily within the technology world, as well as being extended to start-up companies and the health and habits domain. For me, hacking has three distinguishing features. First, it is an unconventional means of solving a problem that often challenges conventional wisdom. It is not necessarily a shortcut (although it can be), but it always involves some creative means of addressing the issue. Second, and related to this unconventional approach, is that it includes some degree of limited resource or constraint, such as doing the same with less, for instance, in a company process that suffers from budget cuts. Such an instruction has been commonplace in company austerity measures the past few years and can result in employees stretching themselves to conceive new creative solutions. This logic is at the core of lean start-up methodology, which forces established companies to find solutions with constrained resources similar to that of a new company. The third aspect of hacking is that it involves some iterative loop. Fast cycle time is necessary to experiment and learn from failure. This iterative exploration, together with an unconventional and creative approach to problem solving that succeeds in spite of constraints, is hacking and can be characterized as a design-based approach, as we discussed in Chapter 3, "Design Your Life."

When we apply such an approach to ourselves and our own daily lives, there is an opportunity to identify and improve the key habits, often the small actions, that have a large impact on our health, well-being, and performance. I apply all the content of the SEP program on myself and try to find out what works for me. I don't always get it right. Indeed, I never get it right first time. I gain deeper insight only after a period of experimentation where a balance between action and reflection is the core process.

More Sophisticated Tracking

Tracking was not alien to Drucker's approach to self-management. Indeed, returning to the basics of reflecting on practice—for example, writing in a journal over a period of time, as advocated by Drucker to identify strengths—is a greatly positive practice in a world of complex technology and lack of reflection. Yet the opportunities provided by modern technology, from various apps to big data sets, cannot be ignored. Previously invisible parts of our lives, or at best hard-to-measure parts, such as sleep, the calories we consume or burn, and the moves we make, are accessible measures for everyone and have the potential to offer deep insight into work performance as well as health and well-being. More sophisticated tracking also allows us a clearer view on where we are allocating our resources, something that Christensen calls for. Many of us are often drawn toward work because that offers a clear view of progress—a new customer, product, or presentation—yet progress in other areas of our life has traditionally been less tangible and more difficult to measure.

The anticipated 2015 launch of the Apple iWatch may at last bring wearable technology to the masses. This increased sophistication of tracking and measurement technology has led us to the age of the Quantified Self and is the lubricating oil of the new self-management.

From the Managed Self to the Quantified Self

For Socrates, the threat of exile from Greek society and the loss of involvement in the deeper reflection and examination of life filled him with such dread that he believed life to be unworthy of continuing. It is perhaps interesting (though certainly frivolous) to reflect on what he would make of the myriad opportunities to examine one's life through today's measurement technology.

We are surrounded by measurement. Ever since enlightenment philosophers developed theories of human progress, we have looked to measure the world around us. Adam Smith looked at how wealth could be increased on a national level through improvements in productivity, and Robert Owen looked to balance this thirst for increased productivity with progress on a true human level. Drucker also said, *"you can't manage what you can't measure."* Yet this belief is rarely applied to the field of personal mastery that became his focus in later years. The result is a whole menagerie of Key Performance Indicators (KPIs) and metrics—customer churn, employee turnover, operational capacity, EBITDA (that is, earnings before interest, taxes, depreciation, and amortization), and countless others—in an attempt to increase company competitiveness.

Yet what happens to the often invisible parts of our own executive reality that affect performance? Our mobility? The calories we consume and burn? The quality of sleep during a demanding project? We have looked at measuring and progressing along all of these and many more in the SEP program since 2007. The Ancient Greeks had two concepts of time: *Kronos*, the conventional and contemporary focus that we measure in seconds, minutes, and hours, but also *Kairos*, which was the experience of that time. So perhaps rather than just an hour for lunch, we should measure the experience of that lunch for better health, well-being, and performance. Instead of six hours of sleep, an efficient sleep with sufficient deep sleep and no disruptions may help us to better cope with that 14-hour day ahead.

The Quantified Self movement has grown rapidly in the past few years, building on these areas, using ever more sophisticated and accessible technology, marked by the rapid growth of smartphone apps that measure different areas of our lives. Digital health is a growing market, and I believe we can exploit this movement for professional performance. Individuals are empowered, whether it be downloading an app, buying a pedometer, or investing in a more expensive accelerometer-based wristband. A whole range of personal data can be generated, yet that doesn't mean we are automatically better managing ourselves or indeed progressing; that data and measurement process must be managed correctly. Challenges also exist, including the accessibility and ease of use of technology and wearable computing in general, the ethics of use, and the problems associated with the sheer quantity of data.

Elite sport has long measured the performance of athletes as a means of improving performance, from heart rate during and after training sessions, to body fat and oxygen consumption. Medical science has also used a variety of measures in the health domain, with Michael and Juliette McGannon[4] bringing such measures to the executive context, including cholesterol and urine and blood acidity, principally through management development programs at INSEAD. The line between health practitioner, elite coach, and curious individual is also being blurred. Technology such as the Zeo sleep monitor, which was the world's first home EEG (electroencephalography) monitor, was developed in response to a growing call from the curious individual yet was also used by elite sports teams, including the U.S. Olympic cycling team in the lead up to the London 2012 games.

However, the ethics of this Quantified Self data must be treated with care. GPS locations of where people run, heart rate profiles, and body-fat percentages are private information that flood the public domain, and which could be used for Machiavellian purposes by certain parties. It may be advisable to retain balance in measurement. We can use those tools, which make sense to improve the visibility and management of certain areas of executive life, especially as a means of moving toward specific objectives, while treating with care the data that is produced. Who indeed, owns the data collected on an organizational level? Is it the employer who, for example, supplies its workforce with an accelerometer to track movement and incentivize health as part of gamification, or is it the individual?

Measurement need not be complex. Progress can be gauged by the simplest means, with a tape measure as one of the most effective tools for weight-management purposes, and a $10 step counter able to effectively measure mobility as well as raise awareness of the mobility choices during the day. I recognized the importance of measurement in my own athletic career from an early age. Although fascinated by my Polar Coach Heart Rate Monitor in the 1990s, on reflection the most important tool at my disposal was my training diary. And that is true of athletes at all levels. Having a diary where one can reflect, add notes on physical and mental states, the weather, opponents, and of course the quantitative stuff—miles, seconds, centimeters—is the data on which progress and motivation is based. This is why tracking can be so powerful. Progress is fuel. It is the energy for continuing with practice.

Transferring this to the professional domain, a training diary is recommended, or perhaps it is just called an executive journal. Studies have shown that keeping a journal has major mental health benefits for the modern day professional. It allows us to be more mindful and offers a pause (normally at the end of the day) to reflect, be grateful, and think about where we've been and where we're going. I've found such a practice absolutely critical to both my athletic and business development; whether it's writing one word or one page, opening that journal at the end of the day has enormous benefits.

The Sustaining Executive Performance (SEP) Model

Within the context of the Quantified Self and integrating the new factors of self-management, I developed the SEP model for management development. Tracing core development back to 2007, I have had the fortune of building a client base that has allowed me access to thousands of leading managers worldwide. In addition to my own company clients, I teach and train managers through their business school attendance and have taught more than 200 classes in the past four years at four of the leading schools worldwide—IESE, IMD, CEIBS, and IE.

SEP is a design-based framework that allows twenty-first century professionals to better manage themselves. Personal mastery is developed in health, well-being, and performance, and is guided along the lines of the Quantified Self where an understanding of personal data, causality, and experimentation is encouraged. In the same way that Robert Owen considered the basic human needs of his workforce in the New Lanark Mills, I consider the basic human needs, starting from the physical self, of the professional in a demanding business environment.

SEP has five elements: MOVE, RECOVER, FOCUS, FUEL, and TRAIN, each with a dedicated chapter in the next part of the book. Instruction is delivered in both class and field settings, with the necessary in-class theory and discussion acting as a basis for action, experimentation, and measurement in the field. In the same way that work doesn't happen only in the office—it's not about being chained to the desk anymore—learning and development not only happens inside the classroom. It has been said that design cannot be passively learned, and the aim is to maintain an active and experiential approach that nevertheless maintains the professional conduct necessary at the core of management practice. A design approach is also maintained in the iterative loop of awareness-legitimacy-action. Taking into account the low level of exposure to SEP elements, as well as various misconceptions of its aims and validity for management education, we consider the steps of awareness and legitimacy critical for moving to action (see Figure 5.1). With action, mostly within the field of practice, subsequent awareness and legitimacy is increased.

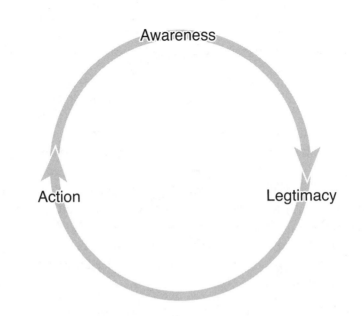

Figure 5.1 The iterative SEP action model

Toward the Sustainable Leader

Like the three levels—individual, organizational, and societal—of the Triple Lens of Sustainability, there are three levels, or layers, built up during the SEP program. First, in *Human Being*, we remind professionals that they have a body and consider basic human needs—primarily mobility and recovery—that are often compromised in the workplace. We also demonstrate by making the link to business that such needs are necessary not only for health but for increased, and sustained, performance. Next, in *Business Athlete*, we consider the energy requirements necessary in a demanding career, using primarily the lens of elite sport to build positive practice that fits with business. Finally, in *Sustainable Leader*, the end of the journey and overall objective of the program, we integrate all concepts at the individual level to consider how change may occur across the Triple Lens, reflecting on and affecting change at the organizational and societal levels. The link may be both literal with respect to personal habits and leadership of teams, as well as conceptual in the holistic, long-term mind-set that influences a more responsible view of business. We therefore move from a position of *self-awareness* to *social-awareness*, and from the *taskwork* to the *teamwork*—on a work, family, and community level.

This chapter concludes Part 1 of *Sustaining Executive Performance*. With the building blocks now in place, we move on to the content of the SEP model (Part 2), a mostly individual-level focus on change for improved health, well-being, and performance that will be interspersed with Part 3 on the practical and conceptual links of such content to the macro level. The wider significance of the SEP elements within Part 3, I hope, will clearly show the logic of continued action and help lock in change at the individual level. We also switch between a mostly pre-scriptive treatment of individual change in Part 2, offering practical takeaways, to a more descriptive narrative on societal factors to affect a change in mind-set in Part 3.

Content is derived from leading research, contemporary trends, and experiences—with elite athletes and also elite business professionals. After teaching thousands of business professionals over the years, I hope to offer insight into what works. The good news is that the knowledge gained from elite athletes is accessible and within the reach of us all, irrespective of previous exposure to sport, the physical self, or health and fitness in general.

Socrates, Aristotle, Plato, and the rest would reflect on the big questions of their *examined life* in the gymnasium. We are now in the new age of self-management, which allows us to examine ever deeper the small changes and their impacts on our day-to-day life. As we begin Parts 2 and 3 of *Sustaining Executive Performance* and a reflection toward becoming a Sustainable Leader, what is the present state of that day-to-day—your energy, stress, satisfaction, performance, and happiness? Let's examine that present state and aim to transform it through simple change and the new self-management.

6

MOVE

When I see someone at their desk all day, it's suspicious how they pretend to work.

—Tom Kelley

We were born to move. Scientists have found that our ancestors moved up to 12 miles per day. Every day. Why? It is perhaps fairly obvious on reflection that they moved to survive, either to hunt for food or escape from predators. I'm not sure what would be the worse ending from not moving—starving to death or being eaten alive by a sabre toothed tiger!

So movement is in our DNA. It is part of the survival imperative, yet what happens today is that we sit. All day. Every day. This has garnered much attention in the medical profession in recent years; doctors call the phenomena *sitting disease. The Washington Post* brought much of this research together in an alarming graphic in 2014[1] highlighting the effects of excessive sitting time on muscle degeneration, poor circulation, and excessive insulin production, which may result in different cancers.

So given that the modern professional workplace is characterized by a distinct lack of movement, having an office job becomes one of the most dangerous professions we may pursue! *Harvard Business Review* blog picked up on this at the beginning of 2013 with the post "Sitting Is the Smoking of Our Generation."[2] The focus here is our lack of awareness of the dangers of a sedentary lifestyle in today's society, just like our lack of awareness of the dangers of tobacco 50–60 years ago. The rapid changes we have experienced as a society in terms of movement and mobility are traced in the following chapter. It is always surprising to find newspaper advertisements from the 1950s in which medical practitioners would support the sale of well-known cigarette brands. I'm sure the advice for coping with the pressures of the workplace would be much different today, because we have long known that smoking tobacco is not a wise choice for relaxing and combating stress. Yet we cannot afford any smugness. What may seem obvious with the benefit of hindsight often takes time to emerge. How might the "second-nature" practices of future generations look? Especially considering that some studies have shown sitting disease to be so severe that it has the same effects on life expectancy as smoking.[3]

The good news is that dramatic changes to one's life are not required. We need not convert ourselves into marathon runners. Australian researchers[4] measured the movement of office workers and then carried out a series of health checks related to their cardiovascular (heart) health, weight, and related measures. What they found was that workers who moved just a little bit more, even just a minute every hour to hour and a half, were at significantly reduced risk of health problems associated with heart disease and being overweight. So the small things can make a big difference over time. Again, sitting disease can be so powerful that even runners can be in danger of it.[5] Even the most serious runners may run only 2 to 3 hours per day, yet the day has 24 hours and running this amount often means minimizing movement during the remainder of the day. So the key is continual movement throughout the day.

The First Law of SEP

Yet because we sit all day doesn't mean we don't get tired at the end of it. The great temptation when we arrive home is to remain static, often converting ourselves into true "couch potatoes," and so the sedentary lifestyle of the office environment becomes a vicious circle. Here is where I want to share the First Law of SEP:

When we move, we create energy.

A common misconception is that physical movement spends energy. We often say or hear, "I'm tired, I need to sit down," or "I'm tired,

I need a nap." At times this may be the case, but within the context of the modern professional workplace, I would suggest that when you are tired, stand up. When you are tired, go for a walk, get outside, get some air. Because we were born to move, because movement is part of our survival imperative, when we move, we generate energy. And the path to making the change can be straightforward. The commonsense benefits for the whole self of physical movement may be best illustrated by a quote from David Livingstone, the nineteenth-century missionary and explorer:[6]

> Brisk exercise imparts elasticity to the muscles, fresh and healthy blood circulates through the brain, the mind works well, the eye is clear, the step is firm, and a day's exertion always makes the evening's repose thoroughly enjoyable.

Contemporary research—mostly within the domain of healthy aging, the battle against cognitive disease, and learning efficacy for children—seems to advance along three principal areas of brain benefit from physical movement:[7, 8, 9] first, the oxygen advantage provided to the brain, providing extra energy through the transportation of blood (which also helps with repair functions); second, the activation of the brain in terms of neuron development associated with exercise; and third, the release of hormones that help growth. The mechanisms that mediate the benefits of exercise at the cerebral level are associated with changes of neurotransmitters and neurotrophic factors. All of them contribute to improved cognitive performance and counteract the deleterious effects of the aging process in the brain. A further interesting benefit related to healthy ageing is the concept of "cognitive reserve,"[10] which refers to the protective effects against dementia and other brain disorders in older people who maintained higher levels of activity throughout their lives.

Although the context for brain-body research has rarely focused on executive performance, such research lines clearly show much promise for the business professional in order to sustain performance during a long, happy, and healthy career. We now turn our attention to the workplace context and, especially, the clear business benefits of moving more.

Escaping Sedentary Traps in the Workplace

So what changes could we make in the workplace to move more? Think first about the culture of work and the habits that make up your day. How do you communicate with your colleagues? Why do we email or phone someone who is on the other side of the room? Or separated by a couple of floors? Putting aside for one moment the stress-inducing volume of email that we receive (which we cover in Chapter 10, "Focus"), why don't we simply get up from our desk and go to see that person? Of course, documents may need to be shared, but often we need to communicate clear messages, and a message is often better delivered face to face—with no ambiguity and no misunderstandings.

I came to understand the criticality of face-to-face communication in my doctoral research on virtual teams, design, and creativity.[11] Teams have been conceived as distributed if separated by as little as 50 feet.[12] We are often changed by our built environment in ways we fail to recognize immediately, which nonetheless offers opportunities to design an environment for positive behavior. Robert Kraut, a social psychologist at Carnegie-Mellon, studied proximity and communication patterns as far back as 1990[13] leading to an awareness of the value of accidental encounters—where people may be indulging in general chit-chat that could lead to discovering valuable information, such as a project from another function with similar features to their own, a client request, or available technology. This became known as the "watercooler effect," and companies then began to design spaces to encourage such encounters that could lead to these unexpected synergies. Today, such a dynamic results in many companies, regardless of their technology capability or prowess, such as Google, actively discouraging remote and telecommuting work.[14] By having more of their talent physically collocated, they are convinced of more opportunities for high-quality creative work.

Delivering a message face to face may run the risk of not finding the other person at his or her desk. You can, of course, call ahead, although the temptation is that you convey the full message via phone. However, the likelihood is that the person is part of the same sedentary sitting trap that affects most of us, and you'll find your contact there. Regardless of your destination, the accidental encounters along the way may provide you with valuable insight. I think this is the dynamic nature of work today—especially creative work—which builds on the Tom Kelley quote that opens this chapter. Taking time away from your chair and having greater visibility in the workplace also helps builds personal relationships, and senior staff may benefit from spending more time using the Management By Walking Around (MBWA) method—an accepted management method, principally in the context of quality, where managers raise their awareness of the front line of operations through unstructured wandering.

So to "beware the chair" offers us many more benefits than simply combating sitting disease. But what other changes could we implement? How about just standing more? For example, during simple short tasks, as inferred by the 2012 *New York Times* article, "Stand Up While You Read This!"[15] Yet standing for longer periods may work also. Ernest Hemingway (at least when he was sober!) wrote all his books while standing up, so why do we have sitting desks anyway?

Standing desks have come to prominence in the past couple of years, with sophisticated solutions provided by major office furniture companies such as Steelcase and others, which have motor control to be able to switch between seated and standing positions. Yet "hacked" versions can be done for free, by simply propping a laptop or computer on several stacks of paper. This is one of the major changes I have integrated into my home office: I found an inexpensive architect-style desk from Ikea and raised it to its maximum height, which was still a little low, so I propped my *Oxford English Dictionary* underneath my keyboard and also raised the monitor and mouse in a similar fashion. I found my own productivity and task attention to improve greatly. It also improved my posture—back and core strength, critical areas for a busy professional that we cover here and in later chapters. We also burn more calories standing—an extra 50 per hour, according to researchers at the University of Chester[16]—the equivalent of running 10 marathons a year, by standing 3 to 4 hours per day at work. Another potential advantage is less distracted time from co-workers. If colleagues have a habit of approaching your desk or entering your office and taking a seat when you want to continue with focused work, a standing desk may help to cut the time they distract you. I think it's always good to have a seating option for you to read or meet people in a relaxed fashion. If you don't invite your guests to take a seat, you may find they begin to get "twitchy" by remaining standing, and so leave you alone to work much sooner!

To Hemingway, add Abraham Lincoln, Donald Rumsfeld, and William Lever as exponents of standing while working. As we covered in the previous chapter, however, it is critical to maintain a level of awareness of any new practice, measuring, reflecting, and adjusting. At the beginning of my own standing working practice, I began with such gusto that after several months of standing for several hours a day, I began to develop a heel compression injury. This may or may not happen to you—I was training for a marathon around the same time, and so my running habits meant my heel wasn't getting sufficient recovery. The lesson was obvious for me—have a clear view on the effects of any change and implement that change step by step. Standing for an hour or two with sitting periods in between is probably better than standing all day, at least at the outset. Being on our feet all day may not be the best—ask any waiter or bar staff!

A strong business case exists for challenging the sedentary culture of the workplace, and the biggest potential benefit of them all is changing meetings. Next, I'll share one of my experiences of changing meetings, and culture, in small business.

Hydrafit

Hydrafit Subsea was a successful small company in the energy capital of Scotland, Aberdeen. I had started consulting for them after meeting the senior manager during one of my cycle tours in Girona in 2005. Suffering up one of the cols (mountain passes) used by Tour de France riders as part of their winter training, our conversation had turned to small business strategy and innovation. The company had experienced rapid growth and was fantastically successful on a turnover and profit level, but was not without its stresses and strains. Known for hard work and reliability, it was a trusted partner to some of the oil majors and manufacturers, such as BP, Chevron, and Vetco Gray.

The energy of the three men who comprised the senior team was impressive, yet the health of the senior manager started to suffer. A back operation to address a disc hernia was only the beginning, and his increasing waistline mixed with a pining for former athletic prowess complicated our personal coaching and wider organizational change. I focused first on the simple matter of bottlenecks. Small and medium-sized enterprises (SMEs) with about 50 people or fewer can function well with a single line of command to the manager at the top. And so it was in this case; a very paternalistic, small company driven—yet also limited—by one man. Meetings were the order of the day, every day, all day—either with the other two managers, wider company staff, or clients. They were often poorly focused, with no agenda and beset by distractions of the senior manager, who was thinking on several matters at once. Decision making and action started to slow in the company, yet the answer to a more lean, focused operation was next door in the workshop. The engineers who serviced the subsea equipment would hold frequent "toolbox talks" during the day; the talks were short, focused, actionable, and, crucially, standing. Lean manufacturing principles were practiced in the workshop environment, and this had extended to the communication between the engineers, meeting for a maximum of 10 minutes to discuss the high-priority jobs "on the floor" and raising potential problems to their successful completion. So why didn't we practice those same lean principles across the road in the management space? Standing meetings were then implemented in the office space, along with several other Golden Rules of having meetings, with copies of the following ten steps to better meetings posted around the company:

1. Don't call a meeting unless you have to. Make sure—really sure—that the meeting is needed.

2. Invite only those people who will get something out of the meeting. Only have people come if they are going to contribute and/or get something out of the meeting.

3. Cancel your meeting if you think you no longer need to have it or if everyone is not prepared. Never have a meeting just for the sake of having it.

4. Have a leader. Every meeting should have a leader who can hold everyone involved accountable to keeping things on track.

5. Announce at the beginning how long the meeting is going to last. Set a time limit. Then think about cutting it in half. Put a clock in plain view. If you have droners at your meetings, establish a time limit for how long any one person can talk.

6. Maintain a zero-tolerance policy toward latecomers. Punish them in some good-natured way. Charge them money; make them serve the coffee.

7. Set a crystal-clear agenda, and stick to it. If other issues come up, make a note of them, and then get back to the agenda.

8. Ban toys. No BlackBerries, iPods, laptops, or cell phones.

9. Schedule the meeting for first thing in the morning when people are more alert and still intending to get something done that day.

10. Try holding meetings standing up. Standing meetings are shorter than sitting meetings!

It was a simple change that had a good impact on a coherent company culture as well as those bottlenecks. Those back disc problems had also been a symptom of the increasing amount of sitting time in the manager's life, from his early morning 40-minute commute to work, followed by meetings all day long, and a "sofa crash" at night, his back had becoming increasingly weaker over a period of time. Standing more, in addition to other back and core-strengthening exercises that we implemented, helped to strengthen the back again. In the Hydrafit case, health, well-being, and performance from a small change, and also business coaching of the senior manager, helped to drive organizational change and culture.

Standing meetings are a quick and easy win in a business age where meetings represent more than one-third of an executive's weekly time—almost 20 hours.[17] What percentage of that time is wasted on people playing with their electronic toys, arriving late and leaving early, or simply not listening to what is going on? The Agile Programming movement in the United States has been characterized by a wave of standing meetings,[18] which helps cut down on inefficient wasted time, making meetings more focused and people more *mindful* (mindfulness is a core topic of discussion in Chapter 10). People report on the current status of their job, and what they are doing that day, before moving on to the next person.

Walking meetings could be viewed as a natural progression in this line of thought—another simple physical action with many repercussions on the performance, as well as health and well-being levels. Steve Jobs was a well-known advocate of the walking meeting, believing in the value of getting to know someone on a walk and being able to drill down on a tough problem. Why indeed do we have the orthodoxy of a meeting where we often sit across from one another at a desk? It's quite an adversarial position to begin with. I've suggested walking meetings for several years now, and they tend to go well! Whether that comes from the fact that both people have the same view, or because they are simply happy to be away from their desks, I'm not sure, but they do work. Of course, there are limitations; with more than two people, they can be tricky (you don't want to look like the cast of *Reservoir Dogs!*) or where reference to key data is required, yet management is often about critical, intimate conversations that occur frequently between pairs of people. The nuance of those critical conversations often makes the difference. Perhaps you've thought of the sensitivity of a conversation you needed to have and so have taken it out of your own office to counter any "power-play" dynamics. Maybe you've suggested having coffee to have an informal chat or a breakfast or lunch meeting to take the pressure off. Next time, make a suggestion to go for a walk and see what happens.

Another common practice is to take a conference call and go for a walk—at last fulfilling the potential of the "mobile" phone in the workplace! Sometimes our focus is so intently placed on the conversation that we are not even aware, or mindful, of the movement and exercise, or even the route we have taken. Attention is therefore placed on the mental activity at the expense of the physical. The physical movement, fresh air, and associated blood and oxygen movement can have a powerful impact on our thinking process along with our well-being. For many years, we have believed in the power of mobility for the thought process, and more generally the performance of the brain, and only now are we beginning to understand so much more on a scientific level to back up these long-held anecdotal beliefs.

Brain imaging scans allow us to compare the brain activation that results from mobility as compared to sitting at our desk. Psychophysiologist Dr. Charles Hillman has shown that we essentially "switch ourselves on" by moving. Much of his work has been with schoolchildren in an attempt to correlate fitness with academic performance, and he has found that better fitness equals better attention and better results.[19] Yet quality thinking, so often at a premium within a busy, distracted workplace, can also be supported. In the *Harvard Business Review* blog, Dan Pallotta talked of going for a walk but not calling it a break,[20] citing his own preparation for an important assignment that required hard focus, which progressed much more rapidly during the process of walking. A recent Stanford study[21] also found that walking improved creativity by an average of 60% as compared to sitting. For executive health, well-being and performance walking isn't quite a panacea, but I think it's as close as one can get. As twentieth-century historian George Macaulay Trevelyan said, "I have two doctors, my right leg, and my left."

Designing Our Environment for Health, Well-Being, and Performance

We can, of course, push back against a non-optimum workplace through simple practices, yet we may also design our workspace to better support health, well-being, and performance. Another Stanford piece of research, linked to the Design School, looked at different types of sitting and how this affected a common creativity method, that of brainstorming. Specifically, they found that the design of the chair affected peoples' behavior regarding their criticism of other ideas.[22] One of the key rules of brainstorming is that we build on the ideas of others, even the wild and/or unrealistic ones, because we may construct a point of departure on which a more feasible, innovative idea may result. The researchers found that when people were sitting on comfortable sofa-type chairs, resting back, they would criticize the ideas of others and the sessions wouldn't go so well. By replacing these comfortable chairs with more uncomfortable stools with people perched on edge, they tended to support more ideas, and the brainstorming would improve. Along similar lines, the link between posture and defensiveness has been investigated by researchers at the Olin Business School.[23] Comparing the work of groups having a table and chairs compared to having no chairs, they found those who remained standing were less territorial, more collaborative, and more excited about their work. So, simple body posture was shown to affect the quality and output of teamwork.

Treadmill desks have also gained attention in recent years within the context of sedentary dangers and workplace redesign. My own view is that they could be an option depending on the context of work—for example, in call centers where people are required to be at their own workstation responding to external clients 100% of their time. I don't think they should constitute the go-to option on a general level. Where is the credibility for managers conducting an indoor walking treadmill meeting? There are simple means of improving health, well-being, and performance, in MOVE, and the remaining SEP elements, in which your professional conduct is maintained, even improved. Treadmill desks, in my view, don't always fit within that professional conduct. Make movement a more natural, accidental concept and build a dynamic culture where we are not chained to our desk.

The topic of stretching is also considered within a reflection on workplace movement and professional conduct. Movement in terms of walking, and the number of steps we take in a day, is a primary consideration together with the time we spend sitting. Thinking about stretching and posture, particularly during seated periods in the workplace, is also important. Yet this doesn't mean we ought to start an aerobic session in the office! Subtle, small body movements and good practice can make a big difference. I believe the world of dance to offer the best lessons. As I mentioned in Chapter 4, "Day-to-Day Reengineering,", my wife trained as a dancer, and I've spent a lot of time with dancers over the years. Putting aside their strength for a moment (ballet dancers, for example, are arguably the strongest athletes in the world), I believe there to be two main lifelong takeaways of dance training. The first is related to discipline, respect, and good manners, and the second to posture. Dancers know how to carry themselves, how to stand tall, how to sit, and when and how to stretch. Sample stretches are available on the book website at mysep.net. For example, moving one's head from side to side and up and down can help to alleviate tension. Our heads weigh up to 11 pounds (5 kg), and if we don't move it all day, tension can build in the neck, shoulders, and elsewhere. Rolling the shoulders or extending the arms backward are simple movements that can provide benefit during a long day and need not draw attention in an open workspace environment. Finding a private space to conduct more of the floor exercises to help back pain and core strength is a worthwhile pursuit that only requires 5 minutes practice a day to gain real value.

The wider context and implications of our built environment are discussed in the next chapter, but first we'll consider another simple aspect on the architectural level—stair use. Volkswagen created a popular series of "fun theory" video shorts a few years ago; one of those was piano stairs, where they built a piano on a set of subway stairs in Stockholm, which resulted in a 66% increase in people taking the stairs instead of the escalator. This case highlights the barriers and attitude toward movement in society and the fact that *we've engineered movement out of our lives*. We've been too clever, designing machines that allow us to minimize movement, to the detriment of our health and, ultimately, performance.

Subway stairs are a common example in research related to improving citizen health, and building design may be another. Why should the elevator be the first thing we see when entering a building instead of the staircase? Even finding the staircase in many modern-day buildings, and especially hotels (think of your business travels), is a tough task. An opportunity for movement, and the associated benefits of heart health and weight management, is missed, and we waste time waiting. Even using the stairs is not permitted in certain companies that are afraid of accidents in the stairway—this is "health and safety" with a narrow, short-term view! Lack of movement in society can also be linked to advancement, as we discuss in the following chapter. With increased status in an organization, we often enjoy the services of a chauffeur or are given a reserved parking space. Again, challenge conventional orthodoxy and do yourself a favor by parking in the spot farthest away from the entrance. This extra daily movement will be beneficial, especially if you have sedentary traps in other areas of your life.

So we have engineered movement out of our lives because we view it as an inconvenience. Yet I hope to have made the case so far in this chapter that it is, rather, an opportunity—an opportunity for improving health, well-being, and performance. Always taking the stairs may be considered trite and insignificant, but it can have a large impact on weight management. It may also create an important mental break, for example, in a busy day going from meeting to meeting where stress levels increase during the email focused elevator rides that serve as the only break between those meetings. We look in detail at habit-forming and behavior change in Chapter 16, "Leading Change in the Triple Lens of Sustainability," and even the simple change of taking the stairs can be a challenge—made easier by taking the right approach.

So look for opportunities to move more in a busy professional life, understanding that *movement creates energy*, even when those opportunities are not entirely obvious. Let me give you an example:

I teach three to four times a year in China, and given that I live in Barcelona, it's a long trip. I normally have a stopover in Dubai. Flying from Barcelona to Dubai takes around seven hours, after which I have a short two-hour layover before flying the nine hours or so to Shanghai. Of course, during the flights, I'm mostly immobile. I'm seated or sleeping, and I can't move so much. What I've started to do the past few years during that two-hour layover in Dubai is look for opportunities to move. Even on those flat "moving sidewalks" and escalators, I keep moving, which often requires gently nudging aside half-asleep travelers. During those two hours, I walk, and I walk. I take advantage of any opportunity to move during that time. I've felt my energy increase and also make my body truly tired for the next flight, on which I attempt to sleep. When I get to my destination, I've found my jet lag to be greatly decreased. Let's think about jet lag: on a layover, people often rush to find an opportunity to sit down or sleep—yet we've just been sitting or sleeping for hours during the previous flight, and will do so again on the next one. Or we may have a desire to eat and drink—yet we've just been eating and drinking for several hours on the preceding flight, and will do so again. We get to our destination and say, "Jet lag's killing me!" This isn't jet lag, it's a hangover!

There will always be a degree of jet lag due to a misalignment of our circadian rhythm (we discuss this and other tips for minimizing jet lag in the next SEP element, RECOVER, in Chapter 8), but we can impact greatly on its effects through small changes—hydrating well, paying attention to food and drink, and most of all, moving at every opportunity.

In addition to the wider barriers to movement in our society, the Volkswagen Fun Theory video also shows a possible means by which we can get people to change. In effect, the Piano Stairs acted as a nudge—a gentle push to make people change their behavior. The 66% more people who took the stairs were most likely unaware that they were doing so, their attention instead taken with the fun of the piano simulation. Yet such a simple practice may have become a habit in the long run. There are different ways of designing environments to nudge people toward different behavior. A UK government department is nicknamed the "nudge" department, given its focus on peoples' behavior related to environmental recycling and other areas of government interest. I have tried to create similar nudges to that of the Piano Stairs, in subtler, lower budget ways through signage, which again challenges conventional orthodoxy (see Figure 6.1). Why should we wait for an emergency before taking the stairs? It helps to put a question mark on long-held practices from time to time.

Figure 6.1 Workplace staircase nudge by The LAB (Leadership Academy of Barcelona)

It's worth repeating. Taking the stairs whenever possible, often viewed as a trite, insignificant action, may have a powerful impact on your life.

Top Ten Takeaways: MOVE

1. Movement is part of our DNA. Our ancestors moved to survive.

2. Beware the chair. Our current society is characterized by a lack of movement and excessive sitting time, which is putting in peril our survival.

3. Movement creates energy, in the oxygen-rich blood that is transported through the body and brain, activating neurons and releasing hormones conducive to better cognitive performance.

4. Get away from your desk for more direct communication and the accidental encounters that drive innovation.

5. Stand for longer during individual work, to improve focus, productivity, and core strength.

6. Conduct standing meetings for improved focus, more collaborative teamwork, and less wasted time.

7. Conduct walking meetings to build relationships and cover sensitive subjects.

8. Go for a walk to tackle tough problems and advance quality work.

9. Maintain your professional conduct in change practices to allow the best chances of changing the company culture.

10. Push back against societal norms that look to minimize movement. Stand out from the crowd and thereby *nudge* others to follow your lead.

Measurement, as we traced fully in the previous chapter, can be another powerful nudge. So what can you measure for movement? What changes will you attempt to implement? And do you have a clear view on the effects of those changes? Scientists found that our ancestors moved up to 12 miles per day (incidentally, the same distance that Jagger moves in one concert!). We may not have to move that distance to find food or escape from predators, but finding out the distance—and practices that form the basis of that distance—for your own health, well-being, and performance imperative can lead to life transformation.

7

On the Changing Patterns of Mobility Worldwide

I'd rather cry in the back of a BMW than smile on a bicycle.

—Ma Nuo

Accusations of performance-enhancing drugs, riots at an overcrowded Madison Square Garden to watch sports celebrities do battle, professional gambling on a massive scale, and dirty tricks campaigns. Welcome to the 1870s and the world of competitive walking. Pedestrianism was the world's first popular spectator sport where athletes would often walk distances of up to 500 miles and more around loops of a dirt track in front of sold-out arenas. And such sporting fervor can be traced to one man.

In 1796, at the age of 16, Robert Barclay Allardice won his first competition against a "London gentleman" walking 6 miles in an hour for 100 guineas.[1] His father, a Member of Parliament, thought nothing of walking the 500 miles from the family home in Stonehaven to London. His son would go on to accomplish a feat that would capture the attention of a nation: walking 1,000 miles in 1,000 hours for 1,000 guineas. A mile walked every hour, day and night, for almost six weeks. With no more than 40 minutes uninterrupted sleep during all that time, he would start at 10 minutes to the hour, and walking briskly, he could finish before the hour struck, before continuing for a further mile in the first 10 minutes of the next hour.[2] The total amount of side bets was astronomical, some $60M at today's prices, and rivals would shoot out the gas lamps that Barclay had installed on the Newmarket Heath track where he carried out the bet. Barclay, a soldier and huge man, nevertheless carried two pistols with him at all times and also counted on the services of bodyguard Big John Gully, a prize fighter who would beat him with a stick if he didn't wake up for the next two-mile stint. The Celebrated Captain Barclay. A name well deserved.

Nowadays, walking 1 mile, never mind 1,000, is out of the ordinary. Changing patterns in mobility have had profound effects on human health and society the past 50 years. Whether that is actual physical human movement, motorized transport, or even the transport associated with our food system, macro-level changes will continue to offer critical risks and opportunities into the future. As we saw in the previous chapter, we were born to move, or let's say *designed* to move. Yet we have designed and constructed a modern world in which that movement is harder than ever. *The irony is that we're more mobile than ever, but never have we actually moved less.* The repercussions for this are manifold and damaging—and we discuss them here and in future chapters, particularly Chapters 12, "Fuel," and 13, "On the Systematic Change Required in the Global Food System," on the micro and macro treatment of how we feed ourselves.

This is the first chapter in Part 3, which looks at the wider consequences of individual action—in this case, the SEP element of MOVE. With the integrated placement of Parts 2 and 3, I hope to further legitimize the individual action suggested in each part of the SEP model—to recognize that small changes can have big impacts on our own health, well-being, and performance—but also *beyond ourselves* to the organizational and societal levels.

For mobility, the message is getting through about the peril we are in. We cover several areas of policy and urban design through the course of the chapter, and a concrete example of a current awareness-raising campaign comes from the White House. Michelle Obama launched the Let's Move! initiative in 2010, which recognized the rapid increase in childhood sedentary levels in the United States and the corresponding increase in obesity. Childhood obesity is not a danger only in the United States; the same problem is evident around the world. More than 40 million children worldwide under the age of 5 were either overweight or obese in 2012. A variety of issues are at play, and the other main area is the food that we eat. This all results in our children representing the first generation in human history where their life expectancy is actually lower than that of their parents. The Let's Move! campaign, supported by a YouTube video that shows Barack Obama and Joe Biden going for a run around the White House, looks to push back against this complex issue through simple changes in sedentary habits. Active kids have also been shown to score up to 40% higher on tests (see Chapter 6, Reference 15), highlighting the movement for performance imperative for future generations.

Mega City One

Fans of the comic strip character Judge Dredd will be familiar with Mega City One, the fictitious futuristic cityscape that provides the trials and tribulations of Dredd and his fellow judges. And we are moving ever closer to the age of the Mega City. Urbanization, the demographic transition from rural to urban, is associated with shifts from an agriculture-based economy to mass industry, technology, and service. For the first time ever, the majority of the world's population lives in a city. As of 2010, more than half the world's population lived in a city, up from 33% in 1960. By 2050, this will increase to more than 7 out of 10 people. The growth of mega cities (more than 10 million people), often traditional hubs with great prestige, such as London, Paris, and New York, are at the forefront of a balancing act between business and life, with the Economic Intelligence Unit commenting in 2013 that "prestigious hubs have the big city buzz but they pay for it with more crime, greater congestion, and inferior public transit."[3]

Although it is not a mega city, my home city of Barcelona faces similar challenges but seems to be doing well, often figuring in global city rankings according to entrepreneurship, technology, and quality of life. Indeed, Barcelona has the stated aim of becoming a world reference for Smart Cities, and is working to merge urban planning, ecology, and information technology to ensure that the benefits of technology reach every citizen. Yet it is not without its problems; it has a bad reputation among tourists for pickpocketing in well-known tourist areas and has challenges in merging increasing volumes of bicycle traffic with existing car and pedestrian spaces.

Here, the broad topic of "liveability" is of interest—essentially, the quality of life as a city dweller. This may include macro topics such as transport, health care, and culture, with other concepts able to make a contribution, including design against crime, walkability, cyclability, and technology connectedness. So what makes a city liveable? What products, services, and policy can we design to increase this liveability? Is worsening liveability always a by-product of increasing scale? Following the logic of The Triple Lens of Sustainability, what is good for the individual is also good for the organization and society. So quality of life for a citizen should equate to a better way of doing business, as well as creating a more sustainable and flourishing planet. Amid the talk of smart cities, it is important to remember that technology development should not take place just for technology's sake—but that the overarching aims of liveable, sustainable cities are considered. I was recently involved in the successful bid for a major European research project on sustainable lifestyles in the year 2050. The four areas of research into this future world, in order to design better policy today, were transport, food, energy, and living in general. With the exception of energy, all are covered in *Sustaining Executive Performance*, and transport, in particular, is covered in this chapter.

Future scenarios on urban living, such as those offered by Siemens in its sustainable cities initiative called The Crystal (thecrystal.org), highlight issues that include local food production and high-rise development. Most future studies concur that with ever-tightening space in the urban center, the only way is up. Asia, the world region with greatest population and economic growth in recent years, accounted for three-quarters of the 53 newly built skyscrapers over 200 meters in 2013.[4] In general, we see an exponential rise in the completion of buildings 200 meters and taller, with the number of completions in 2004 of 18 rising to 90 a decade later. Does that mean that we will spend even more of our time in elevators? Yes and no. We will have veritable parks in the sky, a trend that has already started with more and more green spaces evident in large-rise buildings, particularly in Asian countries such as Singapore. Living higher up may also affect the quality of the air we breathe. So does that mean we are heading toward a future such as that represented by Ridley Scott's 1984 movie classic *Blade Runner*? Future scenarios do not always paint a positive picture of the future, but they can be used positively to show the likely extension of our current choices. The Forum for the Future created different scenarios for its Megacities on the Move project.[5] In the dark future of Sprawl-ville, people are shown to spend most of their lives in traffic, traveling around in motor homes that double as a working space. A range of factors combines to turn future visions of our society into reality, including urban design and government policy. And our own habits combine to influence this as well.

An Advancing Society?

Nowhere has the change in societal habits been more marked than in China. Once the land of almost a billion bicycles, it is now home to the largest automotive market the world has ever seen, surprising the U.S. market in 2009.[6] According to the Earth Policy Institute, between 1995 and 2005, China's bike fleet declined by 35% from 670 million to 435 million, while private car ownership more than doubled, from 4.2 million to 8.9 million.[7] Although growth has slowed in recent years in line with an overall slowing of the economy, it remains the focus for global manufacturers, with Volkswagen alone currently developing production to manufacture 4 million vehicles per year. Annual sales of passenger vehicles in China has risen from 4 million in 2005 to more than 17 million in 2013 as part of a total sale of 22 million automobiles, when including commercial vehicles.

And here is the most dangerous part: A lack of physical human movement in favor of machine-movement is seen as advancement by the society at large.

In 1950s-70s China, people aspired to own SanZhuanYiXiang (三转一响), meaning a wristwatch, bicycle, sewing machine, and radio: the markers of a modern life. A predominantly agriculture-based economy resulted in much higher levels of physical movement than we see today. After 1980, the bicycle, a cultural icon, came to represent backwardness. As China looked westward for the secrets of economic success and social sophistication, the post-1980 generation developed a subliminal shame toward things intrinsically "Chinese" as well as an appetite for consumption.[8] The perception of affluence that comes from not having to walk, or ride a bicycle, was powerfully illustrated by Ma Nuo, as we see in the opening quote of the chapter. A contestant on a Chinese TV dating show, "If You Are The One," this was her response to a question asking if she'd like to go on a romantic bike ride. In general, riding a bike, once a staple of Chinese life, is now seen as "something for losers."[9]

Chinese capital Beijing, once the global reference for bike use and as synonymous with bicycles as Venice is with canals, has seen bike use drop from 60% in 1986 to 17% in 2010. At the same time, car use has grown 15% a year for the past 10 years. Many people may have stopped cycling practice given the severe pollution problems experienced by the city in recent years, and this leads to a vicious circle whereby less bike use and more car use leads to greater pollution, which in turn makes it more difficult to use the bicycle. My own observations in Shanghai has been that the only people I see on bicycles (and usually electric ones to boot!) are evidently some of the poorest people in the city. The roads also seem to function according to the law of the jungle—irrespective of traffic lights or road rules, it seems that the larger vehicle has the right of way! China is, of course, a huge country with massive investment in building new roads matched by investment in high-speed trains and other public transportation. Cutting journey times and making it easier for people to get around may be viewed as signs of progress the world over, yet we ought to be vigilant about taking it too far. Some city governments in China have closed bike lanes, blaming cyclists for increasing accidents and congestion. Instead we should consider aspects of city design and individual action that are better for the health and well-being of our planet as well as ourselves. Let's look at such factors now.

Power in Our Hands (Well, Feet)

Commuting is an example of a simple practice that may affect all areas of the Triple Lens of Sustainability. Beyond use of the bicycle discounted in recent years by so many Beijing citizens, all modes of commuting other than private car use have been shown to have benefits. Research published in the British Medical Journal[10] found that men and women who commuted to work by active and public modes of transportation had significantly lower Body Mass Index (BMI) and percentage of body fat than their counterparts who used private transportation. In total, the BMI of 7,534 people and the percentage of body fat for 7,424 people was checked with men who took nonprivate transportation about 1 full point lower and women around 0.8 points lower. Changes in body fat were of the same magnitude, which equated to weight loss of around 7 pounds (3.2kg) for men and 5.5 pounds (2.5kg) for women. However, the most interesting takeaway from the study was that the positive effect wasn't limited to those who walk or ride bikes but also those who took public transportation. Evidently all those walks to the bus stop and climbing stairs through the subway add up to significant physical exercise. The effects observed for public transportation were very similar in size and significance to those for walking or cycling to work.

I recognize the barriers to nonprivate car use around the world, such as pollution problems in Beijing and chronic traffic congestion in Jakarta. Making things easier, simpler, or *frictionless* is an overarching aim of a healthy and productive business life in the Triple Lens. What of the chaos and stress of a daily London Tube commute, for example? Or the dangers of riding a bicycle on the overpopulated and traffic-congested streets of Mumbai? Yet we ought to push back and help to change attitudes. I remember my stay at Stanford in 2001 when, much to the amusement of my colleagues, I didn't have my driver's license at age 24 (which I didn't get until the age of 35). *"What, you get the bus?"* was the common incredulous refrain, and where once inside, only one narrow demographic was ever represented. Flexing in the way we move ourselves will not only improve our physical health but also our resilience in experiencing low-level "shocks," a concept covered in Chapter 9, "On the Criticality of Resilience for Our Future World," the next chapter that composes Part 3.

Urban infrastructure is generally planned, built, and used over decades— and in response to the common practices of the day. So by pushing back and changing our own mobility habits, we may make the case for a new urban infrastructure that will help meet the challenges of the next 50 years, making our future mega cities more liveable. A critical mass may be achieved easier than we think. Let's consider a little closer the following cases of "'two feet" and "two wheels."

Walkonomics

Adam Davies founded the Walkonomics initiative, which looks at rating the *walkability* or pedestrian-friendliness of every street in the world. Combining the power of big data, crowdsourcing, and social media, he aims to create a movement to influence better urban design. The Walkonomics project has highlighted several interesting research findings from different sources that show the wider benefits of having a more walkable urban space:

- Walkable neighborhoods improve the affordability of city center homes by 30%.[11]

- People who walk to work are the most satisfied with their commute.[12]

- Compact walkable cities reduce diabetes by 42%, obesity by 33%, and high blood pressure by 13%.[13]

- Retail rental values are 54% higher in walkable neighborhoods than in car-dependant areas.[14]

- 90% of Americans and 93% of Canadians want cities to become more walkable and to add more parks.[15]

- Making Times Square in New York more walkable increased footfall by 11% and cut accidents by 35%.[16]

- GDP is 38% higher in walkable parts of cities than in car-dependant areas.[17]

- Walkability can boost home values by up to 200%.[18]

In countless studies, walkability has been shown to increase health, happiness, and commerce. However, in widely distributed cities, there may be limits to the feasibility of walking and the benefits accrued; proximity is a large factor in realizing those benefits. But an increasing number of young people are showing a strong desire for walkable cities and other features, including parks, so it may be that we see the end of the "car city" and migration toward those cities that are better designed and more able to deliver the many advantages of a walkable city.

Cyclability and Lead Users

From two legs to two wheels, cycling has benefitted from a range of measures in recent years as cities aim to reduce the reliance on cars while also reducing the burden on public transportation. Studies have shown that cycling increases by 75% on streets with dedicated bike lanes,[19] and city bike rental schemes have exploded in recent years, including new systems in today's mega cities of London, Paris, and New York.

City bike schemes, however, are not without their problems. Much may depend on local climate—how may we expect a business commuter to bicycle to work in 86°F (30°C) heat and 90% humidity, such as on the streets of Singapore at 8 a.m.? The geographical layout of Barcelona, with some large differences in elevation from *Mar to Muntanya* (sea to mountain) results in many people taking the bicycle to roll down the hill in the morning but find an alternative means to make the return journey. The motorized transport required to replace these bicycles has resulted in a net increase in carbon emissions.

Citi Bike in New York has experienced financial difficulties since its inception in early 2013. A call was made for public cash to be added to the privately funded scheme to extend it beyond Manhattan to Brooklyn and Queens, as well as improvements to the first-generation "buggy" software.[20] Despite various controversies, it counted on more than 100,000 annual members and seven million trips taken after its first year of operation. Although still tiny compared to other modes of transport, it has been noted as having an effect on the safety of all users on New York streets; the increasing visibility of bicycles has a calming effect on other road users, particularly drivers.

We are moving in the right direction, but there is a long way to go. In the United States, there has been a 60% increase in biking to work in the past decade, but the most popular city, Portland, OR, still has only a total of 6% of commuters who bike, compared to over 50% in Copenhagen.[21]

Technology and investment may help play a part in ironing out the problems encountered in the Barcelona and New York schemes, as part of an overall push to changing the habits of a greater percentage of the population—and looking at lead-user cases may also help. Copenhagen, a recognized lead user in city bike use, has twinned with Beijing within the context of sustainable city development. And the *cool* of Copenhagen cycling may be helping affect a U-turn in attitudes. The Chinese government is now making a concerted effort to promote bike use around the country. Even the relatively recent transformation[22] of Copenhagen into a global reference may offer hope to China and other cities around the world. Traditionally, a strong cycling culture existed in the nineteenth century, but city planners ripped up much of the cycling infrastructure in the aftermath of World War II, all in the name of progress toward private car transportation. Barely any pre-war cycling infrastructure remained by the early 1960s, with an all-time low of 10% of the population using bikes for transportation. The energy crises of the 1970s then resulted in a wave of protests and a rebuilding of the cycling infrastructure, beginning in the early 1980s.

Scandinavian countries in general show an enlightened attitude to city transport. The Swedish city Gothenburg started a scheme whereby people were given free bikes if they promised to stop driving for at least three days per week.[23] A powerful *nudge*. The "unique genius" of Hong Kong's system shows that public transportation can also work in a dense, populated area.[24]

Another example of a lead user, at the city administration level, is Tallinn in Estonia. This northern European city on the other side of the Baltic Sea from Helsinki has offered free public transportation to its 430,000 residents since December 2012.[25] Its reasons included guaranteeing mobility for unemployed and low income residents, stimulating economic activity, and decreasing the modal share of private motorized transportation. The city Mayor claimed that the free transportation would equate to a 13th month of salary. The loss of revenue from fares was to be made up by municipal revenues from personal income tax, because people are encouraged to register their residence in Tallinn in order to be eligible for free public transportation. Since April 2012, the registered population of Tallinn grew by 13,000. The operating cost of the new ticketing system, to be used interchangeably for trams, buses, and metro, is much lower than the old system and helps to simplify the collection of public transportation usage data so that the public transportation network can be optimized.

However, the stated aim of a 20% increase in public transportation use hasn't been achieved. Researchers at the Royal Institute of Technology in Sweden found only a 3% increase in passenger demand and also a decrease in walking in favor of public transit. Yet it has improved substantially on a social scale—for example, passenger rates have increased 10% for a densely populated district on the edge of the city with high levels of unemployment and a large ethnic minority. It may not have achieved its stated objectives so far (after only one year), but such policy experiments ought to be applauded and given the chance to grow. The insights gained may help other city administrations on a larger scale as they look to create a more sustainable future.

We highlighted the First Law of SEP in the previous chapter as an understanding that *Movement Creates Energy*. Several fascinating technology start-ups are taking this beyond the biological level to actually creating energy from our physical movement, and so turn the human advantage into real energy advantage. For example, Pavegen, a London-based start-up that spun out of research at Loughborough University, manufactures flooring that converts the kinetic energy from footsteps into renewable electricity. So with our own changing habits, we may help create a future society that perceives physical movement as the sign of affluence (and simple common sense) following in the footsteps of the Celebrated Captain Barclay, but where that physical movement doesn't win the wager but rather helps power the sustainable city rising above us.

8

RECOVER

Sleep that knits up the ravell'd sleave of care, The death of each day's life, sore labour's bath, Balm of hurt minds, great nature's second course, Chief nourisher in life's feast.

—William Shakespeare *(Macbeth)*

"Much of our focus is on the sustainability of the plane, yet many of our decisions are affected by how sustainable the pilot is!" I was sitting in the main hall of IMD Business School in Lausanne, Switzerland, listening to the story of Solar Impulse, an initiative started by Bertrand Piccard and André Borschberg to build the world's first solar-powered airplane to fly nonstop around the world. Millions of euros invested, dozens of sponsors, pioneering innovations in aircraft construction, composites, adhesives, and energy efficiency, both pushed and limited by who we are as human beings. New-age design created, and limited, by our own human design.

So how many times do we push ahead in the world of business, in whatever domain, yet neglect the basic human needs that will indeed make or break the success of the venture? For a nonstop flight around the world, in an aircraft that is as light as possible, with the cockpit as small as possible, how can the pilot move? Go to the toilet? Sleep? Depriving oneself of sleep for 24 hours can result in hallucinations, or at the very best result in a vastly compromised mental ability—not ideal when Bertrand, the first man to circumnavigate the globe in a hot air balloon, is expected to cope with any matter of unexpected occurrences and react at a moment's notice. The armed forces carry a book with them at all times that informs them of the decrease in performance with sleep deprivation. More conventional aviation pilots often enjoy the use of a nap pod in the cockpit, and professional sportsmen and women count recovery as one of the key things in their life—transforming what looks like a part-time commitment to their graft regarding the total hours spent on the field or in training—to an all-consuming *craft* that affects choices related to any activity, no matter how small. Recovery is a key aspect of performance in all. But in business? All but forgotten.

The Universal Law of Stress and Recovery

The point of departure for a deeper consideration of recovery is the fact that *we are rhythmic beings*. Recovery doesn't exist in isolation; rather we mix, or switch, between some mode of work (in its broader sense) and recovery. We breathe in and out, are awake during the day (normally!) and asleep at night; oxygenated and deoxygenated blood is pumped around our body. But too much work and the system doesn't function. In the context of business, this can lead to suboptimal performance and even burnout. Maybe you've seen it in a colleague—it's not a nice thing to see. But neither is too much recovery a good thing. On a muscular level, if you've had the misfortune to break a bone in your body, for example, if the muscle is not used, it will atrophy. In the management domain also, we sometimes need an edge to perform, something that elite sport has used to its advantage for years, whether that be the stress of an approaching competition or a rival competitor who pushes performance to new levels.

A deadline is a simple example of stress being applied to a work situation. "Stretch-goals" are another, which may be used strategically to improve output, yet are unlikely to work if used on a continual basis. The well-known U.S. composer of *West Side Story*, Leonard Bernstein once noted:

> Two elements are required to do great things, a plan, and not quite enough time.

The lack of time therefore pushes us to perform beyond what we may normally achieve. From my innovation work, I am also convinced that innovation works best with constraints, driving surprising and creative solutions. For example, considering the budget available for company innovation, Steve Jobs once noted, "Innovation has nothing to do with how many R&D dollars you have. When Apple came up with the Mac, IBM was spending at least 100 times more on R&D." Yet living with constant constraints could lead to a downward spiral of disengagement and lower performance. The physical process of training is one where the stress that is placed on the body, whether on a cardiovascular or muscular level, is valuable only when it is followed by recovery. During recovery, the muscles grow stronger after the initial damage of the training, and the heart renews. Many modern heart rate monitors now give you a recovery time after your workout. I'm writing this part of *Sustaining Executive Performance* during one of those periods—22 hours after a hard half-marathon race. *Brain Rules* author John Medina[1] also showed that stress on a mental level, if controlled in quantity or exposure, is good for us. Performance and memory improves. We always remember stressful events in our life—for example, moving into a new house, getting married, the bereavement of a loved one, or attending a tough training course where we learned new things.

Stress and recovery was a primary consideration in the initial development of the SEP program. Observing frequent attendance at such training courses by executives from around the world, but during which their day jobs didn't stop, I saw the investment in *mental stress* on an organizational development level. However, I felt the lack of attention to the physical domain (stress and recovery), as well as the mental recovery necessary during which new knowledge would fully take hold, meant the full value of that investment wasn't realized. The SEP stress-recovery matrix was then developed, shown in Figure 8.1.

The matrix emphasizes that the employer will take care of the upper-right quadrant, but it is the employee's responsibility to continually invest in the other three. For example, physical training, sleep, and meditation are sample content areas that exist in the quadrants of physical stress, physical recovery, and mental recovery, respectively, and that sustain executive performance in the long term.

So recovery makes stress valuable, and waves or rhythms allow us to control it. Following are two examples of the natural rhythms that form part of us all.

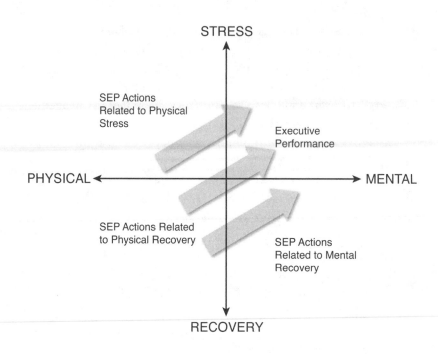

Figure 8.1 SEP stress-recovery matrix

Consider first your heartbeat. In fact, place a hand on your heart and feel that for a few seconds. How often do you pay attention to it, or listen to it? That is the engine room of everything that you do. Every beat of that engine, which may beat up to 100,000 times per day, comes in the form of a wave. Pumping 2,000 gallons (7,500 liters) of blood in a 24-hour period, tiny electrical currents drive the waves of movement that form the beating of your heart. A small electrical shock is first produced by pacemaker cells at the top of your heart. This electrical activity travels down through the muscle, contracting and passing on the current from cell to cell. After each has fired, it becomes momentarily unable to do so again, as if exhausted and having a rest. This delay in cell excitability is called the *refractory period*, lasting between one-tenth and one-fifth of a second, and ensures that the electrical wave can pass only once through the muscle tissue, until the next electrical shock from the pacemaker cells starts the whole process again.

In Chapter 5, "The New Self-Management," we talked about the growing area of the quantified self, and my heart rate was one of the first things I started to measure as a young athlete. These days, as well as the long-established heart rate monitors, you can use a variety of apps that can measure heart rate from the pulse measured through your index finger to the color of your face. Yet you can easily take this manually by placing two fingers, either on the underside of your wrist or at the side of your neck, on the carotid artery. Do you know what your normal resting heart rate is? Go ahead. Take your resting pulse right now.

Count the beats over 10 seconds and multiply by 6. Your heartbeats per minute is your resting pulse (RHR) right now. So what do you have? 60? 70? 80? We are all different, so simply getting to know what is normal for you is of value, because our resting pulse is a barometer of our present state. If you are tired, you may find the resting pulse at 5 beats above normal. If you experience something a bit more serious, such as a virus, it could be 10 beats above. This allows you to proactively manage your health, perhaps take some more sleeping time to fully recover if your RHR is high, which will prevent a dip in performance and having to take time off work further down the line. Elite athletes regularly monitor their resting pulse to gauge their recovery from hard training sessions and their readiness for another, often changing or even canceling a training session depending on the information received. I'm not saying that you should take your resting pulse before a key meeting and cancel that meeting if it is too high! Yet being more aware of it can give us valuable information.

Returning to the number, we are all different, and women have a higher resting rate than men, but it will decrease with age (until it gets to zero, if you know what I mean!) and also with increased cardiovascular fitness. The fitter or stronger our heart becomes, the less hard it needs to work when at rest. My own resting pulse varies from the high 40/low 50 range in noncompetition time to low 40s when I'm in peak fitness. Generally speaking, a resting rate under 60 should be the aim, but don't worry if the value you just measured was much higher! Your true resting comes first thing in the morning, upon waking. Getting into a habit of placing two fingers on your neck and measuring over a few seconds can tell you a little bit more about what's going on—your tiredness, general health, or fitness progress.

You can also try a simple exercise to see how quickly your heart rate will rise. You may have had a RHR of between 50 and 80 depending on age, fitness level, and other genetic factors, or you may have just had a few espressos! The next time you can try a simple exercise, such as climbing a few flights of stairs or even trying 10 squats, try the measure again. A good form squat is standing with your feet just a little wider than shoulder-width apart; raise your arms straight flat in front of you, and squat down as if sitting on a chair, then raise up to the original standing position.

You will likely, very easily, rise above 100 beats. There are a couple of things I want to point out here: first, that squats are pretty hard and they are a great strength exercise that can rapidly increase core strength in a short space of time (discussed in detail in Chapter 14). More importantly, I want to show that your heart rate will rise very easily on even the simplest exercise. On the positive side, by simply taking the stairs at every opportunity, your heart will get an important percentage of the weekly "work" it needs to remain healthy. By taking a few flights, you will easily find your heart rising above the 100 beats barrier. On the negative side, I also want to demonstrate that you will leave, very easily and often, your true resting heart rate which signifies real recovery. Just by going through our normal day, reading emails, stressing about a project, driving to work, our heart rate will rise. The danger then is that many of us go through our lives with our heart neither at the top levels where it is required to work to keep healthy, yet neither at the low levels, where real resting and recovery lies. This middle or "gray zone" is the real danger in a professional business life, neither working nor resting, neither fully on nor off. Part of my coaching work regards monitoring the heart rate of executives over the course of a day and using the more advanced measure of Heart Rate Variability (HRV). Sometimes the insight gained has been that the most stressful periods occur, not at work as one may expect, but at other times of the day—commuting, or at home managing the tension between being with the family yet still connected to work. We discuss further factors related to our heart, in the context of physical fitness and weight management, in Chapter 14, "TRAIN."

The next example of waves is in our head. The now defunct U.S. company ZEO was one of the pioneers of the Quantified Self movement and brought electroencephalography (EEG) recording to the home market with its sleep monitoring device. I bought several of these on launch for my executive programs as well as for personal use. A typical graph of my own sleep from October 2012 is shown in Figure 8.2.

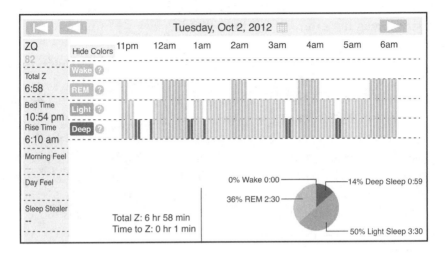

Figure 8.2 ZEO sleep graph

There are several concepts I'd like to highlight with this graphic. First is the different phases of sleep that we experience. Rapid Eye Movement, or REM, sleep is the dream state. This is a shallow phase of sleep, and some scientists believe it helps our mind to recover and put in order all the conversations, cases, and emails of a busy day—one of the possible reasons for having dreams. Deep sleep is when our body recovers from the physical exertions of the day and is characterized by a complete lack of physical movement during sleep. Light is the intermediary stage that connects REM and deep sleep. One aspect of deep sleep links the previous SEP element of MOVE to our present discussion on recovery. We commented in MOVE the sedentary traps that characterize an office-based life and the fact that just because we sit all day, it doesn't mean that we don't get tired. Yet the key is that we are often only mentally tired and not sufficiently physically tired. The result can often be, even if we spend 8 or 9 hours in bed, that we don't get the requisite deep sleep, and we still feel tired upon waking. Sleep *efficiency* has been poor. This is another incentive to move more during the day. Research has shown that those who exercise more achieve a higher percentage of deep sleep.[2]

With more deep sleep, we recover more powerfully during the night and feel more refreshed upon waking.

Another concept that we see in the ZEO graph is the movement between stages. It is not simply the case of achieving more deep sleep with longer sleeping time and moving toward a shallow state in the morning. Rather we move in and out of these phases, lighter and deeper, all the way through the night, with such sleep cycles lasting around 90 minutes. This is where the ZEO sleep graph is misleading, because REM sleep, a paradoxical phase of sleep that was discovered only in the 1950s by a graduate student named Eugene Aserinsky at the University of Chicago, comes at the end of the sleep cycle rather than at the beginning. It is paradoxical because it bears greater similarity (on the brain-wave level) to being awake than being asleep (see Figure 8.3). Indeed, leading sleep scientists have said a more accurate description for REM is that it is not sleep at all, rather a more primitive state where wakefulness is turned off rather than sleep being turned on: "like the screensaver mode on a computer."[3]

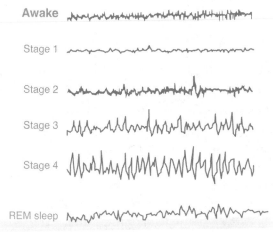

Figure 8.3 Brainwaves during each stage of the sleep-wake cycle

The sleep cycle (see Figure 8.4) begins with phases 1 and 2, light sleep, in which we spend about half the night. Brain waves are small and similar also to a drowsiness state. We then move into stages 3 and 4, deep sleep, which is characterized by large, slow waves. This takes a total of around 10–20% of total sleep time and is loaded to the first few cycles of sleep where recovery is required, primarily on the cortical level of the brain. This is also affected by the length of prior wakefulness and the resultant homeostatic, or sleep, pressure—the longer we've been awake, the greater the pressure, and the greater need for recovery. After stage 4, around the 90-minute mark, we then enter the REM phase, which actually includes characteristics of both light and deep. Because the brainwaves are so similar to being awake, additional defining features are the eye movements and the fact that tension in the muscles around the chin and jaw disappears, which is not true in the other stages. REM takes around 20–25% of total sleep time, with more evident in the latter sleep cycles. Given the placement of REM and the fact that its percentage increases greatly if we oversleep, it is probably not as critical as generally assumed—certainly in comparison with deep sleep. It does play a more important role before we are born, with over half of our sleep time taken by REM—more than at any other time in our lives, around 8–10 hours—in the month or so before we are born. The world we are then born into takes over the stimulation our forming brains require.

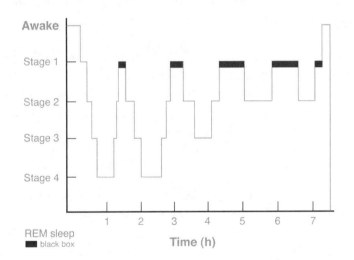

Figure 8.4 Sleep cycle (Hypnogram) for a normal adult

So *sleep is a process*. We do not merely fall asleep or go to sleep; we go *toward* sleep. The 90- to 100-minute rhythms that characterize our sleeping cycle can be interrupted by various factors, which then requires our sleeping process to start again.

Shallow sleep at different points during the night also means it can be easy to wake up at different points, for example, due to some external noise. Raising awareness of such factors and, for instance, changing the location of our bedroom within our home, or even moving to another house, can lead to a more restful sleep. Brief awakening periods can account for around 5–10% of our total sleep time. We are often not aware of such disturbances, yet our recovery is still compromised. REM is also characterized by a different type of stimulus toward awakening. Because it is not true sleep, our brains are still watchful to a certain degree, and we may awake easily given a meaningful word or noise (such as someone speaking your name) if even of a low volume, yet remain "asleep" with a louder noise, but one with no meaning, such as a train traveling past as part of a nightly route. Indeed, REM sleep has been compared to a submarine periodically surfacing to periscope depth in order to scan the environment.[4]

The sleep cycle shows it to be a perfectly natural occurrence to awake during the night, and history shows us that people would generally sleep in two blocks of four rather than one large block.[5] In the middle of the night, people would engage in different activities, and Shakespeare's characters would indulge in their deep reflection, communicated to us through the soliloquies of his plays. The industrial revolution meant that work time was increasingly focused during daylight hours, and so we changed as a society, better planning our rest and taking our sleeping time in Robert Owen's "middle 8."

So when you wake at night, accept it as a normal thing. Waking several times, on the other hand, is symptomatic of other issues, such as excessive stress and severe fatigue. So what do you do when you wake up? Try to get back to sleep, I suppose? Research has shown this may not be the right thing to do. Paradoxical intention (if I say, "think of anything apart from pink elephants," what comes to mind?) shows us that actually trying to stay awake may be the better option. Researchers at the University of Virginia found that "the ironic effects of sleep urgency"[6] meant that the more we try to fall asleep, the more stress we place on our bodies, and the less likely we are to fall asleep in a timely fashion. Now don't try and stay awake with a typical "alpha-business task-driven" approach that means you may actually achieve it! Get up if you wish, visit the bathroom, drink some water, then get back to bed and close your eyes. Focus on your breathing, as we detail later in the chapter, and try, in a relaxed fashion, to stay awake. Ideally, before you know it, you'll wake a few hours later at the time you desire.

A further practical takeaway from the sleep cycle science, made possible by modern sleep monitors and apps, is the concept of the smart alarm. Detecting at what part of your sleep cycle you are in, and with a programmed range of, for example, 40 minutes set by you, the smart alarm will wake you at the end of your sleep cycle, in the most shallow stage of sleep closest to being awake. The result is that you awake feeling alert in contrast to awaking from a deeper part of the sleep cycle that results in a "heavier" feeling, termed *sleep inertia*.

A Key Professional Skill

A deeper understanding of the sleeping process as an example of our rhythms offers us insight to the things we can change. World-class athletes, for example, are world-class sleepers! You may not include it on your curriculum anytime soon, but if you can improve your ability to sleep, you can transform your work and life. Amnesty International found that the most common form of torture worldwide is sleep deprivation. It can have disastrous effects and was one of the factors in the Challenger shuttle disaster. Yet sleeping is a vastly neglected area of business and life, recognized by those in the medical profession, as we see from the following *British Medical Journal* (*BMJ*) editorial:[3]

> The subject of sleeplessness is once more under public discussion. The hurry and excitement of modern life is held to be responsible for much of the insomnia of which we hear; and most of the articles and letters are full of good advice to live more quietly and of platitudes concerning the harmfulness of rush and worry. The pity of it is that so many people are unable to follow this good advice and are obliged to lead a life of anxiety and high tension.

Sound familiar? This was indeed the *BMJ*, yet from September 29, 1894! More than a century ago, yet we may detect the same factors that result today in the same basic lack of respect for the value of sleep. Humans have progressed in the past century without a doubt, but perhaps not in every way. *Plus ça change.*

In 1997, *Nature* published a study where sleep deprivation was shown to have a similar effect on work performance as blood alcohol concentration.[7] So the conclusion is that if you go to work consistently sleep deprived, you may as well go to work drunk. Hey, maybe you try both at the same time! But seriously, this goes against the whole culture of high-flying business, entrepreneurship, and industries such as investment banking, where a lack of sleep is seen as a badge of honor, or where high performance means more waking time and less sleep; again, it's the complete opposite of sports performance, where recovery is highly prized. I'm realistic. Business is business, and if a hard deadline is approaching, we may need to work all night. Family life, too, also means that a young family may be sleep deprived for a couple of years. Yet try to mitigate that deprivation and take sleep a little more seriously. Don't make those business all-nighters the norm. The *Harvard Business Review* blog picked up on the *Nature* research in 2012, with its piece titled "Get to Bed by 10pm and Change the World."[8] I know that if you live in Madrid, for example, you're eating your evening meal at 10 p.m., but the rationale remains. Take sleep a little more seriously. Try getting a half-hour more during a week and observe the effects. Watch less TV. Sleeping is a key professional skill. If you can get more sleep and become less sleep deprived, if you can fall asleep faster, wake up less often during the night, get a higher percentage of deep sleep, and follow clean sleep cycles through the night, you can transform your work and your life. It is particularly beneficial for the modern-day executive who is required to be agile and innovative. What science tells us[3] is that procedural thinking, using tried and tested strategies, can proceed relatively unhindered, even with chronic sleep deprivation, but responding to unexpected events is greatly affected. "Executive thinking," which requires us to be flexible, agile, and innovative, responding to a changing environment, is the type of thinking that suffers most with sleep deprivation.

So are you getting enough sleep? Traditional wisdom (and research) shows a bell curve distribution where around 90% of us need between seven and eight hours on a daily basis.[2] Although we may need extra sleep after a hard training session in order to fully recover, oversleeping can cause just as many health problems as sleep deprivation, so finding out how much you need is a worthy exercise. This is best done during a period when you don't need to get up at a certain time, such as when you're on vacation. Without using an alarm, simply go to bed when you are tired and get up when you feel like getting up. You will need three or four days to pay off any sleep debt, and the following three or four days then offer insight into your own pattern. Of course, replicating your normal day, without late-night dinners and excessive exercise or alcohol, is required to identify that pattern. So maybe you can take a different type of vacation then! Finding your own pattern, or rhythm, is a critical concept here, and we revisit it later in our discussion on the circadian rhythm.

I have met many people during my programs who are concerned because they sleep only 4 to 5 hours a night. The first question I ask them is: *Do you feel OK?* If they say yes, then I say congratulations! Of course, we can experiment by changing the amount of sleep we get and observing the effects, but some people exist in this percentile and need only a short amount of sleep—not me, unfortunately!

Sleep quality can be improved by the preparation we afford it. Prepare for sleep as for any important task. Call it a key meeting, with yourself, and follow a few simple steps. We often go through a busy day at work and at home, become aware of the late hour, and then get to bed in a hurried fashion. Some executives I have coached have created an alarm clock to remind them to go to bed. We have one for waking, so why not for sleeping?

The first thing is to create the right environment. The bedroom should be for sleeping and one other thing not covered here! So no electronic devices or TVs. Take care of the basics to ensure the best chances of a good night's sleep—light and noise. This may sound trite, but the simple fact of having blinking LEDs from a TV or alarm clock, or light from underneath a door, can easily disrupt a night's rest and is the first sweep I do of a hotel room when traveling on business.

The next key aspect is to have a gradual wind down of at least an hour, preferably 90 minutes before going to bed. Gradually let go of the chaos and activity of the day, and steer clear of everyday stimulants or depressants such as TV, email, coffee, and alcohol. Aim to create a ritual of preparation that will allow your waking brainwaves to more closely resemble the theta waves of stage 1 sleep. Even caffeine after midday can be problematic for people with sleep issues. The ubiquitous use of smartphones, which is covered in greater depth in the FOCUS element of the SEP model (Chapter 10), creates the temptation of email checking being the last thing you do before going to bed and the first thing upon waking. This is viewed as necessary for an increasing number of managers, especially those engaged with globally distributed teams, yet it is one of the most serious sleep saboteurs. Do you really want to dream about your boss at night? Red wine in particular has fantastic health benefits (primarily as a powerful antioxidant), but alcohol close to bedtime can result in a very shallow experience of sleep, even if you think you get the benefit by falling asleep faster.

Electronic devices in general can also scupper sleep through the blue light they emit. So even if you think that you are relaxing by reading on a tablet, the blue light will suppress the production of melatonin in your brain, and melatonin is required for healthy sleep. Indeed, when we are jet lagged, the primary cause is a severe deficiency of melatonin, as we cover later.

The final aspect worthy of mention for sleep preparation concerns breathing. During the day, we breathe through our chest. It is a high breath. At night, this changes to a lower breath, where we breathe through our belly, centered on our diaphragm. Watch a baby sleeping and the relatively large movement of their small stomach to appreciate this. To prepare fully for sleep, we can change our primary mode of breathing from our chest to our belly. Lying in bed, simply place one hand on your chest and the other on your waist. You will notice that the hand on your chest will rise first. Over a period of 30 seconds or 4 to 6 breaths, change your breathing so that the hand on your waist is rising first. You are now in nighttime breathing mode, and you will find it much easier to fall asleep. Being skilled at changing to belly breathing can also be very useful in other situations, such as waking in the middle of the night and trying (but not too hard, remember!) to fall back asleep.

In general, it's a mode of breathing that we tend to forget about, after almost purely breathing this way as infants. Trying it during the day can bring about a sense of deep relaxation. Students of yoga will be familiar with such an exercise. Simply place your hand on your belly/waist, in even a standing or sitting position, and breathe deeply in and out through your nose, and aim for the maximum extension in your belly.

Regardless of the preparation we afford it, some of us may still find it difficult to fall asleep and/or awake at certain times. We are all characterized by different sleep patterns—generally as either early risers, Larks, or late risers (and therefore late to bed!) who are Owls. Such specific patterns exist within the general domain of the circadian rhythm, our biological clock that governs different physiological processes in our day.

Finding Your Own Rhythm

Circadian is taken from the Latin *circa dia*, meaning "around a day." Independent of when we go to sleep, our circadian rhythm lasts about 24.5 hours, during which time our body temperature will rise and fall together with various other body functions. This internal clock preempts each part of the day. It ensures that sleep, wakefulness, alertness, and various hormones will be at their most suitable levels. Body temperature varies only around 0.7 degrees, yet it's enough to affect the suitability of certain actions, including exercise. Most world records are broken in the afternoon or evening, when body temperature is highest, blood pressure is lowest, and lung function is more efficient. Alertness tends toward its lowest level between 2:00 a.m. and 6:00 a.m. and its highest between 6:00 p.m. and 8:00 p.m. This clock therefore gives us clues as to how to lead, or "reengineer" our day-to-day activities. Exercise, improved focus, and the need to recover are all daily actions that can be better aligned by considering this rhythm. Thousands of years of human evolution have conditioned these physiological processes according to the rise and fall of the sun. The light that our eyes receive helps to set the circadian clock. The invention of the light bulb fundamentally changed this, as did global air travel, yet we are still limited by this underlying pattern. The pineal gland (positioned between our eyes) secretes the melatonin necessary for healthy sleep toward bedtime, with the fading of the day. Human Growth Hormone (HGH) is the critical hormone released when we sleep in order to carry out the various repair functions necessary, and when we awake, adrenalin is produced to kick start our day. These cycles are repeated each day and are another example of the powerful rhythms that govern us.

On the simple action level, a basic understanding of whether you are a Lark or an Owl may allow you to change your habits. Owls, of course, have the hardest time fitting in to the business and wider social convention of starting work early in the morning and getting to bed at a time that allows them to rise early, which is much easier for Larks. I use a basic questionnaire on finding your type in LAB programs, and Professor Roenneberg of the Ludwig-Maximillians University in Munich, Germany, offers practical advice or "hacks" for adjusting your type as part of the Munich Chronotype Questionnaire. For natural Owls, gaining the maximum amount of sunlight (or at least outdoor light if you live somewhere like Scotland!) during the first half of the day will help to ensure that your clock begins to wind down a little sooner each day. On the other hand, Larks may experience difficulties coping with different late-night activities such as business dinners or parties. The same hack holds—aim to stay indoors during the first half of the day and gain as much outdoor light exposure during the afternoon to improve alertness toward the second half of the day.

Varying alertness as part of the circadian rhythm leads us to the concept of the *nap zone*—generally between 2:00 and 4:00 pm. The urge for a midday nap, therefore, is not a matter of how well we slept the night before or having just eaten a large lunch, although these can be contributory factors. More car accidents occur during the nap zone,[1] and research from NASA[9] has shown working memory to improve after napping. General acceptance is still a long way off within the workplace, although Google has $60,000 nap-pods for its employees as part of a wider approach to workspace design to improve productivity and happiness. Yet even if taking a nap in the early afternoon is not an option, and it rarely will be for the majority of us, simply being aware of that danger period and mitigating that dip in performance is valuable. Be careful what is scheduled for 3 p.m. and try to push mission-critical tasks toward more high-energy periods of the day (which may differ from person to person), yet also consider your reenergizing options if important work has to be carried out during the nap zone. Don't simply fight it at your desk and compromise your performance. Take a five-minute break, preferably outside; meditate, eat a healthy snack, do some light exercise, such as a few flights of stairs or some standing squats, to get the blood moving around the body. Or just close your eyes and take some deep breaths.

Napping can be used strategically to mitigate sleep deprivation. As mentioned at the beginning of the chapter, pilots have nap-pods at their disposal to maintain alertness on a long-haul flight, yet napping for too long can cause *sleep inertia*—feeling groggy on waking—which has been the cause of some airline accidents. So keep it short to gain a refreshing boost. Sleep cycles show us that by napping too long, we may enter a deep phase (slow wave) stage of sleep from which it is difficult to surface. Caffeine may be used strategically, because it takes 15 minutes to absorb into the bloodstream, and sitting on a chair holding a spoon allows one to nod off for a few minutes, with the dropping of the spoon acting as the alarm. Although napping for blue-collar workers, especially in Asian cultures, is generally accepted, within management circles it is still perceived negatively. So perhaps think of doing it privately, for instance, in the car. Even having a few minutes with your eyes closed and allowing your heart rate to come down to its true resting level can be immensely valuable if the actual sleep is unfeasible. Repeating more than once during the day can be valuable for those in high-pressure situations or with severe sleep deprivation, such as young parents. Polyphasic sleep practitioners take up to six naps during the day, replicating the sleeping strategy of young babies—something also considered by the Solar Impulse pioneers.

Jet lag, when discounting the common "hangover" effects as discussed in Chapter 6, "MOVE," is almost wholly due to disruption of our circadian rhythm. Our body expects to be shutting down for the day, and suddenly finds itself in another location at the beginning of the day. Of course, the farther you displace your normal "clock" by traveling across more time zones, the worse jet lag will be. Traveling east is also proven to be more problematic—we adjust only 1 hour/day compared to westward travelers, who adjust 1.5 hours/day. This is because the circadian rhythm has a tendency to lengthen the day (being 24.5 hours) and westward flight also lengthens the day, fitting more with the natural rhythm of the clock as compared to eastward flight, which shortens the day. If the trip abroad is of a very short duration, there may be the case to suffer for the entire visit and remain on "your own clock." However, even on short trips, this may be difficult because you will be expected to conform to local hours and perform at your best during them. Several tips for dealing with jet lag include the following:

1. Anticipate the change by moving toward the destination time over a period of days. There is no need to go all the way, yet some movement will minimize the adjustment when you arrive at your destination. This movement may also be done during the travel if, for example, you have a layover, or even on the plane. Since light exposure is the key in moving toward the destination time, I've found strategic use of the window blind on a plane to be immensely valuable.

2. Ensure that you are well rested and not sleep deprived before your trip. A large homeostatic (sleep) pressure will exacerbate jet lag effects. If possible, try to sleep on the plane—and so make your body tired before traveling by doing some exercise.

3. When you arrive, switch to the local time immediately. Get outside and get some sunshine. This will help your natural circadian clock to reset as quickly as possible.

4. Common sense and planning go a long way. Schedule that important meeting for when you know you will be most alert, and follow the practice as detailed in all the SEP elements.

Recover Like a Professional

So if these waves or cycles are a natural part of who we are, why then do we have a very linear, machine-based view of work? The 90–100 minute sleep cycles are also present during the day in the form of ultradian rhythms. Think for a moment how much this machine-based view pervades our everyday language. We aim to *leverage* advantage and look at the *nuts and bolts* of a problem. Yet we are no longer in the industrial age where clocking in and out was of paramount importance and where the human resource was often considered as another tool or machine. Such a linear approach to work results in quickly diminishing returns. Staying true to our rhythms, even when we have a good level of energy at the beginning of the day or week, is the path to sustaining higher performance. Cultivating that energy is at the core of the corporate athlete concept developed by Jim Loehr and colleagues at the Human Performance Institute in the United States.[10]

An interesting case in breaking free of this linear, machine-based approach comes from CEO and Chairman of Procter & Gamble, A.G. Lafley. In a Fortune interview,[11] he talked of his approach to work:

> I'd be up in the morning between 5 and 5:30. I'd work out and be at my desk by 6:30 or 7, drive hard until about 7 P.M., then go home, take a break with my wife, Margaret, and be back at it later that evening. I was just grinding through the day. Now I work really hard for an hour or an hour and a half. Then I take a break. I walk around and chit-chat with people. It can take five or 15 minutes to recharge. It's kind of like the interval training that an athlete does.

Lafley returned to the head of P&G in May 2013 at age 64. He knows how to manage his energy and talks about interval training, a staple of athletics for more than half a century and a key part of the TRAIN element of the SEP model, covered in Chapter 14. Consider this as a mental, work-based form of an interval session, allowing deep concentration and quality work before changing focus and recharging, then reentering the fray. The 90–100 minute rhythms that characterize our sleep and waking day therefore govern our ability to focus during the day. It is with good reason that most classes in universities are 1:15 in duration; this is about the maximum we can hold deep concentration before needing a break.

And such a break need not be wasted time. As we have seen in Chapter 6, accidental encounters can lead to innovation, management by walking around can increase an awareness of what's going on in the company, and face-to-face contact builds relationships and a positive culture. Maintaining such a work rhythm or flow allows for deep recovery that drives performance. We discuss flow in work as a high level of performance in Chapter 14. Yet another case from sport and further work from Jim Loehr and colleagues show us that the recovery necessary to drive performance can be done easily and in a short time frame—ideal for the busy professional.

Breathing

Much of Loehr's original work was with elite tennis players—star players of the 1990s, such as Pete Sampras and Jim Courier. One key research insight came after exhaustive video analysis on the difference between good professional tennis players and the stand-out champions or greats of the game. They found that the champions would take just a little bit more time to fully recover between points.[12] This increased time was small (there is a maximum of 30 seconds between points) yet consistent across all cases. They would ask for the towel to rub down, even if not strictly necessary, or take a few seconds extra on ball selection. Witness the difference the next time you watch a tennis match, or even earlier footage of current tennis greats. Part of their development is learning how to take those valuable extra few seconds to fully recover and refocus. Today, Nadal, Federer, and Djokovic rarely lose a run of points or games, such is their ability to return to high performance. Such insights led Loehr and his team to develop a method for deep recovery between points. Termed "the 16-second cure," they worked with players to develop a ritual of recovery in the short time available, combining physical actions with mental cues to move their attention fully to winning the next point.

So if this is a means of valuable recovery for elite tennis players, how may elite professionals better recover in small time frames? In a busy chaotic day, perhaps with everyone's eyes on you "on court," what is your equivalent *16-second cure*? The answer is in something that we do every day, but which is often not leveraged for full benefit: breathing. It may sound strange, but in a busy, stressful day, we forget to breathe. Athletes often breathe intentionally and deeply on the starting line to control nerves, and taking 30 seconds out to do the following can be immensely valuable:

1. Be aware of where you are. Feel your feet on the ground, and sit or stand upright.

2. Breathe in through your nose to the count of three, filling your lungs and raising your chest high.

3. Hold.

4. Push out through your mouth to the count of six, emptying all air.

5. Repeat 3 times (nice and noisy if in an appropriate place!).

Of course, the appropriateness of such an exercise must be gauged for the right place and time. A heavy breathing exercise in a client meeting or open-plan office may not be the wisest choice! Yet the benefits of such an exercise cannot be overstated. Take 30 seconds for real recovery from a stressful situation, as a means of controlling nerves before a key presentation or meeting or as a means of keeping your emotions in check before a key decision. I've also worked with executives who have employed this exercise in a quiet fashion, also using belly breathing as we have already covered, during a stressful meeting where it is difficult to actually leave the room.

When we stop breathing, we stop thinking, and the primal part of our brain takes over. This is referred to in sport psychology as "monkey brain," and learning to control it through reconnecting with deep breath is fantastically valuable.

Distinguishing Between Active and Passive Recovery

As we discussed in Chapter 6, movement creates energy, and so the best means of recovery may actually be to move. Chapter 6 content and related sketches, together with Chapter 14 may help identify movement most appropriate to your needs. Athletes are well versed in the art of *active recovery*. Sometimes the best thing to do is light exercise—allowing oxygen-rich blood to travel around our bodies—and help repair any little niggles or injuries. Here, another 2×2 matrix (see Figure 8.5) may help to identify what type of recovery is required. Are you in need of physical or mental recovery? Is it better to be active, or to simply disengage?

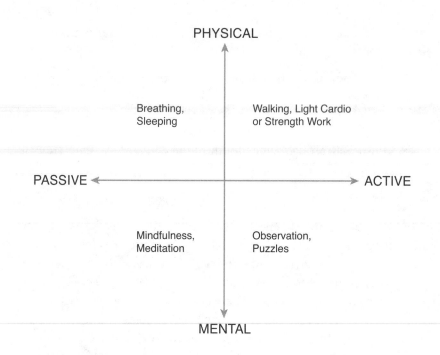

Figure 8.5 Active/passive recovery matrix with sample activities

Paying Attention

Regardless of the action—walking, stretching, breathing—all may involve varying aspects of attention and intention. Walking offers great value for health, yet its mental recovery potential is often compromised by the business habit that results in being glued to our smartphones. Taking a conference call on the move can be beneficial for thinking, as we discussed in Chapter 6, yet for full recovery, focusing on the walk itself offers more. How many times have you bumped into someone on the street because the person was looking at his or her phone? Paying attention while walking is important. We can walk and check our email, or we can walk and stare at the ground, thinking about our projects and our worries. Or we can walk and look around us. Observing powerfully is a key design method for gaining insight, as we showed in Chapter 4, "Day-to-Day Reengineering," and we look at this again within the context of mindfulness in the FOCUS element in Chapter 10. When I'm experiencing a tough week, I make a simple change to a walk: I look above, at the buildings and the sky, and I try to notice something for the first time. It's not always easy; I often catch myself looking at the ground and thinking, but my walking companion, Harry the sheepdog, often reminds me of what I need to do.

Top Ten Takeaways: RECOVER

1. Try to understand your own rhythms and identify the rhythms that surround you.

2. Think about stress as a valuable concept, where greater attention to it will allow it be used positively.

3. Get to know your heart. Feel it beating. Raise an awareness of your RHR at rest and during different activities.

4. Understand that sleeping is a process and a key professional skill that can be hacked.

5. Prepare for sleep as for any important task.

6. Gain insight to your own circadian rhythm: when you feel more alert, when you need a break, how you cope with jet lag.

7. Experiment with napping as a strategic action to sustain performance in a long day.

8. Learn how to breathe: during the day for relaxation and energizing, and at night to improve sleep.

9. Understand the difference between physical, mental, and active and passive recovery, and which is required when.

10. Pay attention to what surrounds you as a means of recovery.

The Solar Impulse innovators attempting to push back the boundaries of what is possible take inspiration from the great explorers and pioneers of the past—those who climbed higher, traveled further, and pushed human limits until they left the atmosphere of Earth itself. There is still so much out there, of course, beyond our planet, our solar system, and indeed our understanding. Yet the next century of pioneers, following in the footsteps of people such as Bertrand Piccard and André Borschberg, may well be confined within the boundaries of our planet. The next great "firsts" and discoveries could improve life on earth, let it flourish, and leave behind the outdated metaphor of the industrial machine age. This would first recognize the great need, with an ever-increasing population, for recovery on both an individual and planetary level.

On the Criticality of Resilience
for Our Future World

*I've... seen things you people wouldn't believe... Attack ships on
fire off the shoulder of Orion. I watched c-beams glitter in the
dark near the Tannhäuser Gate.*

—Roy Batty *(Blade Runner)*

*When philosopher, engineer, and designer Buckminster Fuller faced per-
sonal tragedy in 1922, he resolved to "find out what a single individual can
contribute to changing the world and benefiting all humanity."[1] Sustainability was key to his personal vision and renewed his hope in life. Fuller's
often philosophical—and at times obscure—work on synergetics and his
various inventions distill to one basic precept: create more with less. Over
time, Fuller's work as an individual has influenced and provoked the
way different groups have considered models of transportation, city planning, and home building. Fuller showed incredible personal resolve and
resilience after his personal trauma—the death of his young daughter—
and his work impacts to this day on how cities and societies may be better designed for resilience in the face of twenty-first century challenges,
including climate change, overpopulation, and food production.*

As we face our own future of possibilities, we take inspiration
from Fuller, who designed "arguments" that were never dull.
They caught the imagination of the public at large, challenged
the status quo, and inspired a different way of looking at the world,
but were never fully realized. His best-known inventions include the
geodesic dome, which exploits the geometric nature of the tetrahedron
shape to create strong, lightweight structures, and the Dymaxion car
and house—both of which addressed issues including energy, space,

local sourcing, and cost—all of which are more acutely felt today. Considering some of the individual SEP element concepts noted so far, he also serves as a true pioneer, having experimented with polyphasic sleep and jet-lag effects as well as keeping a detailed log of his life—the Dymaxion Chronofile takes up a total length of around 270 feet (82 meters) at its home in Stanford University.

Some may see an impending future in which sustainability requires a compromised life on all levels. I think sustainability, inspired by Fuller's actions and arguments, provides a powerful context for accelerating innovation—recognizing that innovation often works best with limitations. Abundant resources, be they natural, monetary, or human-based, continue to drive society forward, yet my own experience of design has shown me that a reduced solution space and a focused mind can yield significant breakthroughs. The *frugal innovation* field works along similar lines. By drawing on Fuller's personal experiment in discovering how a single individual can make a difference, we too can adopt a similar outlook and help create system-level change that leads to an inspiring future.

Learning to Change Ahead of the Survival Imperative

So what is resilience? There are different ways we can look at the term, and for this work in the context of the Triple Lens of Sustainability, I think it is useful to look at resilience on the individual, organizational, and societal levels.

As a point of departure, consider the tale of the Moscow Dogs. I came across this story in the *Financial Times* a few years ago,[2] being particularly sensitive to the issue of dog abandonment since my Mexican field studies in 2008. Moscow has a big problem with starving dogs on the street—a common sight for locals. The amazing change in recent years has been these dogs, in their search for food, *learning to ride the subway system*. A tragic, yet amazing tale, it shows the resilience of those animals, which I think can be extended to us as human beings. We can survive under even the harshest of conditions.

We find a way to survive, yet this is sometimes not in our favor because we discount the need for change—with change being hardwired into us on an ancestral level as a threat to our survival. Our ancestors would have experienced change as a threat to food supply or security from predators. So the key is moving from surviving to thriving, and also *learning to change ahead of the survival imperative.* Legendary football manager Alex Ferguson was a prime example of this practice during his long career with Manchester United. I was often taken aback when he would take apart his winning teams, yet he knew that to keep winning, he had to rebuild on a continuous basis. If he had waited until he *needed* to change, he wouldn't have sustained his success.

The SEP framework for health, well-being, and performance was designed for personal resilience. Recognizing that as busy professionals, we have a demanding career during which we will fail and fall—indeed, where failure is healthy because that is how we learn—I was interested in how quickly we get up after falling. Considering resilience on the personal level—or perhaps *bouncebackability*—there were several connection points to the more frequently visited resilience at the organizational and societal levels. As an example of personal resilience, Lane4 consultancy in the United Kingdom, with a history in elite sport, has looked at the resilience traits of Olympic athletes, aiming to transfer elements of their mind-set to the world of business. We look at such aspects of the athletes' mind-set in Chapter 14, "TRAIN." So can the rituals and culture of the individual offer clues to resilience studies and insight at the macro level?

Bouncing back concerns some element of intentional action. How will we react to setbacks? Yet even in the most alarming of situations, we are often reluctant to act. Nando Parrado is one of the survivors of the Uruguayan rugby team air disaster of 1972. Popularized in the movie *Alive,* Parrado tragically lost both his mother and sister in the plane, which crashed into the Andes, killing 29 and leaving 16 survivors in the middle of a savage mountain range. I've heard Parrado talk to groups on several occasions, and he often highlights the point at which they were moved to action. Despite the tragedy of the crash and the real danger they faced in merely surviving near the wreckage of the plane—an avalanche would kill eight of the survivors after the plane crash—a greater danger was perceived in venturing out into the wilderness. Surely the rescue party would come? And then they picked up a radio broadcast that said, "the rescue mission for the Uruguayan rugby team has been called off." It was then, according to Parrado, that they realized they needed to act. No one was coming to save them, and they themselves had to act if they wanted to live.

I also believe that resilience includes a deep consideration of *recovery* and the ability to recover in response to some shock. This returns to the concept of rhythms or waves that we introduced in the preceding chapter. Waves and rhythms are an integral part of ourselves, as we demonstrated there, and also in the world around us, both natural and designed. From the behavior of the sea to the basic principles of light and sound, as well as machines like X-ray and microwave ovens, waves are the foundation of their existence. This supposes some rhythm between two states, on and off, high and low, or action and recovery. For innovation, frameworks such as the industry life cycle and technology S-curve, discussed later in the chapter, give us insight into the rhythm between incremental and radical innovation, between a focus on product or process. Some degree of ebb and flow must therefore be recognized at the organizational and societal levels, as well as on the individual level, and in this regard resilience offers us an actionable view of recovery.

One man who has done much in recent years to connect resilience at the individual, organizational, and societal levels is Andrew Zolli.[3] He defines resilience as

> how to help vulnerable people, organizations and systems persist, perhaps even thrive, amid unforeseeable disruptions.

Resilience is therefore viewed in some quarters as a response or even replacement for sustainability, in a world where a more practical treatment of society's "wicked problems" is required. The difference, according to Zolli, is that sustainability looks to put the world back into balance as well as looking to stop the cause of that imbalance—for example, unethical behavior or rampant capitalism that may result in, for instance, abuse of workers' rights or rapid deforestation. Resilience, on the other hand, looks at adapting to the reality and managing the imbalance that exists. According to Zolli, rather than providing tacit acceptance to those that cause the imbalance, it provides practical, if imperfect, adaptations to those who are vulnerable and require action now.[4]

An element of *hacking* the solution at different levels is therefore apparent, recognizing the need for those "practical, imperfect adaptations," and design, again, has a part to play. An imbalanced world supposes a non-optimum solution space, and design has been used to address, as we commented in Chapter 3, "Design Your Life," some of the wicked problems of the developing world. The iterative approach of design where cycles of experimentation, exploration, and failure help to advance toward a solution also fit with the disequilibrium of the modern world, where trying, failing, adapting, learning, and evolving is the norm. It is for this reason that the most resilient places on earth are often those that experience these shocks. As long as such shocks are mild enough to allow recovery, and are not catastrophic, such societies may grow stronger. The same can be said for the individual; *by experiencing failure and practicing change, we are better prepared for each time such shocks occur.* Let me give you a couple of examples.

The severe weather of December 2012 caused massive disruption to the South of England, including the closure of Heathrow airport. Contrast the harsher weather yet lack of disruption in Scandinavian airports or even New York. By experiencing these weather shocks on a continual basis, they are better prepared for when they occur. I sometimes marvel at the effects that heavy rain has in Barcelona in comparison to what I grew up with in Glasgow! The esteemed Glaswegian sports journalist Doug Gillon often commented that the best Scottish cross-country runners also had outdoor jobs that made them tougher, more resilient. Is the marked decrease in British distance running as a whole the result of an "easier" professional or civil life? The hunger and resilience of a Masai, like 800-meter Olympic champion and world-record holder David Rudisha, is certainly greater than many Western suburbanites. The same principle of experiencing shocks on a societal level applies also to the physical self. When we exercise, we force our bodies to become more resilient to stress, paradoxically through stress itself. This is best displayed in the interval training method discussed in Chapter 14.

Given the massive urban shift we are experiencing, how can we design cities to be more resilient? One example of the difference between sustainability and resilience approaches in urban design is the rebuilding of Lower Manhattan after the 9/11 terrorist attack. The area contains the largest collection of LEED-certified, green buildings in the world, designed to generate lower environmental impacts, but not to respond to the impacts of the environment. Having in addition redundant power systems would have enabled the city to better cope with the recent climate shocks, including Hurricane Sandy in 2012.[4]

Such shocks are increasingly commonplace. Whether they come in the form of flooding, pandemics, terrorism, or energy shortages, individuals, organizations, and society must be better prepared so that they are able to recover. Disruption, therefore, is inevitable. It is how we deal with it that sets us apart. Although we cannot predict the future, we can use certain frameworks and tools that allow uncertainties, at least in the organizational context, to be a little less uncertain.

Dealing with Disruption

Disruption has been examined within the management domain, principally within the context of discontinuity and radical innovation. Disruption at its basic level is something that affects a revolutionary change in the way we do things, in contrast to evolutionary, low-level change that continues along the same path.

At the technological level, discontinuity has been investigated by Christensen in his work on the innovator's dilemma.[5] Companies at some point, no matter how successful, must leave behind the old way of doing things and make the switch to a new path. Even if that new path is seemingly of no value, in terms of both market and performance, it will have the potential to eventually overtake the existing solution. Technological disruption therefore occurs when an innovation emerges that offers superior performance along a new dimension, even if performance on conventional measures is initially poor. Incumbents will tend to dismiss the new innovation as no importance, yet it may create a new market that eventually supersedes the existing one. The industry life cycle, shown in Figure 9.1, is a common frame for thinking about such discontinuity and allows a company to design and test the robustness of its strategy.

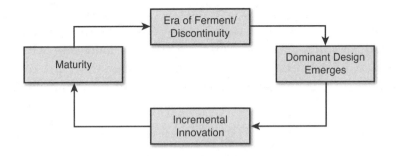

Figure 9.1 Industry life cycle

The life cycle shows that discontinuity will occur when an existing path or solution has run its course and approaches maturity. A period of radical innovation replaces incremental innovation, and the industry will experience an early experimental period—characterized by a diversity of pioneering design, experiments, design improvements, and crude and expensive products—before moving toward a dominant design. Introduced by Abernathy and Utterback,[6] a dominant design is a broadly accepted core design principle from a number of competing principles. After a dominant design emerges, innovative activity is directed to improving the process by which it is delivered. Examples include the QWERTY keyboard and the IBM PC. It may also exist for some time, even if it does not represent the best technical solution. For example, in video cassette tapes, the better technical solution was Betamax, yet VHS was more effective at securing the industry infrastructure to make it the winner. A dominant design helps to integrate the industry *as a system with a specific solution*. It concentrates the efforts of participants in the industry onto refining that solution and bringing down the cost of production with firms' specialist roles coordinated around leading designs. Industry concentration will result in fewer more powerful firms. Yet with concentration, the maturity of an industry comes closer. There follows a lower relative growth of new demand, productivity reaches limits, and there is a reduced rate of innovation. Competition intensifies and becomes more international before profit margins fall. These are the signs that another big disruption and discontinuity may be around the corner.

The stages of the industry life cycle can also be represented as an S curve, shown in Figure 9.2. It was introduced by Foster[7] to describe how the performance of a technology varies over time, or more strictly how it varies with increased research and development effort or investment. Technological performance increases with effort but eventually hits an upper limit or plateau where further improvement would either be impossible or prohibitively expensive. To achieve higher performance requires a discontinuous switch to a different technology, in turn following its own S curve. The new S curve may start at a performance level below the old one but has potential to overtake its predecessor.

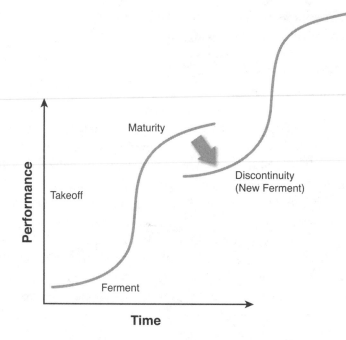

Figure 9.2 Technology S curve

Examples of these S curves include, for joint replacement: metal, then plastic, and then human tissue itself. For music, a classic example: LPs were substituted by CDs and then by digital downloads. Major transitions occur between the stages of ferment and takeoff, takeoff and maturity, and maturity and discontinuity. They provide extreme challenges but also major opportunities. The nature of technical work changes, but this affects also the marketing and organizational challenge, and the way that a firm captures value.

Both the industry life cycle and technology S-curve are not scientific realities, but useful frameworks to think about the rhythm of innovation that will test the resilience of the organization. Although they focus on technological change, they highlight some of the questions that must be asked to better deal with uncertainty. In a technology-driven world, they also offer insight as to the pattern of change that affects many other walks of life. For example, Singularity University, a privately funded education institution sponsored by organizations including Google and Autodesk, looks at the evolution of technology through similar frameworks, considering decreasing cost and increasing performance. They believe we are entering an age of unprecedented disruption in many fields of technology that will have profound effects on all areas of society—such as the increasing sophistication of robots, which will soon replace a large percentage of jobs currently done by humans, and the imminent mainstream use of 3D printers, which will take custom manufacture to a revolutionary scale. They consider the rate of change so fast that they do not maintain a curriculum that remains unchanged long enough to gain accreditation.

So what of this future? We do not have a crystal ball, but we can use tools to help gain a better view of what that future may look like. The field of foresight science uses tools such as scenario creation, forecasting, Delphi models, and trend and data extrapolation. Delphi models, in which we ask a range of experts their view, and the similar Lead User theory are surprisingly simple. Because these people are experts living on the extreme edge of practice, they are often years ahead of current day-to-day practice. So their current reality is often reflective of the future reality of society as a whole. Lead users like Solar Impulse pilot Bertrand Piccard allow us to view a future world even beyond surviving and thriving to that of *flourishing*. Future scenarios, such as those developed by the European SPREAD project on sustainable lifestyles in 2050, test the robustness or fragility of our current response—and so give clues as to the new policy, technology, products, and services required for this future world. SPREAD developed four future scenarios: Empathetic Communities, Governing the Commons, Local Loops, and Singular Super Champions.[8]

And here is where it gets really interesting: *advancing technology for the masses is potentially able to make lead users of us all.* For a truly sustainable future, instead of viewing consumers as (more or less) passive recipients of sustainable products, what are the emerging productive, innovative, and entrepreneurial roles of users in developing new sustainable products, services, and systems? While acknowledging the value of companies, the path toward a true sustainable and *resilient* society, with the requisite impact on the wicked problems of today, is likely to be more user centered and user driven.

Inspiring Futures

It is critical, therefore, to construct an inspirational view of the future, where sustainability is the powerful context of creating a better world for us all, and getting more with less. As Buckminster Fuller once said, adapting the original call to arms from Abraham Lincoln, *"the best way to predict the future is to design it."*

Science fiction has been incredibly accurate over the years in predicting our future. "If we can imagine it, we can build it" seems to be the logic. The touchscreen interface that seemed so futuristic in the 2002 movie *Minority Report* (based on a Philip K. Dick story) became ever more real with the launch of the iPad, a functionality that in short time we have taken as a natural everyday part of our lives. Tesla founder Elon Musk has recently tried to advance such functionality in the engineering design world—not quite at the level of another contemporary movie, *Iron Man*, but impressive nonetheless.

Another Philip K. Dick story has turned into arguably the most accurate of all. *Blade Runner*, based on Dick's "Do Androids Dream of Electric Sheep," presented a dystopian future, more pessimistic than optimistic, but in the view of Dick (who was delighted with the film adaptation) also realistic. In a letter he wrote to the producers, he believed that the movie was "not escapism" but "super realism, so gritty and detailed and authentic and goddamn convincing."[9] The 1982 movie, which opened to mixed reviews, has become more popular as the years have gone by, perhaps as a result of our realization of how accurate it was. Perhaps the ever-nearing world presented wakes us up to changing our habits so as to create a much brighter world.

Buckminster Fuller called himself a "comprehensive anticipatory design scientist," which simply meant that he was willing to think systematically and across the usual disciplines for future possibilities. He was also a proponent of goals and aspirations that served community needs. Most of Fuller's ideas were never truly realized, yet that does not prevent us from learning what we can from an earlier dreamer, and then supporting how the next generations may carry his zeal forward into meaningful actions as part of the never-ending cycle of sustainable innovation. More importantly, we must fully exploit the democratization of technology and knowledge in today's society, recognizing that our own actions create a more inspiring, and resilient, world.

10

FOCUS

Effective executives do first things first and they do one thing at a time.

—Peter Drucker

Pep recognized the signals. His mind started to wander. He couldn't stop his hands fidgeting. His heart started to beat a little faster in anticipation, and he felt a bead of sweat begin to trickle down the side of his head and past his ear. My God, he thought, when did it get this bad?

Mr. Pep Vicens was an addict, and it was affecting his work and life. Yet his was an addiction both depressingly familiar and socially accepted in today's world and workplace—that of smartphone addiction. Whether it was going online to check his social media status, email, or simply to ask Google or Wikipedia to answer a nagging question, he wasn't able to retain concentration for any meaningful length of time.

Nuria Oliver and her team at Telefónica Digital in Barcelona investigate such concepts, and she compares the use of smartphones to eating a piece of candy or chocolate—short, sweet, and satisfying an urge that quickly returns. Technology can be seen as *candy for the brain.*

Dr. Oliver is Scientific Director at Telefónica where she leads an extended team of ten full-time researchers, augmented with a similar number of PhD students who intern in the team for three months. She has been working for almost 20 years in closing the gap between humans and machines by building smarter cities, homes, cars, offices, and mobile phones. Her goal is to understand people and people's behavior and build systems that incorporate such understanding, be that on the individual or aggregate level. An important source of human behavioral data are the *digital footprints* that we all leave when we interact both with the physical and the digital world. Her dream is to build technology that not only understands people, but adapts to us, and can have positive impact in our lives, both individually and collectively. With interests ranging from big and personal data analysis, artificial intelligence and machine learning, persuasive and wearable computing, user modeling, and personalization, her team's work has taken various forms: from applications that characterize and understand human mobility in a city, region, or country to inform better policy and decision-making to persuasive mobile social games that help people take their medication properly, and sophisticated recommender systems that are able to take into account context to recommend relevant friends, mobile apps, or movies. And of course, in the case of Pep, the reasons why he is addicted to his phone.

The focus of the research project with Pep, and the lens through which Oliver and her team consider addiction, is *boredom* and *attention*. Inspired by the emerging prevalence of ephemeral or nonpermanent communication, they are investigating more fluid dynamics between users and their phones. Companies such as Snapchat, an extremely popular ephemeral messaging app that enables sending messages with an expiration time often measured in seconds, shows a possible future where not all of our digital footprints are left behind, or at least not so easily visible. As a by-product of their investigation into the use of Snapchat, they collected empirical evidence that people use mobile technology to combat boredom. With over 100% mobile phone penetration in developed economies and more mobile phones than people on the planet, gone are the days when we let our minds wander while commuting or waiting for an appointment, or when we initiated a spontaneous conversation with our neighbor in the subway or bus. We all carry a powerful computer in our pockets and purses, a computer that is connected 24/7, enabling us to access a wealth of information and potentially learn anywhere, anytime—but also meaning that we live in a world of constant entertainment and distraction.

We are all bored at times, and within this newly created world, we have found many ways to kill it. Fisher[1] describes boredom as *"an unpleasant, transient affective state in which the individual feels a pervasive lack of interest and difficulty concentrating on the current activity."* Psychologist John Eastwood, from York University in Toronto, has recently studied all scientific theories about boredom and concluded that boredom is best described in terms of attention: a bored person is not just someone who does not have anything to do; it's someone who is actively looking for stimulation but is unable to do so. Eastwood describes this state as the "unengaged mind."[2] Interestingly, in Eastwood's definition, boredom can correspond to both high and low arousal states.

Yet does boredom have a use? Is it necessary to pass through such an unpleasant transient state to achieve other benefits? Some studies have shown that boredom can lead to creativity. Researchers at the University of Central Lancashire found that people who first carried out a mundane task were more creative in the next compared to those who moved directly to the creative challenge.[3] The way that we kill boredom, through constant distraction, has been noted as one of the principal "creativity killers" by noted expert Teresa Amabile, who notes that *"interrupted people are unable to get deeply involved in the problem they are trying to solve."* My own previous work on creativity was centered on the virtual teams domain[4] and attempted to address the apparent oxymoron of virtual teams creativity by better controlling such interruptions and ensuring the human factor remained to the fore.

Boredom does have a purpose. As American poet Dorothy Parker once remarked, *"the cure to boredom is curiosity."* It is an emotional state that signals that your current activity or goals do not satisfy your needs or sufficiently motivate you. It is through the process of being bored that we look for other more interesting, fulfilling, or challenging activities. Today we flee from doing nothing and are increasingly subjecting ourselves to continual stimuli. This may defeat the actual purpose of boredom and lead to behavioral states including addiction, anxiety, and adult attention deficit disorder (AADD), which as Kass et al.[5] found increases with one's *proneness* to being bored together with sleep disorders.

In the Telefónica boredom research, Oliver and her team also look at one's *boredom proneness,* or propensity to being bored, which is considered to be a trait similar to personality. Yet many other factors are at play. Through the use of experience sampling, they have carried out a study where volunteers provide information about their emotional state throughout the day—namely, happiness (valence), excitement (arousal), and boredom levels—together with information about their context and mobile phone usage. Oliver and her team are beginning to correlate the operating context at that time—including information on location, movement, temperature, humidity, screen time, and so on—with the ultimate aim of predicting the user's state and associated needs and then providing content and appropriate suggestions. This doesn't mean, however, that the aim is to "kill" boredom or provide constant stimuli. By better understanding boredom, Oliver's team may better help people when they need to disconnect and so rather than endlessly cycle through social media and other frequently visited sites, provide nudges to other interesting and relevant content, or even suggest to turn the phone off, relax, or engage with the real world instead. The overarching aim is to develop technology that adapts to people, and not the other way around.

Addicted to Distraction

So is smartphone addiction simply a symptom of a deeper malaise? Broader questions are worthy of reflection. If we are bored, is it because of a lack of interest in the work we do? Who is responsible? The employer, by providing a more stimulating and challenging work environment, or the workers, by recognizing their own responsibility of doing the work they are paid to do in a disciplined and diligent manner? There is also the question of passion. Although not everyone has the choice, shouldn't we just stop following a career that fails to stimulate us—and simply do what we love? Whatever the answer, technology addiction is becoming more and more prevalent, and it's affecting the quality of work we do.

The ubiquitous nature of the smartphone allows us to take advantage of small time pockets during the day, leading to benefits including micro-productivity—killing some emails while waiting on a bus or the coffee line, finding some key data during a meeting—or diversion—playing Angry Birds or connecting with friends on Facebook—or basic utility, such as setting a morning alarm clock. And that ubiquity means that it is always there. Studies have shown that 79% of 18- to 44-year-olds have their smartphone within reach 22 hours per day.[6] Yet there is often a tipping point where that productivity, diversion, and utility becomes detrimental and even dangerous. How many people now check their email or Facebook status walking down the street, or while driving a car stopped at a traffic light (or even while driving), or the last thing they do before trying to get to sleep? Like similarly addictive drugs like alcohol, tobacco, and sugar, any perceived benefits can quickly evaporate, yet many of us cling to the illusion of advantage.

The Economist previously talked of being a "Slave to the Smartphone"[7] with the "slave" in question shown to be chained to the phone in the article header image. This is reflective of the fact that so many of us always have our smartphone at hand, as noted previously, and it also leads us to two key questions: First, do you feel the stress and strain of always having your smartphone within reach? Can you, for example, leave it in another room of the house when you go to bed at night, thereby resisting the temptation to check your email as the last thing you do before trying to fall asleep, or checking it if you wake up in the middle of the night to go to the bathroom. Buy an old-fashioned alarm clock! And second, are you in control? Many drug addicts are in denial (and just like drug addicts, people nowadays are checking in to clinics suffering from smartphone addiction—the Betty Ford clinic for the new age!), but can you make it through a family meal or business dinner without checking it? Try just the first course for starters! During drinks with friends? The sight of groups of people in a bar where each one is in the virtual world instead of the physical is increasingly (and depressingly) commonplace. Of course, there is often a good reason for checking in, but as Nuria Oliver and her team are finding out, it is not always beneficial to do so.

Such "slavery" affects health and well-being, yet also, critically, performance. In her work "Sleeping with the Smartphone,"[8] Harvard professor Leslie Perlow investigated the work of senior consultants at Boston Consulting Group, finding them to suffer from "always on dysfunction." This affected their health, well-being, and quality of client work, given that they were trapped in a never-ending cycle of responsiveness. So she asked them to switch off. Yet simply switching off is rarely an attractive proposition for many of us. There is often an anxiety that we will miss something important—an instruction from our boss, order or information request from a key client, a family member in need. However, they made a small change to their offline time, ensuring that when one member of the team was offline, all of them were. Termed Predictable Time Off, or PTO, they unplugged with less anxiety, safe (or at least safer!) in the knowledge that they weren't missing anything important, thereby redressing the balance and improving once again the quality of work.

I put *safer* in parentheses because there is a limit to the control we have over our external environment. Who knows when a client will look to close a deal or a family member is in urgent need? There are simple fixes. Putting aside the fact that much of our work stress these days comes on an internal level, we may simply redefine what urgency or emergency means. Perhaps having two phones makes sense, with one for private family matters and the other for business, or two email accounts. Or kill email altogether on your phone, making clear that a phone call is expected for "urgent matters." My doctoral research from 1999–2002 on virtual work looked at the mix of synchronous and asynchronous communication modes at the disposal of design teams (see Chapter 6, Reference 11). Part of the problem of the smartphone revolution has been the misuse of email, transforming it from an asynchronous mode of communication to synchronous. Think for a moment on the absurdity of an "urgent e-mail!"

Related to this point is the way in which we use technology in a company. Can you push back against a culture that expects 24/7 availability? Could you create a protocol for your team that defines how they are expected to use communication technology in a responsible and productive fashion? Think clearly on how messages should be communicated and who should be copied on an email, as well as the times those communications should be sent. There are increasing examples in business today that show elements of all of these, and that have been proven to improve health, well-being, and performance.

Intel in Germany found that its engineers were suffering stress from their email usage over the weekend, so the company unplugged the servers. Predictable Time Off in one fell swoop! Such approaches are commonplace in Germany; for example, certain parts of Volkswagen do not forward emails sent after 5 p.m. There was wide misreporting in April of 2014 regarding legislation that France had passed on banning emails after 6 p.m. There was no such legislation, merely a labor agreement that protected autonomous workers. The gusto with which the nonstory was picked up worldwide is perhaps symptomatic of the mass need for more offline and less distracted time. Some of my own client work has focused on (either technically or culturally) not sending emails between 10 p.m. and 6 a.m. That time, as we have seen in Chapter 2, "The New Lanark Mills," used to be reserved for rest—Owen's third "8." Yet just because we can't email doesn't mean that we can't work. Email is not work. More time writing and thinking will help us redress the balance of rigor, depth, and attention that is so scarce today. And even if we write an email late at night, saving it as a draft is often best. As we cover later in the chapter, our judgment can often wane late in the day. Have you ever sent an email late at night and immediately regretted it upon wakening? Further, by sending emails late at night, we often create pressure and expectation on others, especially more junior members of an organization. Google's Dublin office experimented with "going dark"[9] whereby employees checked in their phones when leaving at the end of the day, picking them up on their return the following morning. Increases in happiness and well-being were measured.

Attention Economics

Distraction addiction affects performance in many ways. Meetings are a prime example—overlong, poorly focused time killers where no one is sure what the conclusions or actions are. Through constant distraction, we reduce the quality, depth, rigor, and attention of our work and relationships. Nicholas Carr, in his work on *The Shallows*,[10] investigated the effect of constant distraction on the learning process, showing that memory consolidation, the process by which we transfer new things from our short-term memory to our long-term memory is affected by emails, phone calls, and people coming into our office.

Daniel Goleman's work on focus[11] combines many of the factors that have risen to the surface in recent years through our changing work and technological environment. He stresses the importance of improving our abilities in the focus domain, something that can be improved through training, and to be aware of the three types: inner focus, which concerns our thoughts and feelings, often known as cognitive control; empathy, connecting with others, as we have seen in Chapter 3, "Design

Your Life;" and outer focus, which concerns our understanding with the external world and the way we see and interact with that on a system level.

Work engagement and distraction have been investigated in the management literature. As touched on earlier, Eastwood and colleagues[2] proposed that boredom be defined in terms of attention in their paper on "The Unengaged Mind," arguing that attention on both an internal and external level comes from our satisfaction of that stimuli. Jett and George[12] discuss four key types of work interruptions—intrusions, breaks, distractions, and discrepancies—showing which are within our own control, and those within the organization's control, as well as the positive and negative nature of each.

It is with such a contemporary context that the words of Herbert Simon in 1971 retain an even greater significance. Talking on the subject of attention economics, Simon said:

> What information consumes is rather obvious: it consumes the attention of its recipients. Hence a wealth of information creates a poverty of attention.

These words came before the invention of the World Wide Web and about 40 years before former Google CEO Eric Schmidt talked of the exponential growth of information online, saying that we create as much information every two days as we did from the dawn of civilization up to 2003. Much talk in the business world focuses on the VUCA world where Volatility, Uncertainty, Complexity, and Ambiguity are the new normal. We ought to understand that more and more data is not necessarily a good thing. The concept of information overload means that the very technology that is causing the distress in the first place also has the potential to be our savior—through features including filters and intelligent recommendation systems. As I learned during my engineering education and particularly from the work of Professor Alex Duffy at Strathclyde and his "KID" typology—Knowledge, Information, and Data are distinct concepts often erroneously clubbed together for convenience. A simple example is the treatment of knowledge—a complex, implicit phenomena that combines the varied experiences of a human being—as if it were merely information; explicit, tangible, and easily transferred. The knowledge management field of the late 1990s and early 2000s never quite recovered from the inherent paradox it contained. As a consequence, organizations need to understand that more and more complexity, omnipresent in an era of Big Data, is certainly not the same as deep insight or knowledge. In the same way, Peter Drucker's conception of the "knowledge worker" should not be confused with a data or information worker. Just by having access to data and information through myriad sources such as YouTube and Wikipedia does not give us the deep insight and knowledge that Drucker noted as necessary to progress non-procedural thinking.

In my virtual design teams research, I created an awareness and switching framework for geographically distributed designers to better manage their work cycles and understand the effects this would have on their colleagues in another country. A necessary compromise of virtual team work is that our awareness is reduced, and so I proposed that greater focus be placed on different elements of awareness, such as the workspace, the goal of collaboration, and shared knowledge, and that they pay attention to balancing their own cycles, such as the switch between synchronous and asynchronous work, formal and informal work, and explicit and implicit communication. In the 10 or so years since that work was published, technology has altered these work cycles, putting them out of balance so that we constantly switch between communication modes and tasks throughout the day, with very little awareness or planning. This work behavior of constant switching has gained significant coverage the past couple of years and is more commonly known as *multitasking* (a slight misnomer because we never actually do more than one thing at the same time; rather, we switch rapidly between things). The original belief now being pushed out is that in a professional life with ever-increasing demands, doing more than one thing at a time was the only coping mechanism. Nowadays, however, multitasking is being recognized as a myth—a belief that is supported by research in fields from management science to neuroscience.

A well-known YouTube clip in recent years is the London Transport's "Awareness Test"—a campaign for cyclist safety.[13] If you are not familiar with it, try the test first before reading on!

It asks you to count the number of passes that a street basketball team makes, which normally results in the requisite focus to get the right number of 13. Just as you're patting yourself on the back for "passing" the test, it then asks if you saw the moonwalking bear, which passes through, rather brazenly, as the team passes the ball. This is based on the seminal "invisible gorilla" research in psychology,[14] which expertly illuminates the limits of our peripheral awareness. Simply put, when we focus intently on something, we miss what's going on around it. For my work with executives, I use it to emphasize the dangers of dividing our attention, and that under a multitasking protocol, the time taken to complete a given task, as well as the accuracy of it, can suffer greatly. The principal reason for this is the way our brains are wired. They are serial processors, not parallel processers like a computer, and are not capable of processing information-rich media simultaneously.

Mihály Csíkszentmihályi, whose work on Flow we discuss later in Chapter 14, "TRAIN," also comments on the bandwidth at our disposal for processing that information. At 110 bits/second, we are sadly just shy of the required bandwidth for holding two conversations at the same time (each would require 60 bits/second), although many do try!

Two common perceived outliers I receive in my classes regard childrens' and womens' abilities to multitask. Yet this is not just an adult male malaise! When we are surrounded by distraction and change our focus between multiple tasks, we need time to refocus fully on the previous task. Consider working on a document, or even reading this text. If you allow your email to ping, or a telephone call to disrupt your attention, you will lose "switching time" as you switch between tasks. Women are better at refocusing and lose less time on switching, but they still can't multitask! Regarding the younger generation, I believe that the giant leaps in usable technology in the past 20 years, from researchers like Dr. Oliver, are beginning to show the real potential of what we can do and how efficient we may one day become. Our brains are rewiring (and not always for the best—when was the last time, for example, that you remembered a phone number?), yet fundamental limits exist. Research at Stanford[15] found that the younger generation who believe "multitasking as the only way to get things done" were just as terrible in task completion in laboratory testing when multitasking. Even when the millennials consider something like email as prehistoric, the notion of advancement is far from guaranteed.

So although I considered switching from a positive planning standpoint in my virtual teams research, it has become the source of much wasted time and low-quality work where "firefighting" is the norm. With certain menial tasks, and even in exploration mode, multitasking may even be beneficial, yet for tough problems, only our undivided, focused attention will do.

This can also affect the quality of relationships. How many times do you talk with someone while really paying attention to something else, such as email? When was the last time you had a telephone conversation with someone and heard the gentle tapping of the keyboard? Either they're not listening to you, or they're writing a very bad email!

So how do we retain the quality, focus, and rigor in this increasing age of distraction? I've found simple changes to make a huge difference.

Positive Switching

Unplugging is key, but on its own it may be detrimental to well-being and performance. Following the rationale that we developed in Chapter 8, "RECOVER," on our rhythmic nature, having a more global view of switching between online and offline work, between hard focus and daydreaming, between exploring and refining allows us to maintain balance that leads to great work. From our discussion of design in Chapter 3, we see that such cycles or switches occur in creative work, through the stages of convergent and divergent thinking, which characterize the creative process. So positive switching is not about doing less work, it is about doing more human work. We are not machines that are designed to be "on" all the time in a very linear fashion.

The A. G. Lafley example in Chapter 8 shows periodic downtime, working to set rhythms during the day, while the BCG consultants in Professor Perlow's work benefitted from downtime that was predictable in order not to suffer from unrealistic expectations. These examples show that a large amount of time offline is not always necessary—Lafley talks of the 5–15 minutes required to recharge. So Lafley's protocol was just as much about the hour or hour and a quarter of focused quality work with no distractions as it was about the recovery. One would not work without the other.

Small, frequent unplugging is what is required. The times of being offline or uncontactable for a two-week vacation are long gone for many professionals—if they even take their vacation in the first place![16] So strategies such as "killing emails" for an hour or so in the early morning of a family vacation when everyone else is still in bed, and then unplugging for the rest of the day can help people stay connected but still enjoy the off time. Many of the executives we have worked with at The LAB can't actually relax without having dealt with their correspondence on a daily basis. Creating focused time with no distractions can be very valuable and allow high-quality work to be completed. Consider long-haul flights when many professionals fill their briefcase with key work that has been pending, and enjoy the uninterrupted reflection that the flight affords. And now they tell us: "Fantastic, we now have onboard Wi-Fi!" Please, no!

How can we create such an environment in our day-to-day lives? Even planning two or three 90-minute slots during the day (a very low percentage of your total working day) with no email, phone, or meetings can be highly productive. What is your closed door policy? Do people know to phone you only if it's an emergency? Perhaps you even have two phones, with a special "emergency phone" always on, and known only to a few people. Do colleagues know not to email at 11 p.m. or at least not to expect a response at that time? Of course, being a manager is about being responsive and reacting to crises—steadying the ship—yet some degree of proactive, quality focused work is also critical.

So switch positively between online and off, between hard focus and fun, between email and real work. Seriously, how about a simple change such as checking email in blocks, four times a day, or ten? How many times do you currently check it? As well as the carousel of social media and other favorite websites? Boredom perhaps has a role to play here, but also a lack of awareness of the way our work patterns and habits have changed with technology advancement over the past 10 years. What time do you disconnect from technology at night? As we have seen in the RECOVER element of Chapter 8, even if we think we are relaxing by reading a book on a tablet, for example, the blue light will affect the quality of our sleep.

Considering our rhythmic nature, quality is required in "off" as well as "on." What is the point of taking a break if you're still checking email? Are you fully present when having a meal with a loved one? Or do you complain about work? At times, the catharsis of discussing work matters with close family and friends is important—I believe successful people have such a network who act as trusted advisors for all aspects of life—yet I think being aware if this is the norm is important. Enjoying deep disconnect, if only for a short while, will allow you to sustain high performance when returning to "on" mode. The best performers that I have come across in life, whether in business or sport, are fantastic at recovering.

So positive switching may enable us to cultivate our energy and focus during a long day and week, allowing us to get more high-quality work done.

Mindful or Mindless?

Greater attention to our different states leads to the concept of *mindfulness*, which has garnered much attention in executive development circles in recent years. Being mindful simply means being in the present moment. Many of the stresses of modern day professional work come from the fact that we are stressing about something that has already happened, such as an unpleasant conversation with a colleague or client, or something that is yet to come, a key presentation or talk with our boss that is pending. Stress occurs because, generally, these things are out of our control. We can control the present. And this is not only a symptom of our time. The society of the day will always tend toward stress and chaos as part of the "modern way"—consider de Coubertin's correspondence communicating the overwork in the Paris of 1887 and the 1894 *British Medical Journal* editorial on the factors affecting sleeping disorders. Can you therefore set yourself apart by getting the necessary mindful reflection in between the action?

Meetings, again, are in the firing line! We often spend our day flying from meeting to meeting, without a break in between. Have a look around you the next time you're in a meeting—if people aren't playing with electronic toys, their mind may very well be in the meeting they've just come from, or even the meeting they're going to next. Body and mind are not always aligned.

Mindfulness has three main tenets, which can help us reconnect to the present. First are the physical sensations. Feeling yourself physically sitting on a chair, and your feet planted on the ground, is a first step in many mindfulness practice sessions. Feel your heart beat, and the inhalation and exhalation of your breathing. For me, mindfulness fits perfectly with my focus on the physical self as the point of departure for health, well-being, and performance. It is called "mindfulness," yet it often starts with the body. From feeling your body to engaging your senses: what are the things you hear, smell, or feel? These could be in the internal environment, or ideally outside, such as the wind on your cheeks or the warmth of the sun on your body. In addition to the physical senses, the second and third tenets of mindfulness are ideas and emotions. Perhaps being fully conscious of a scene that surrounds you will give you an idea to redesign a work process, or paint your bedroom a different color. Being fully mindful of a familiar smell may fill you with joy or excitement. If you're Scottish, feeling the sun on your face will ensure you make the most of that moment!

You can practice mindfulness in many situations. These can include taking the pause or time-out upon waking and before starting another busy day, or in the car in order to create the necessary *switch* between office time and family time. Creating an internal, mental space when all around you is increasingly frenetic can be a very valuable tool, as shown again by A. G. Lafley (see Chapter 8, Reference 11):

> I've tried to teach myself to meditate. When I travel, which is 60% of the time, I find that meditating for 5, 10, or 15 minutes in a hotel room at night can be as good as a workout. Generally, I think I know myself so much better than I used to. And that has helped me stay calm and cool under fire.

We've been using mindfulness practice in our executive programs since 2009, and it is another example of a specialist field that we have studied and attempted to "operationalize" for busy, skeptical executives. I have a lot of respect for mindfulness-based practitioners who dedicate 100% of their time to this discipline. I believe in certain circumstances that

Mindfulness Based Therapy (MBT) is of great value—and is proven to help in cases where severe stress, depression, and other mental health issues are at play. The British National Health Service is an example of a highly pragmatic institution that prescribes MBT. Yet as a guest observer on other executive training programs, I have witnessed a room full of managers revolting against a one-hour body scan when they have only a few hours to spare. As such I have tried to take some of the value of mindfulness and apply it in shorter time frames as well as frame it within the real context of a professional life. A common tool is trying a 50-second mindfulness-based exercise, which most attendees feel to be at least 2–3 minutes, or simply trying a group mindfulness walk or lunch during programs. These are simple, time-efficient, and easily replicated in the field.

By advocating increased mindfulness in our daily lives, I do not mean always applying hard focus to our working day. Being mindful may simply mean paying more attention to our surroundings, rather than being glued to our electronic devices or staring at the ground and ruminating on the myriad issues that comprise our life, work, and ambitions. As we discussed in Chapter 8, paying attention while walking can have a positive impact on recovery. Beyond the simple definition of mindfulness as "being present," we have the more advanced conceptualization as the "nonjudgmental observation of thoughts and feelings." As we saw in Chapter 4, "Day-to-Day Reengineering," observation plays a key role in gaining deep insight to a phenomena. When was the last time that you observed something deeply? Perhaps even something that you have passed or "seen" a hundred or a thousand times. By taking just a few minutes out of your normal day, observing something powerfully, as designers do in their daily work, we can yield some surprising results. Challenge your assumptions and long-held beliefs! Linked to this train of thought is a quote I often show in my classes, together with some video clips on disconnecting from technology. It comes from a letter that the artist Jackson Pollock received from his father, which I found via the excellent Brain Pickings website:[17]

> The secret of success... is to be fully awake to everything around you.

At first glance, it may seem a little strange, since as a generation we are more sleep deprived than ever before and always awake! We are awake, but we rarely pay attention. Instead, we multitask our way through a constant minefield of distraction. So what are the "weak signals" you are missing through a *mindless* day? Mindlessness comes from the fact that we rely on our underlying patterns, because we have experience and because we have knowledge and skills. Such an autopilot mode is dangerous because it doesn't allow us to question and change the things that we are doing, with the added detriment to time becoming indistinct. So even in following the same routine each and every day, such as a daily commute, observe and notice something for the first time. In a meeting or presentation, do something different. Do something for the first time. This allows us to be more mindful instead of mindless, and also to slow down time. Positively switch between work and play, between focus and daydreaming, and being more mindful can play a role in each.

Decision Fatigue

Being on 24/7 affects performance, and one of the key issues is the quality of our decisions. Advancing through a managerial career is often measured by the increasing quantity and quality of decisions, and being the "decider" can leave a mark. Yet decision fatigue is hard to detect. It is not like physical fatigue where one is conscious of being tired. Suffering from decision fatigue will simply result in making bad decisions. As we noted earlier regarding the regret that surrounds sending a late night email, many of us may have experienced it. As reported by the *New York Times*,[18] "the best decision makers are the ones who know when not to trust themselves." The article describes research by Shai Danziger and colleagues (see Chapter 1, Reference 14) on the case of a jury panel in Israel, where the chances of getting parole were 90% less in the afternoon. The judges were suffering from decision fatigue through having to rule all day on cases without sufficient breaks. The system was subsequently redesigned to give all prisoners a fair hearing, with this redesign including greater attention to recovery as well as the food the judges were eating. Judicial decision making, where stereotypes and heavy caseloads can create a challenging environment for consistent, high-quality decisions, has also offered a context in which the benefits of mindfulness has been investigated.[19] Much of the routes of decision fatigue can be traced to Baumeister and colleagues and their research on willpower as a muscle.[20] This research looks at the energy requirements of the brain, which, like many muscles in the body, requires glucose to function. Part of their findings lead us to the catch 22 situation of dieters. To lose weight, you don't eat (or eat less), yet in order to get the glucose for the willpower not to eat, eating is necessary!

And the decisions don't have to be complex to take their toll. All decisions big or small, private or professional, use up the energy we have. This explains why supermarket shopping is so exhausting and why food companies place sugar and chocolate products at the checkout. Creating automatic routines, as we discussed in Chapter 4, can remove the need for decisions and therefore help reduce the load on decision fatigue. Barack Obama mentioned this research in an interview with *Vanity Fair*.[21] Talking of his routine and habits that supported his performance, he said:

> You'll see I wear only gray or blue suits, I'm trying to pare down decisions. I don't want to make decisions about what I'm eating or wearing. Because I have too many other decisions to make.

Now, I don't want you to wear the same clothes every day, or eat the same food every day! Rather, we may look at how even seemingly insignificant small changes to our daily focus may have an effect on how we perform. If someone like Obama is looking at reengineering his day and essentially "hacking" his routine, then maybe we all can.

Top Ten Takeaways: FOCUS

1. Ask yourself if you are addicted to your smartphone, or the online world in general.

2. Recognize doing nothing, including boredom, as serving a valuable purpose.

3. Reduce the ubiquity of the smartphone, for example, through using an old-fashioned alarm clock.

4. Manage expectations on a professional level before unplugging.

5. Create a positive culture in your team by creating and sharing a protocol on communication and technology use.

6. Recognize multitasking as a myth and cultivate more focused time with distractions *designed out*.

7. Again consider your rhythms, in terms of your workflow, through *positive switching*.

8. Try mindfulness, even for short periods, recognizing that it begins with the body.

9. Think about the quality of your decisions, when you normally make them, and take care when making decisions in the latter half of the day.

10. Look for more simplicity in your work and life.

It is important that we take a pause and cut away much of the complexity in our professional lives. Historical wisdom is again at our disposal. The opening chapter quote from Peter Drucker was part of his writing in 1966 on *The Effective Executive*, and I believe we need to revisit such aspects of prioritization and focus almost 50 years later. In 2002, *Harvard Business Review* asked us to "Beware the Busy Manager," with the question: "*Are the least effective managers the ones who look like they're doing the most?*" Just because we run around like crazy, answering emails within a couple of minutes, does not make us an effective executive. Being busy does not mean being successful. As Ernest Hemingway said: "*Never mistake motion for action.*" Focus is essential for our well-being, our creativity, our learning ability, and the quality of our work, and it can be easily cultivated by us all. Even Pep.

On Building a Systematic, Continuous Innovation Capability

Out there in some garage is an entrepreneur who's forging a bullet with your company's name on it.

—Gary Hamel

Janus was the Roman god of beginnings and transitions. Having two faces, one to look ahead to the future and one looking back at the past, he is with us to this day in the name that the Romans gave to the first month of the year, January. He was also associated with gates, travel, and endings. On an enterprise level, how may we consider such aspects of tension between the old and the new? How to build on the successes to date without being trapped in the same way of doing things? How to maintain a sense of urgency within the workforce? How to balance the optimum nature of existing operations with starting again and innovating a brighter future? Short term or long term? Or both? In short, what to focus on, and when?

Longevity is a difficult thing to pull off in companies. The changing face of the Fortune 500, FTSE 100, and other tradable indexes is testament to this fact. Innosight reports that the average company lifespan of companies in the S&P 500 index was 60 years in 1960 and 18 years now.[1] Microsoft, celebrating its 40th birthday in 2015, is a veritable veteran seemingly bereft of agility and the ability to change in recent years. Even those companies that began to show Microsoft as an aging technology company, including Facebook and Google, have not always found the scaling process to be smooth and have themselves faced pressure from a new generation of entrepreneurs ensconced in their garages. Having two faces is a difficult thing to manage. The requisite organizational focus is required on various levels—on leveraging previous experiences, on fully exploiting current strengths, and on addressing the gap for future success.

Tushman and O'Reilly (see Chapter 4, Reference 5) considered such factors in their work on *ambidextrous* organizations, a line of development reframed by various management scholars, including Govindarajan and Trimble[2] with their work on strategic innovation. They examine the dual purpose of organizations to exploit existing business and to simultaneously explore a related new business—by forgetting what has helped the corporation thrive yet borrow its resources. Learning, forgetting, and borrowing are the three key actions, with learning being the most difficult, which concerns the ability of the new organization to learn how to predict new business outcomes. Another key aspect of learning is that the rationale for making decisions and working actions is more visible.

There are three different challenges then: forgetting assumptions, mindsets, and biases that may no longer be valid or relevant; borrowing assets and resources with concrete value; and learning how to improve predictions of business performance. They use the terms "CoreCo" and "NewCo" to illustrate their examples. Planning is also of a different nature because not all actions will be completed. They note that "though accountability to plans is an effective practice in mature businesses, it can be crippling in new high-potential businesses." This links to some of our previous discussion on dealing with disruption in Chapter 9, "On the Criticality of Resilience for Our Future World." As noted by Bowers and Christensen, a new mind-set and culture of an emerging business must learn to get excited again by the "$50k sale"[3] Govindarajan and Trimble also highlight that the means of evaluation of the new organization is key, which should not always be based on financial output, as is the case for the existing organization. Beyond the conventional financial metrics, how may we fully evaluate the new way of doing things, often within a broad range of options? Innovation metrics ought to constitute a key area of focus.[4]

Innovation Metrics

Innovation metrics are the set of measurements used to track the development of a new idea toward a final form. The measures can be used for issues such as creating a staged research and development (R&D) model, measuring the cost of R&D, ranking innovation investments inside the company, developing a portfolio view, forming codevelopment partnerships, and analyzing internal and external intellectual property.

They are a topic of prime interest to countries, economists, companies, teams, and individual innovators. Across this spectrum of interested parties, the measurements comprise all manner of the quantitative and qualitative, strategic and tactical, knowledge oriented and profit oriented. The challenge is in knowing how innovation metrics affect behavior. The best metrics will align priorities and provide focus on key activities. Examples of innovation metrics currently in use within industry include the following:

- IBM deployed a beta software download site (http://alphaworks. ibm.com) that measured the number of downloads and source-code licensing requests per software package. This quantitative data offered the company an indicator of future demand for individual packages.

- Intel measures the dollars spent on its university-based research versus the dollars spent on bringing any university-developed technologies developed into the company. The company uses this financial measure to define the success of its academic research partnerships, with a deliberate focus on lowering the cost of absorption.

- Eli Lilly "variabalizes" the cost of new drug discoveries by offering bounties on hard research problems. The company aims at an ROI of $2 million for a "standard" problem (10% of postings) and $50 million for "roadblock" problems (90%) that Lilly staff has been unable to solve.

- Emerson sought to decrease the costs of adopting new technologies while increasing the value of adopting these same technologies. The company implemented a program to reduce the time elapsed between the first and last adoption of innovation-enabling technologies in the company's business units.

The most successful approach is to use multiple metrics that integrate general measurements (head count, patents filed, or number of projects in development) with metrics that are specific to the area of innovation being pursued. For example, a company beginning a New Product Development (NPD) program should search for existing technologies and create a make-versus-buy analysis, making sure to include the time savings that a license offers. NPD also typically includes three types of metrics: portfolio, project, and process.

Muller, Valikangas, and Merlyn[5] discuss the importance of innovation metrics for improving the management of innovation in organizations. They highlight the degree of change within the top of every industry, contrasting the range of companies cited as best practice in seminal publications in 1982 and then again 12 years later, different again from the present-day innovation "leaders." They state: "Such high turnover at the top suggests that the real problem isn't a lack of innovation—it's sustained innovation. Companies may seize upon a good idea that gives them an advantage for a while, but sooner or later, they cede this advantage to a competitor who has found an even better idea."

From time to time, companies will manage to put in place all pieces of the puzzle necessary to successfully innovate. In the past, such a one-shot success, especially for smaller companies, was enough to sustain a competitive position. Today this is no longer the case. Companies need to pursue a portfolio of initiatives to provide a continuous flow of innovations. A consistent stream is needed to become a regular innovator, to sustain the business in the short, medium, and longer terms.

When developing the metrics for a firm, it is useful to review competitors' metrics, discuss industry best practices, and even work with partner companies to develop a more holistic viewpoint. Metrics should be reviewed at the start and end of new projects, or at recurring intervals to add (or remove) specific measures.

Different companies and industrial sectors each focus on different mixes of the dozens of currently available metrics. The challenge is in finding the right metrics to fit the business needs. These may focus on measuring the project, risk, financial aspects, or the customer.

Operationalizing Innovation

A better understanding of measuring innovation together with the dual view on past and future will help to build a systematic, continuous innovation capability.[6] That dual view of today's operations with tomorrow's innovation may be viewed as *operationalizing innovation*—an oxymoron because the innovation of today becomes the operations of tomorrow—yet signifying a systematic approach that makes innovation an organic ever-present within the organization without compromising the efficiency of scaled operations.

The top management function in a company therefore needs to take closer order of such an activity, better understanding how various streams of innovation pull in the right direction and serve strategy thrust. This calls for a reappraisal of what innovation is, and how we approach it. There is no doubt that the main focus of innovation in recent years has been on technology, and to a lesser extent, the product. Yet it is necessary to depart from this technology/product-centric view of innovation. How do companies foster innovation in any business aspect, beyond technological innovation and new product introduction? What approach and what combination of innovation elements leads to business success? How may that be measured? These are just some of the key questions necessary to deliver the right focus and build a systematic and continuous innovation capability.

Innovation means different things to different people, yet it always implies transforming new ideas into renewed sources of value. This is much more than just new products or technology—a common misconception. Products and technology often lead to relatively short-lived benefits, with the results open to quick imitation and the loss of competitive advantage.[7]

Many of the most well-known innovations in recent years—the Starbucks customer experience around coffee, Amazon's broad offerings, the Cirque du Soleil concept, nimble and fast organizations built on the network and federal forms, low-cost air travel, flexible supply chains, or total customer solutions—have had little to do with technology or new products in the traditional sense, and more to do with the actual delivery of new sources of customer value. Furthermore, by looking closely at one of the most successful products of all time, the Apple iPod, it is clear that the overall value emanated from much more than just core MP3 technology, or even good product design. These were the foundations from which other types of innovation, including service, experience, and marketing, reenforced their strength and ultimate dominance in the market, moving beyond the MP3 player sector to the online music industry in general.

By overly focusing on technology inside the business, companies will be unable to produce their own iPod success story. Muller, Valikangas, and Merlyn[5] state that poor innovation management and performance have resulted from metrics overly focused on technology, stating that such metrics, although useful, offer a limited view of a company's innovativeness. "They don't measure the company's overall innovation capability. In emphasizing technology development, they neglect business-concept innovation," the authors state. "And their focus on R&D and products makes them less suitable for service companies and companies outside the high-tech sector." In sum, product and technology innovation can be viewed as important elements within a family of innovation types— from innovation in any business process or activity to the transformation of the business model.

In *Dealing with Darwin*, Geoffrey Moore[8] considered such a broad family of innovation types highlighting that different types get *traction* at different points. He showed the need to change innovation focus over time, depending on market performance and competitor behavior, which may be linked to the stage of the business life cycle. For example, following a focus on disruptive innovation and then product and platform innovation at the beginning of the life cycle, he advocates a focus toward line extension and then experience. Coordination of activities and integration of goals in different business areas are key to the wellbeing of the innovation outcome. As stated by Moore, if many types of innovation are implemented without a common thrust, the net benefit will be zero. Strategy becomes the common ground, or glue that holds the pieces together.

If innovation is to be broad-based and continuous, it cannot be left to natural, emergent processes or people's heroic efforts. There must be a systematic approach in place, one that fits the current state of the company. Peter Drucker aimed to demystify innovation, stating that it rarely sprung from a flash of inspiration but rather a "cold-eyed analysis of seven kinds of opportunities."[9] He added to the understanding of innovation as a system that could be managed, classifying these opportunities as: unexpected occurrences, incongruities, process needs, industry and market changes, demographic changes, changes in perception, and new knowledge.

Innovation becomes a change program for many companies, and change needs to be guided, directed, focused, well thought-out, and pro-active. It follows that firms need a system in place to transform the underlying processes, mind-sets, attitudes, and competencies that support innovation. This may result in some form of framework, structure, or process, suitable for the specific company needs. Talented individuals may be able to pull it off every now and then, yet in order to be consistently innovative, there has to be a system in place built around an innovative process.

So, broad-based, continuous, and systematic innovation is a requirement for business excellence, *giving innovation the right focus at the right time.*

This demands a different approach to innovation thinking as compared to traditional product and technology considerations. Professor Mohan Sawhney at the Kellogg School of Management defines the narrow focus on product, R&D, and platforms as directional myopia, an "innovation pathology"[10] and details the "innovation radar." It displays 12 dimensions of business innovation, including brand, platform, and customer experience, that encompass all aspects of a business system and that are developed along four principal lines:

- The offerings a company creates (WHAT)

- The customers it serves (WHO)

- The processes it employs (HOW)

- The channels, or presences, it uses to take its offerings to market (WHERE)

The innovation radar is presented as a diagnosis tool to identify and pursue neglected dimensions, and the basis of a business innovation system.

Building a systematic, continuous innovation capability takes a more strategic view of innovation, and a number of implementation challenges exist:

- **A holistic view of drivers of business innovation capacity.** The right approach is an overall management system, including management drivers (such as leadership, strategy, or organizing practices), enabling factors (such as culture), and a process to manage strategic initiatives and individual contributions.

- **An innovative culture.** One which is continuously shaped by introducing evolutionary changes in management principles and practices, specifically designed to foster innovation. This cultural change builds on several levels: high levels of ambition and even stretch in selected areas or strategic issues. New sources of support for intrapreneurs and innovation leaders. And, finally, management commitment to develop trust and discipline along the innovation process. This entails an appreciation of the softer side of innovation—from values to emotions and relationships, in addition to management practices, which jointly shape culture.

- **A systematic innovation process.** One which translates ideas into strategic initiatives and turns them into results. The three building blocks of the process are: an initial strategic thinking effort to provide guidelines for creativity, focused idea generation, and the implementation of a balanced portfolio of projects and initiatives across the business. This is a general management approach to the innovation process, linking strategic thinking and action.

- **Removing obstacles to change.** At the core of implementation is the need to reinvent core management processes and principles that are often taken for granted. In addition to the *forgetting* element of Govindarajan and Trimble's work on strategic innovation, Gary Hamel's work on *Management Innovation*[11] looked at redesigning some of the standard management practices that no longer apply to the innovation and wider organizational challenges of today.

- **A people-based approach.** This includes recognition of the critical value of peoples' willingness to contribute. Commitment by people in different positions will make a difference to the quality of ideas provided, levels of participation in project teams, and the support and resources offered to innovation activities that differ from daily tasks.

- **The involvement of the wider community in the innovation ecosystem.** This includes stakeholders within the value chain and even the involvement of external players (co-innovation) may help to foster broad and regular innovation.

These management challenges may be addressed by assuming two types of focus already touched on in *Sustaining Executive Performance*. First, recognizing constraints as an opportunity, and second, copying best practice from the small enterprise.

We have already discussed the view of design, especially in the context of social need, that looks at turning limitations into opportunities. R&D dollars do not always convert into more innovation: the era of technology push and resultant feature creep products with poor usability are, thankfully, a thing of the past. Lean start-up methodology shows the potential of such an approach and work around reverse innovation (follow-up work by Govindarajan and Trimble) and frugal innovation shows pioneering cases in the developed world as well as emerging economies. GE has been a big disruptor in this space, with CEO Jeff Immelt as one of the pioneers of reverse innovation. *Business Week* reported on the case of developing the MAC 400, a portable ECG machine for the Indian market.[12] The design brief in itself is instructive, both in terms of the creative "stretch" provided to the design team as well as the value for other markets around the world:

> Take a 15-lb. electrocardiograph machine that cost $5.4 million and took three and a half years to develop. Squeeze the same technology into a portable device that weighs less than three pounds and can be held with one hand. Oh, and develop it in 18 months for just 60% of its wholesale cost.

Regarding the second area of focus, the notion of limited resource is at the core of the small- and medium-sized enterprise (SME). Yet the SME also has several defining features that may be replicated by the larger organization. A lack of scale and available resources forces the best small companies to open their doors, to collaborate across their supply chain and with customers, and embrace change more readily. Agility is therefore a key feature of the small enterprise and they value, and fully expect, contribution from every single person within it. The small enterprise also has an affinity and trust with the local community, fully recognizing the role they play in society, and are humble—knowing they don't have all the answers and so are willing to learn and work with others.

In sum, if a company wants to innovate systematically and continuously, it needs a comprehensive effort to align a number of drivers of innovation capacity. It also needs to nurture a culture of innovation and overcome major obstacles to change. Even more, these endeavors have to balance the demands of daily execution and innovation development. This is a major reason why a general management view is much needed, and a narrower approach will fall short. Implementing a systematic, continuous innovation capability is rising up in top management agendas. Building such a capability will help the organization deal with disruption, the unexpected—and forecasted—shocks of a VUCA world that require resilience on multiple levels. This does not mean reinventing from scratch but building on the resources already present within the company. It also recognizes that resource scarcity on a planetary level may affect a more lean mind-set in the organization where creativity and innovation is the de facto result from constraint and limitation. By operating with the humility of the small enterprise, increased agility and the collaborative nature typical of such organizations will result in societal as well as business benefit. This will fuel the organization in the longer term, turning the right *focus* into sustainable success.

12

FUEL

We never have business meals at El Bulli. If it's about business, you're probably not paying much attention to the food.

—Ferran Adrià

I just managed to take the win on the line. The tall Basque, who looked more like a basketball player than a runner, had charged down my lead on the finishing straight, forcing me to dig deeper for a last, final surge, and the line came just in time. It was my first road race in San Sebastian, a 5k in 2003, and I paid little attention to the "dinner for two" voucher that nestled inside the trophy. "What? You won dinner at Arzak?" was the disbelieving reply when I told my colleagues the following day. And so my wife and I trotted along to meet Juan Mari Arzak and his daughter Elena the following week. With Michelin stars going back 20 years and widely considered one of the world's top chefs, it was the start of my gastronomic tour (quite by chance) of Northern Spain. They told me Woody Allen had been at the same table the week before while visiting the city for the annual film festival, and I went home hungry because there was little on what I perceived to be an overly fussy menu to satisfy my simple palate at the time—philistine! I would later cycle past the remaining San Sebastian Michelin stars on a frequent basis, before moving to Girona and doing the same past Adrià's El Bulli in Roses then getting to know the Roca brothers (and sister Encarna!) during my wedding preparation in 2008, expertly catered by El Celler de Can Roca. My background, growing up in the west of Scotland where the local high-starch diet is often a result of braving a harsh climate, was as far from the world of haute cuisine as one can get, but I came to understand several aspects of that world—how we eat and prepare meals—that make such universal good practice, both for ourselves as individuals, and also for the planet. Local sourcing, top-to-tail eating, tasting portions, mindful eating—all staples of the gastronomic world that allow us to consider eating beyond the primal or mechanistic survival view of ingesting calories.

Y et we ought to combine such an art and experience-based view of food with the functional performance view taken by athletes. So how do you fuel yourself? I remember a cartoon from *The New Yorker* a couple of years ago showing two office-based professionals standing next to the coffee machine. One, pouring himself a cup, says to the other, *"I try to keep my coffee buzz going till the martini buzz kicks in."* This shows the tactics employed by many of us simply to survive professional life. It is like A. G. Lafley's previous approach to work when he said he was *grinding* through the day. So rather than merely considering food as an essential element for survival, I believe we can pay more attention to the things we eat to fuel our performance—in much the same way that an athlete does. Let me give you an example.

In the 2008 Beijing Olympics, I remember the press attention that Michael Phelps received regarding his diet. In fact, Phelps said at the time that he could do only three things: "eat, sleep, and swim"—a real swimming machine! If we consider any athlete, particularly at elite level, these actions represent their "holy trinity" of performance, substituting swimming for their own discipline. They recognize the critical importance of sleeping and recovery in general, as we have already discussed in the professional business context in Chapter 8, "RECOVER," but they also elevate food as fuel. In Phelps's case, it was fuel to win multiple Olympic gold medals and break world records. At the time, this was cited as 12,000 calories daily, as well as presented pictorially on the front page of many newspapers worldwide. Phelps later clarified that he ate nowhere near 12,000 calories on a daily basis, yet the principle was correct. To fuel that level of performance, that stellar output let's say, one must think on the requisite inputs.

So rather than grabbing a sandwich at our desk, skipping meals, resenting the time required to both prepare and consume food, how may we change our mind-set from simply *food for survival* to *food for performance*? The requisite inputs for your own stellar output. One of the authors of the Corporate Athlete work, Tony Schwartz, launched an initiative in Manhattan a couple of years ago called Take Back Your Lunch. The idea was to encourage people to recognize the great importance of taking the time to eat lunch, as a necessary means of recovery in a busy day, and not to value the half-hour or so saved by eating a sandwich at their desk and therefore affecting their performance throughout the remainder of the day.

Are you aware of what, how, and when you eat? A majority of diet advice in today's world focuses on what you eat, and we look at this in the course of this chapter. Yet by simply making changes to *how* we eat and *when* we eat, we may also affect change. By reflecting on these simple questions, you may transform the way you eat and the way you perform—not to mention other valued areas of our lives, such as weight management.

How We Eat

We have already covered the concept of mindfulness in several parts of the book, particularly in the FOCUS element of the SEP model in Chapter 10. And mindful eating is a large and growing area of study. Research has shown that if we are more mindful—simply paying attention to the process of eating—we can better manage our weight. One of the main reasons is the speed at which we eat. As busy professionals, we often eat too fast, given pressures on our time or the fact that we have starved ourselves during a large part of our day. When we eat too fast, we tend to overeat because our stomach takes time to send a signal to our brain to say that it is full. So eating more slowly is important, not only to better control the amount of food we eat and therefore control our weight, but also to better enjoy the experience of eating. We often eat so fast that we don't even taste our food, or are unaware of the food that we have put on our plate—for instance, at a buffet. Food is one of the joys of life, and improved well-being can result if we pay a little more attention. So enjoying the experience of a meal with colleagues or friends or family, through food selection and eating, can have mental as well as physical benefits.

The Alicia Foundation in Catalonia, founded in collaboration with Ferran Adrià, conducts research into such themes as part of its mission to improve the healthy eating habits of the Catalan people, particularly the younger generation. They have found a powerful impact on eating habits and resultant improved health by teaching people, especially young people, to cook for themselves rather than always buying ready-made meals or eating out.[1] The Foundation discovered that when people prepare their own food, they increase their awareness of what real food is and eat more healthily. Food ingredient purchase and meal preparation is therefore part of a more mindful approach to eating. Dr. Elena Roura, senior researcher at the Foundation, says that the benefits of healthy eating through cooking extend to involving children in the process, especially those who may not normally eat the right type of food for their growth and development. Although many of us don't have the time to prepare meals in the same way that a full-time chef or part-time worker may have, small changes in preparation and planning can make such an approach feasible. Dr. Roura has also found that the simple matter of plate design makes a difference to our eating experience. When subjects ate dessert from a white plate instead of a black one, they found it to be sweeter and more pleasant in general.[2] The brain therefore plays a key role in the eating process, and another fascinating concept provides us with an additional example. Look at Figure 12.1. Which of the black circles is the largest?

Figure 12.1 The Delboeuf illusion

Both are the same size, and yet our perception is affected by the outer larger circle, which makes us believe that the black circle on the left side is smaller than that on the right. This is termed the Delboeuf illusion, after the Belgian philosopher who created it around 1888 with the same visual processes in play to that of the Ebbinghaus illusion or Titchener circles, which became popular around a decade later. If the black circles were replaced with bowls of sugar-laden breakfast cereal, what would you be most likely to do? The bowl on the left? And the right? Most of us would probably add more cereal to the bowl on the left and either take some out of the bowl on the right or simply start eating. This phenomenon was shown in the *Journal of Consumer Research*.[3] On a simple level, satisfying hunger has been shown to be reliant on *how full we perceive our plate to be* in other studies, around 70%.[4] So what would be the simple takeaway, based on this knowledge, that could lead to eating less? Correct! Use smaller plates. Perhaps this explains why we tend to leave a high-class restaurant, in which they often use very ornate large plates, still feeling hungry!

The law of the small plate has been exploited in Google as part of its overall focus on improving worker productivity through better health and happiness. Yet they simply didn't replace the large plates with small ones. They wanted to give their employees a choice and provided a nudge toward making a choice. That nudge was a simple sign posted in the buffet area that highlighted the research showing the weight management benefits of taking a smaller plate. Now whether they then went to the buffet to refill on twice as many occasions remains to be seen! But the research and the nudge combined to encourage a new, simple, yet potentially powerful change. A similar nudge was created by Google with regard to the consumption of water. By changing the placement of drinks in a fridge, the consumption of water increased by 47%. If you want to grab a can of soda, it proves more awkward—bending down further, stretching one's arm—than simply opening the fridge door and taking a bottle of water that is placed within easy reach. Now you would think that extending your hand a few inches more wouldn't make a difference to the choice, yet those familiar with supermarket strategy know the large premium that brands pay to be situated on a specific part of the shelf, within easy reach and at immediate eye level.

Athletes take hydration very seriously, and dehydration can affect the brain just as much as it affects the body. Maintaining good hydration levels throughout the working day by sipping small quantities of water on a continual basis can keep the body and brain functioning to optimum levels. Sometimes when we think we are hungry, we are actually thirsty, and so by maintaining good hydration, we may also better manage our weight. The body is approximately 65% water (by weight), and Michael and Juliette McGannon, experts in the domain of executive health (see Chapter 3, Reference 5), have talked about how the aging process is actually a "drying out" process. Much of the food and drink we consume, such as coffee and alcohol, contributes to this lifelong drying out, which can result in numerous health problems. So not drinking enough water is one thing, yet drinking too much soda (soft drinks) is also a danger in itself. I think an ice-cold carbonated drink is a great pleasure, especially on a hot day after a training session—Coca-Cola in particular is a fantastic post-exercise boost—yet consuming it every day can be a serious health hazard. The main problem is of course the amount of sugar—one 12-ounce can contains up to 5 teaspoons of the stuff.

When We Eat

Eating at the right time can also have a massive effect. I'll illustrate this by first telling you the story of the Chinese Walk.

Walking after a meal can be beneficial for health. As a practice, it is nothing new, with anecdotal benefits tracing back hundreds of years, yet I started looking into the science behind the practice in greater detail after an experience I had at Telefónica in Spain. We had a welcome celebration dinner for an executive training program where half of the people were from different parts of Telefónica—half from Europe and Latin America and the other half from China Unicom, with whom Telefónica has a joint venture. It was quite a formal, yet enjoyable, affair, with welcome speeches, drinks, and conversations, and the Chinese business culture of copious alcohol consumption well to the fore! It was my first awareness of the importance of alcohol in Chinese business etiquette, where one must not merely take a sip of one's glass with a neighboring dinner companion during the celebratory toast or cheers, but rather drink the full amount after touching glasses with all guests. Enquiring as to the health dangers for senior executives who may have to attend business dinners on a regular basis, they told me that members of the C-suite often have a personal assistant, who is basically a *drinker*. Wow, I thought at the time, what a fantastic job for a Scotsman!

At the end of the meal, the Chinese party, of around 40, got up as one and went for a walk around the campus—of around 1–2 miles. Everyone else went to the bar! I then said this to the rest of the Telefónica group, chiding them on their more unhealthy choice. They replied, *"No, no, the Chinese people weren't going for a walk! They were just looking for the bar; they didn't know where it was!"*

Jokes apart, I see this practice all the time. I usually travel to Shanghai three or four times a year, and it's a real part of the Chinese culture. After lunch or dinner, a walk is common practice. Let me explain the science behind this. When we eat, our body's metabolism fires up. The body basically looks to absorb the nutrients and energy—fuel, let's say— of the food. Our body doesn't know the exact minute that we stop eating and so continues in this higher rate of metabolism for another 30–40 minutes. This is called the Thermic Effect of Food, which according to McGannon and McGannon[5] has a synergistic effect with low-grade physical activity, thereby converting this 30–40 minute period into a window of opportunity. By walking in this window, you can triple the calorie-burning effect. For example, by walking for 10 minutes in the period after having had lunch or dinner, when you go back to your office to kill some emails, or drop on the sofa to watch some TV, you will continue burning calories at that higher rate for the duration of the walk multiplied by 3, so in this case, 30 minutes. It's simply a metabolic walk, which I call the Chinese Walk in honor of my Chinese friends. It is another example of modern science backing up ancient wisdom. It's nothing new, particularly in China where a well-known Confucius proverb is

Walk 100 steps after a meal and you'll live to be 99 years old.

So even though ancient wisdom has shown the way long before, modern science-based reminders are useful for a culture that tends to discount the past and its customs as being out of date and of no value. Further modern science-based reminders include 2013 research in *Diabetes Care*[6] that showed the benefit of walking after a meal for older cohorts in terms of their control of insulin in the body. As we consider later in the chapter, a better control of insulin can have many benefits.

Another aspect of our body's metabolism gives us further insight to the question about when we eat. Here, we must first consider metabolism—the wider set of cellular chemical reactions that keep us alive, but which have a definitive effect on our weight management given the rate at which these reactions occur, using the energy we take in through food. We each have a basic metabolic rate, which is the rate of these reactions when we are at rest, although our metabolism will vary in response to external stimuli such as eating, movement, and temperature. The commonly held belief is that our metabolism slows as we age. This is not strictly true, or at least unhelpful for us to look for advantage in the business context—slowing is not a simple *fait accompli*; it is a by-product of the aging process because first, we tend to move less as we age, and second, we lose muscle. More muscle results in a higher metabolic base rate, burning more calories at rest. It is one of the reasons that we look at building lean muscle mass in Chapter 14, "TRAIN." So if we push back against the aging process by maintaining as much of our muscle as possible, as well as maintaining mobility levels as consistent as possible, the slowdown of metabolism will be negligible.

Linking movement to metabolism is also worthy of reflection on a day-to-day basis, and leads us to the question of how late in the day we should eat. Although mainstream science has challenged the practice of eating late as a factor in weight gain (a common refrain is that a calorie is a calorie irrespective of the time of day), I do believe that such a habit, almost a norm in the professional business world, does lead to weight gain. Recent studies do show an earlier consumption of calories to lead to weight loss,[7] and researchers at Northwestern University looked at late-night eating within the context of the circadian rhythm to test their hypothesis on why night shift workers tend to be overweight.[8] They found that late-night eating did indeed lead to weight gain. A wider reflection on the factors in play for a business professional is worthwhile. Apart from exercise and eating, when our metabolism rises, as we see in the case of the Chinese Walk, it stays fairly constant throughout the day, dipping slightly at night when we are asleep. Another factor is temperature, which affects a marginal rise with the energy expenditure required to keep us warm in a cold environment. In any case, returning to movement, the habit toward an even more sedentary end to the day when we eat a large evening meal may prove to be the biggest danger to weight gain. Let us fully consider a typical eating day for the business professional.

What do you—or the typical busy professional—have for breakfast? Maybe you skip it, or grab a coffee and pastry on the run. Now there is no definitive evidence that says by having breakfast, you will control your weight better. Studies have shown support for both sides, yet the general truth is that many businesspeople consume a low percentage of their daily calorie intake at breakfast. So lunch is next, maybe a sandwich while sitting at our desk, killing some emails—the commonplace habit that Tony Schwartz's New York initiative pushed back against. So eating is relegated to a necessary survival strategy that fits in between other "more important" things to do. And at night, we have our free time, our family time. We sit, and we eat. A lot. This is often very late at night, after which we rarely move, perhaps fall asleep watching TV on the couch, and then slumber off to bed. So the vast majority of our calorie intake is late at night, after which we have our least amount of movement and perhaps go to bed soon after. Such a routine means we eat by far the largest percentage of our daily food when we are slowing down at the end of the day. As well as the lack of movement, we tend to be starving late at night since we have skipped breakfast and grabbed a sandwich on the run, and we tend toward mindless, fast overeating when we finally do get the chance.

Athletes eat more frequently during the day. Rather than eating three main meals a day (never mind the business person's typical one), they eat five to six times, keeping their energy more constant. If we consider also that the size of our stomach is approximately the size of our fist (of course, it stretches, a lot more fits in there, right?), though a little longer, this tells us we can often achieve satiety by snacking on an amount of food that fills the palm of our hand, such as nuts or dried fruit. Traveling with a pack of such snack food means that you will encounter fewer moments of "starvation," which can affect decisions and result in eating too much of the wrong type of food when you at last find somewhere to eat in an airport, train station, or gas station.

So perhaps try a simple "hack"—eat a healthy breakfast that kick-starts your day. Take some time for lunch and have a ready-made snack pack, so that when you arrive home at night, hunger is under control, and you may eat a smaller, lighter evening meal where the experience of the meal itself takes over from animal instincts related to survival. Redress the imbalance and try to consume a little more of your daily caloric intake earlier in the day. Take into account also that skipping meals will slow down your metabolism as your body's survival mode is activated—meaning it is difficult to lose weight by starving yourself. Fasting may have a role to play in certain contexts (the 5-2 diet, where two days a week are characterized by a strict caloric intake, has for example received much attention in recent years), but be careful of the effects of fasting on your mental performance. The brain needs fuel to function.

Time of eating in relation to physical activity also matters. When we finish exercise, our body releases special enzymes that make the absorption of food, and the vitamins and minerals within it, more efficient. Therefore, to recover more efficiently, especially when training is of a hard intensity, eating a light carbohydrate and protein mix, such as a baked potato and tuna, within that 30 to 40 minutes can aid recovery. Chocolate milk has also been shown to be the ideal recovery drink,[9] with the key factor being the carbohydrate-to-protein ratio of 4:1. Care should also be taken with the consumption of energy drinks, which are often so high in sugars that they result in a calorie surplus that metabolizes as fat. In residential SEP programs where we have a field element, we often make a homemade recovery drink to combat fluid loss, which is especially useful in hot weather. This is advised only for a hard training session where a large degree of sweating results in the body losing salt. By simply mixing 2/3 water with 1/3 natural fruit juice and adding a pinch of salt, you will replace those lost electrolytes and may be pleasantly surprised about how much it tastes like a brand energy drink!

Refueling after working out, by eating the right foods, is an often-neglected area for novice trainers. Although they seem to be improving their offering in recent years, "health club" menu options, with their high-calorie foods and "energy" drinks, often result in a large calorie surplus, leaving the health club member in a futile spin to lose weight. This is just one of the factors behind gym membership tripling in the United States in the past 30 years, the same time frame as the soaring rates of obesity in the country, as reported by *TIME*.[10] The other factors—a societal addiction to sugar, willpower depletion, and the relatively marginal differences in high versus low calorie expenditure days—are covered in this and the following two chapters.

What We Eat

Common sense and balance are the two most important factors in what we eat. Balance with regard to a mix of fats, proteins, and carbohydrates, with a basis of that provided not by bread and potatoes, as we see in some older food pyramids, but rather plenty of vegetables and, to a lesser extent, fruit. A varied diet is the first step in maintaining health, and allowing ourselves to eat what we love is a key factor. Balance also concerns acid and alkaline foods, as championed by Juliette and Michael McGannon. Even if we eat primarily healthy foods, such as Omega 3 rich fish, tomatoes, and red wine in moderation, all are acidic foods and they advocate redressing the alkaline balance. An acid-rich balance has been shown to result in fatigue, ulcers, and inflammation, and so eating more fruit and vegetables, drinking green tea, and drinking water with a slice of lemon can help improve the alkaline balance and counter such health hazards.

There are two principal factors that are putting in peril our own health, and that of the planet. First, an addiction to sugar, which is the focus of some practical takeaways that we cover in this chapter, and second, an ever-growing demand for animal-based protein, which is putting in danger the sustainability of human life on the planet and which we cover in the next chapter.

So what should we eat? Dr. David Katz, a nutrition expert and fellow of the Yale Center for Disease Prevention, looked at the main diets around the world in terms of beneficial health outcomes. In a paper titled "Can We Say What Diet Is Best for Health?"[11] he compared low carbohydrate, low fat, low glycemic, Mediterranean, mixed/balanced (DASH), Paleolithic, vegan, and elements of other diets. He concludes that although there are positive features of several of them, no single one is best; if a diet is a set of rigid principles, health is not optimized. Rather, broader guidelines regarding what we eat that combine the best of each of the diets is best for health. He notes that "A diet of minimally processed foods close to nature, predominantly plants, is decisively associated with health promotion and disease prevention." In plain English, real food. It may seem simplistic, but we have created a system where real food is often not on the menu. The weight loss and diet industry has created a range of processed food products that do the exact opposite of what they advertise. The irony is that the many foods that are labeled as the "low-fat" or "healthy" option have probably caused the biggest detriment to our collective health, because they are food "products," manufactured in a factory setting often with high salt and sugar levels. Although the food industry has delivered massive benefits to the world's population by improving convenience and cost, a higher consumption of natural food, rather than man-made food, would no doubt result in greater health. A clue to distinguishing between food and food products? Food has no ingredients!

Katz's research echoes the thoughts of Michael Pollan and his view on *nutritionism*, contained in his 2009 *New York Times* article.[12] A very simple message to "Eat food, not too much, mostly plants" is in fact quite radical within the global food system that we have created. Pollan created a number of simple Food Rules in his 2009 book,[13] including: Don't Overlook the Oily Little Fishes, Shop the Peripheries of the Supermarket and Stay Out of the Middle, Eat When You Are Hungry, Not When You Are Bored, and the simplest of all, Cook. Often timeless wisdom that we are quick to discount in the modern world.

Although there is a turning tide against the obsessive attention to the calorie-in, calorie-out method of weight management—excess calories are stored as body fat, but it may not be as clean an equation as we are led to believe from the mainstream nutrition community—it is instructive in showing us the slow-creep nature of weight loss and gain. Healthy habits and patience are required for change, here and in the other areas of the SEP model. A highly active day, in terms of calories burned, is not as far removed from a sedentary day as one may believe. Careless eating on the active day may quite easily create a calorie surplus—one of the factors behind the gym membership paradox in the United States. Believing a hard 1-hour workout to have given them substantial margin for indulging in a post-session treat, gym devotees would drop by Burger King or Starbucks on the way home, easily creating a greater calorie surplus to that of a nontraining day. Consider Table 12.1, which compares the approximate calorie consumption for a 150-pound (68kg) businesswoman.

Table 12.1 Calorie Consumption for an Active Versus Non-active Day

Active Day Activities	Calories Consumed	Sedentary Day Activities (Sick at Home)	Calories Consumed
Standing 4 hours	333	Sleeping 14 hours	907
Walking 2 hours	1222	Reading 6 hours	444
Running 1 hour	944	Sitting 4 hours	296
Sleeping 8 hours	519		
Gardening 1 hour	380		
Sitting 4 hours	296		
Reading 2 hours	148		
TOTAL	3842	TOTAL	1648

So the difference between a highly active day and highly sedentary (sick) day (around 2,000 calories) is about the equivalent of a Big Mac meal and a couple of Starbucks Frappucinos. Locking in positive practice around movement and fueling is therefore more important than training hard for one or two hours a week, then eating what you want.

The *New Yorker* cartoon with which I opened this chapter also highlights the role of addiction. Both caffeine and alcohol can result in dependency and addiction, yet there is another substance that we are addicted to, and for which societal awareness is low. That substance is sugar. When combined with the sedentary life that many of us find ourselves trapped in, this has resulted in a worldwide pandemic of Type 2 diabetes. I have worked with people with severe joint pain, fatigue, and of course the corresponding reduced mobility. Making the one change of cutting sugar from their diet has had a transformative effect in six months. Carbohydrates have indeed been demonized in certain contemporary diets, yet this takes a narrow view of the sugar that is most harmful.

Instead, for a busy professional, considering the Glycemic Index (GI) is a useful tool. Although Katz discounted low-glycemic as the answer on its own, he did specify benefits including a lower risk of heart disease. In any case, I'm not advocating the GI as the only diet to follow, but rather a consideration that fits well with the *Sustaining Executive Performance* context of sport and business performance. It also highlights the dangers of sugar and excessive insulin production in a sedentary world.

It's not enough to say that all sugar, and by extension, all carbohydrates, is bad. There is a more complex story at play, and the GI offers us some insight into making the right choices in a busy day. Cutting out carbohydrates, as some modern diets advise, may allow you to lose weight, but it may also adversely affect your mental performance. The brain is one of the most glucose hungry organs in the body, and we need sugar to fuel its performance.

Pioneering work in elite sports by nutritionists and biochemists at the University of Sydney[14] enriched our understanding of the GI of foods and their effects. The GI is a measure of the effects of carbohydrates on blood glucose levels (see Figure 12.2). Carbohydrates that break down rapidly during digestion release glucose rapidly into the blood stream and have a high GI. Carbohydrates that break down slowly release glucose gradually into the bloodstream and have a low GI. All foods that have some carbohydrate are given a value in comparison to the reference of pure glucose, which has a value of 100.

We can be more selective of the carbohydrates we eat by considering whether it has a high or low GI (see Table 12.2). Spiking and crashing our blood sugar can also result in craving a higher percentage of calories the next time we eat. By looking for carbohydrates with a lower GI—brown bread instead of white, basmati rice, which has less starch, cooking pasta al dente, keeping the skin on a potato—we experience less of a sugar spike and maintain energy longer. In a long, demanding day, maintaining that energy without having to look for something to eat, or compromising our performance given a lack of energy, is therefore a key advantage.

Our brain recognizes the high GI foods, the processed white carbohydrates, and we make a beeline for these when we feel tired or stressed. Yet those positive effects will quickly give way to feeling tired and hungry. The irony here is that global trends are pointing toward a Type 2 diabetes pandemic due to lifestyle factors such as poor diet and lack of exercise, and this type of strategic eating is very similar to the way that a diabetic must eat, strictly controlling blood sugar levels.

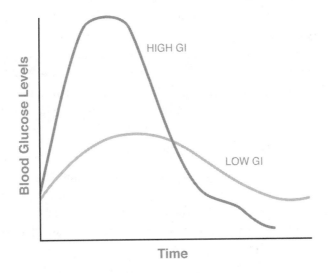

Figure 12.2 High and low GI food effect on blood glucose

Table 12.2 Sample Foods According to Low, Medium, and High GI Values

LOW GI Foods (55 or Less)	MEDIUM GI Foods (56–69)	HIGH GI Foods (70 or More)
Red lentils (26)	Boiled potatoes (56)	Mashed potato (70)
Whole milk (27)	Basmati rice (58)	White bread (70)
Nutella spread (30)	Honey (58)	Bagel (72)
Butter beans (31)	Couscous (65)	Bran flakes (74)
Skimmed milk (32)	Mars bar (68)	Rice Krispies (82)
Fettucine pasta (32)	Weetabix (69)	Jacket potato (85)
Whole grain spaghetti (37)	Whole-grain bread (69)	Steamed white rice (98)

Given the examples previously cited in which the GI may be lowered—such as cooking method and presentation, as well as tweaking your selection between similar foods—it is a much more practical approach to food than merely saying, "Don't eat what you love and eat more of what you hate!" Even different types of chocolate have different GI values.

It is important to note that high GI foods are not "bad;" they just have their place. Eating high GI, for example, after a hard training session can be beneficial and is one of the key principles in elite sports recovery. The dinner and breakfast of a 130 pound (60kg) Tour de France rider, for example, is something to behold, and Michael Phelps would have eaten mostly high GI foods in the eating time at the Beijing Olympics. The key danger for a business professional is starting off a demanding day with a high GI breakfast. If we spike our blood sugar first thing in the morning, we are likely to keep spiking and crashing throughout the day, which results in a very inconsistent level of work performance—affecting emotions, decisions, and physical movement.

It is also worthy of mention the amount of food consumed. Just because a food has a low GI doesn't mean we can eat an endless amount. The Glycemic Load tells us the net effect of blood sugar. A large amount of low GI food will have a similar cumulative effect to a small amount of high GI food.

Making informed choices around the GI, for your breakfast, other meals, and after physical training, will therefore allow you to manage energy and weight, and it will also result in better decision making. Think, for example, about the decision you would make when your blood sugar is spiking after just having had a high GI food compared to the decision you would make during a sugar crash when you are tired and grumpy and looking for something to eat. It would be very different. I've worked in late-night meetings at companies in which we've been unable to make a decision. A pause is recommended, and people find themselves at the company vending machines, which are often full of high GI snacks. Blood sugar spike ensues, the meeting resumes, and a cry of "I've got the solution!" restarts proceedings. This isn't a rational decision-making process—it's blood sugar making the decision! Our decisions are often at the mercy of such small things—a commute to work, a chance encounter with someone in the office—and being aware of this can allow us to improve the quality and consistency of the decisions we make.

Top Ten Takeaways: FUEL

1. Consider the food you eat as fuel for performance, not just calories for survival.

2. Consider eating as one of the great human experiences, with a broader understanding beyond simply *what* we eat, necessary for behavior change.

3. Slow down when you eat. Taste your food.

4. Buy ingredients. Cook more, and involve the family.

5. Recognize the role of the brain in altering perception. Look for easy hacks and nudges, including using smaller plates.

6. Consider your daily eating pattern. Spread out calorie intake throughout the day. Eat smaller quantities and more often.

7. Try a Chinese Walk after a meal.

8. Eat more food and fewer "food products."

9. Consider the Glycemic Index and Glycemic Load of foods, particularly for breakfast.

10. Be aware of the effect that food can have on the decisions made, by yourself and others.

Eating, diet, and weight management are all highly contentious issues, and I don't pretend to have all the answers in this chapter. The science of nutrition is a very young field of study, and we are finding new things all the time. There is much to be said for a commonsense approach: elevating food as a key element of your performance, like Michael Phelps, and being more mindful of food ingredient purchase, preparation, and eating as an experience, like Ferran Adrià. We have created a society where we tend to worry incessantly about some of our choices—*Don't eat sausages!*—but where the worry itself is likely to cause more damage than the actual sausage sandwich ever could. Stress has recently been shown to slow down metabolism,[15] which is particularly relevant for the busy, stressed executive. The resultant increase in weight from a slowing metabolism is likely to cause more stress and create a trap of poor health and lowering self-esteem. Such an acute awareness or hysteria around the odd sausage sandwich contrasts with a low level of awareness of how our choices affect health on a planetary level, as we discuss in the next chapter. So reexamining your day-to-day fueling habits, taking a balanced, yet relaxed, view of what you eat, but just as important when you eat and how you eat, will help drive progress toward being a sustainable leader.

13

On the Systematic Change Required in the Global Food System

Royale with cheese! What'd they call a Big Mac?

—Jules Winnfield *(Pulp Fiction)*

Heinz von Foerster said that "truth is the invention of a liar." The Austrian-American scientist and philosopher was one of the principal founding thinkers in the field of cybernetics—the scientific study of control and communication in the animal and the machine—essentially a study of the systemic nature of things, including ourselves and the world we construct around us. As a simple reflection, who creates the reality or world that we live in? Where does the system that governs the basic needs of a human being, including how we live, move, and eat, come from? It may be alarming to realize the often random, emergent events that occur to create what we may believe to be well-planned, scientific, structured systems—such as the global food system. The prefix sci, as in science, means to separate—and such a reductionist approach to the hard sciences, where things are separated into their component parts, has been highly successful. Yet von Foerster believed that a reductionist approach to a living system spelled disaster. What I am highlighting here is that the global food system is a living system, but that as a society, we have accepted certain scientific results as global truths.

As we discussed in the first chapter of Part 3 (Chapter 7, "On the Changing Patterns of Mobility Worldwide"), personal habits have a massive impact at the societal level. This probably holds most true for the MOVE and FUEL elements of the SEP model. The global food system is designed for us, but to a large extent we can say that it is designed by us—in the choices that we make—with those needs satisfied by food companies and system actors worldwide. And we are getting sicker as a society. And fatter. It is not just childhood obesity rates that are rising, as combatted by Michelle Obama and others. Worldwide obesity has nearly doubled since 1980. In 2008, more than 1.4 billion adults were overweight, and more than 500 million of those were obese, corresponding to 35% of all adults being overweight and 11% obese.[1] Researchers at the London School of Economics and IESE Business School found a positive correlation between rising obesity levels and globalization,[2] specifically the social aspect of globalization on the three primary outcomes of obesity, caloric intake, and grams of fat. Is *Globesity* a by-product of our advancing society?

So why do we seem to be regressing? The changing patterns of mobility and related factors like urban design no doubt have an impact, but the global truths of the food system may also play a part. Nina Teicholz, author of *The Big Fat Surprise*,[3] challenged one such truth of the global food system—namely, the link between saturated fat and heart disease. She traces the history that resulted in the anti-fat crusade, a defining feature of the global food system for over a generation. She believes that nutrition policy has been derailed over the past 50 years "by a mixture of personal ambition, bad science, politics, and bias." One consequence of cutting out fat has been a marked increase in carbohydrates—at least 25% more since the early 1970s, while saturated fat has dropped 11% in the same period. As we covered in the preceding chapter, carbohydrate is a sugar, and a broader view on carbohydrates in terms of the Glycemic Index allows us to make a more informed choice for energy and corresponding insulin levels. Glucose causes the body to release insulin, which is very efficient at storing fat.

Research from Teicholz and others have raised an awareness in recent years of the dangers of our society's addiction to sugar. It may be that the Big Sugar companies today will become the next generation of Big Tobacco, under increasing public pressure and looking for transformation amid questions regarding their license to operate. The World Health Organization, in 2014, is currently reviewing draft guidelines on limiting added sugar to 5% of daily calories, around six teaspoons— equivalent to one can of Coke. Recognizing the increasing pressure, Coca-Cola has acquired smoothie drinks companies in recent years, for which the public perception is closer to one of health, at the same time as advertising the importance of physical movement. Yet the sugar in smoothie drinks is just as damaging to our heath as the sugar in a carbonated drink. However, Teicholz believes that food companies were just following the guidelines laid down to them. Up until 1999, the American Heart Association was still advising Americans to reach for "soft drinks" and in 2001 was still recommending high-sugar snacks instead of fatty foods. Coca-Cola has now released Coca-Cola Life, complete with natural-looking green packaging. Flavored with Stevia, a natural sweetener that has half the sugar and calories of a regular coke, it is symptomatic of the accelerated action now being taken by food companies. Mars recently cut the size of its Mars and Snickers bars to meet a calorie commitment (without cutting price), while Nestlé says it cut the overall sugar content of its products by 30% between 2001 and 2011. Many nutrition experts believe that sugar reduction by stealth, gradually reducing content over time so that the consumer will not miss the taste, is the best strategy, and one that was followed successfully regarding salt consumption in the UK. The Food Standards Agency there has overseen a 30% reduction in added salt to processed food in the past decade.

The other main result of our distrust of saturated animal fat has been the increase in consumption of vegetable oils, yet we now broadly recognize the dangers of such oils, including the manufacturing process of hydrogenation, as a reason for natural butter being a much healthier option as compared to margarine.

The demonization of saturated fat can be traced back to the 1950s, to a man named Ancel Benjamin Keys, a scientist at the University of Minnesota. Dr. Keys was, according to Teicholz, "formidably persuasive and a relentless champion of the idea that saturated fats raise cholesterol and, as a result, cause heart attacks." The Seven Countries study that he conducted on nearly 13,000 men in the United States, Japan, and Europe demonstrated that heart disease could be linked to poor nutrition, but critics have pointed out that Dr. Keys violated several basic scientific norms in his study. These include selecting only those countries likely to prove his thesis and omitting countries such as France and Switzerland where high-fat diets were the norm. Furthermore, the study's star subjects, from Crete, who lived long lives but consumed little meat and cheese, were sampled during Lent, a time of fasting from such foods, and only a very small sample of a few dozen men was taken. A few years later, Dr. Keys landed a position on the nutrition committee of the American Heart Association, whose guidelines are considered the gold standard, and the fate of saturated fat was sealed. Since then, momentum, not to mention energy and investment, has swung behind reinforcing this hypothesis.

What Is Good for Us Is Good for the Planet

So what should we be eating? More butter, cheese, and meat as part of a healthy, balanced diet, according to the research by Teicholz and a growing number of nutritionists worldwide. Meat in particular has come under the microscope in the past few years. For example, the Paleo community advocates a diet that better resembles the diets of our ancestors in the Paleolithic era, which ended around 10,000 years ago with the advent of agriculture and domestication of animals. They argue that humans have been unable to adapt to modern food such as dairy, grains, legumes, and processed foods. Instead, they eat a diet rich in animal protein, fewer carbohydrates, and more fat. Non-starchy fruit, vegetables, and nuts provide a further staple of the diet together with meat and fish. Although it may offer some benefit over a typical processed food diet, Dr. David Katz, whose research we highlighted in the previous chapter, argues that it has provided a convenient banner for eating more meat of any type—often poor quality processed or grain-fed beef that would not have been available to our ancestors.[4] And so the quality of the meat is a key factor. Grass-fed beef contains many more valuable nutrients such as Omega 3 and 6 fats than its grain-fed counterpart. Meat, of the right type, is beneficial for health, but just as with any element of diet, balance is required. In a recent BBC Horizon documentary, a diet characterized by a high daily intake of red meat was shown to have a significant increase on weight and cholesterol. The planetary repercussions of a high meat diet will be discussed later—another example of our own and the planet's health being inextricably linked.

Katz also believes it unlikely to expect any rigorous, long-term studies for finding the best diet that preclude bias. In his work on different aspects of health, he believes that 80% of chronic disease in today's world can be eliminated by simply applying knowledge already at our disposal. As an example, 60% of all Type 2 diabetes cases worldwide—an exploding pandemic—can be linked to lifestyle factors. And our lifestyle factors are a symptom of how we conceive the "modern age."

In several parts of *Sustaining Executive Performance*, we have highlighted historical cases and ancient wisdom—from de Coubertin's views on education to Robert Owen's approach to work, with Ancient Chinese and Greek philosophy in between—in an attempt to show that the modern world does not always have all the answers. We may also understand that the burning questions or issues of the day are not unique to our age. To the *British Medical Journal* editorial of over a century ago talking of the hurried nature of modern life affecting sleep quality, we may add Leibniz and Diderot, seventeenth- and eighteenth-century philosophers who complained of the "information overload" of the day.

Sometimes, our actions to progress cause us to regress. The post-World War II move toward making a car-friendly city of Copenhagen and ripping up the cycling infrastructure, only to replace it 30 years later, is an example. My home city of Glasgow has ever lamented the removal of the city tram system and replacement of the old tenement blocks by high-rise towers. In our quest for advancement, we don't always get it right. I'm not advocating for a rejection of all things modern, but what is the mix of the old and the new required for a sustainable future? An awareness of our basic human need as part of a journey toward the sustainable leader, thereby connecting the three levels of the Triple Lens— individual, enterprise, society— may help us uncover this balance.

The postwar era of the 1950s gave us many aspects of modern life, including the birth of advertising, so vividly reproduced by the TV series *Mad Men*, a reorientation of the female beauty industry and global growth of Christian Dior's "New Look," and the invention of supermarkets. Supermarkets gave us a step change benefit in terms of choice, availability, and convenience—yet it fundamentally altered local production systems and transportation around the world. Furthermore, quality has not always been guaranteed, and local markets and locally grown food have made a comeback in the past 10 to 20 years.

Food transportation has a massive effect on the environment with the result that we have the convenience of seasonal foods during all seasons. A little-known international treaty signed in 1944 to help the fledgling airline industry means that fuel for international travel and transport of goods, including food, is exempt from taxes, unlike trucks, cars, and buses—so tucking into a breakfast comprised of ingredients from the four corners of the earth is the norm. A growing public awareness of local sourcing has helped push back on this impact, with greater transparency and traceability now evident in the food we buy—helping food standards and local economies as well as minimizing environmental impact. A key objective of up-market restaurants to focus on produce from their local larder and connecting deeply with the local environment has been replicated by supermarket schemes such as km 0 (zero kilometers) in Catalan supermarket Bon Preu, which includes a whole range of produce grown only in Catalonia. Taking local sourcing even further, there may be a future whereby we grow more of our own food. Future scenarios around the sustainable city theme, particularly in the context of high-rise buildings, have looked at such self-sustaining production.

Food waste is another symptom of our modern age. Today, we produce about four billion metric tons of food per annum. Yet due to poor practices in harvesting, storage, and transportation, as well as market and consumer wastage, it is estimated that 30–50% (or 1.2–2 billion tons) of all food produced never reaches a human stomach.[5] Some of these factors may be outside the range of us as consumers, but not all. We have moved toward a society where we find it easy to throw out food; sell-by dates, invented around 40 years ago, are one of the biggest points of contention. Recent reports on UK supermarkets has shown that the CEOs of each of the main supermarkets—including Sainsbury's, Morrisons, and Marks & Spencer—frequently eat food that is past their sell-by date.[6] They argue for an overhaul of food labeling, pointing out that the 7 million tons of food thrown away every year in the UK owes much to shoppers' confusion about best-before, use-by, and sell-by dates. Food waste may also be linked to the quantity of food we purchase and eat. The previous chapter looked at how mindless eating results in a practice of overeating, and that we will feel full sooner if we simply slow down. Portion sizes vary greatly around the world, and I remember being astounded on my first visit to the United States in 2000 by the sizes of meals and supermarket items such as potato chips and carbonated drinks. Eating less, by practicing better portion control and following initiatives such as MyPlate (choosemyplate.gov), is therefore good for us and good for the planet.

In general, the professionalization of the food industry has resulted in cheaper food that some believe is the real reason for soaring obesity levels. Roland Sturm, an economist at the Rand Corporation, notes that Americans spent one-fourth of their disposable income on food in the 1930s, dropping to one-fifth in the 1950s and one-tenth today.[7] In Kenya and Pakistan today, people still spend up to one half of their income on food.

An Insatiable, Unsustainable Present

Much of the debate on improving infrastructure, supply chain, and consumer attitudes toward food waste is part of a broader examination of the pressure we are likely to face on a planetary level where the global food system will be required to feed nine billion people or more by the year 2050. Much of that pressure comes from an insatiable appetite for meat. It follows that with greater demand and the corresponding supply pressure, cost will increase—leading people to buy cheaper food—often the processed products of lower nutritional value.

In Chapter 7, we commented on the lack of physical movement and increase in machine movement as being associated with affluence and progress in a modern world—likewise, the increasing consumption of animal protein. The growing demand in the emerging economies for meat has placed a tremendous burden on the global food system. Land is required for cattle grazing, and the methane emissions from those cattle causes stress on a climate change level. One kilogram of beef requires 15,000 liters of water (around 2000 gallons/pound) to produce—in the water required for the cow to drink, to grow feed and hay, and to keep stables and farmyards clean.[8] The pressure on the system that comes from these factors was investigated by a 2014 BBC Horizon documentary that calculated that we can eat, sustainably, up to 3.75 ounces (100 g) of meat per day. Beyond that, and the exponential rise of impacts results in an unsustainable future. At present, 30% of the Earth's usable surface is covered by pasture land for animals, compared with just 4% of the surface used directly to feed humans. The total biomass of livestock is almost double that of the people on the planet and accounts for 5% of carbon dioxide emissions and 40% of methane emissions—a much more potent greenhouse gas. If the amount of meat we produce doubles, a likely current scenario given growing demand in China and India together with overall population growth, livestock could be responsible for half as much climate impact as all of the world's cars, lorries, and airplanes.

So what future are we headed toward if we extend our current choices? Where should the protein come from to sustain an exploding population? Two scenarios that have long been touted as the solution are now approaching the public consciousness. One is manufactured meat and the other, insects.

Insects, a rich source of protein, fiber, and micronutrients such as iron and magnesium, as well as good fats, are eaten in large areas of the world, particularly Asia. Grasshoppers and mealworms are common, yet they remain a niche, and often reviled source of food in most Western countries. The World Food and Agriculture Organization of the United Nations makes the case that insects are key to future food security as the world's population grows, as they are far less carbon intensive than animals and need much less water. A range of entrepreneurs are springing up in an attempt to catch the wave and turn back attitudes to a former age when, for example, insect eating was common in many parts of Europe in the late 1800s. Adventurous gourmet chefs are proving that taste and presentation need not be compromised.[9]

From a simple natural solution to a man-made one. Professor Mark Post of Maastricht University served the world's first hamburger grown from laboratory-grown meat in 2013.[10] Starting with stem cells extracted from a biopsy of a cow, Post's team grew 20,000 muscle fibers over the course of three months. Each tiny fiber grew in an individual culture well, and when ready, were removed individually by hand, cut open, and straightened out. All the fibers were pressed together to form the hamburger—biologically identical to beef but grown in a lab rather than in a field as part of a cow. The total cost of the project was €250,000, a "royal" amount that, even with cheese, *Pulp Fiction*'s Jules Winnfield may have been unlikely to find appetizing. Post sees the future value of manufacturing meat as a means of addressing the poor efficiency in current meat production methods. He says that 3.75 ounces (100 g) of vegetable protein are required to produce only about a half-ounce (15 g) of edible animal protein, so a lot of food is used to feed the cows in order to feed ourselves. Methane and water issues are also addressed by the lab-burger method.

Toward a New Modern System

It may be tempting to look at the complexity of issues in the global food system and throw in the towel. Yet our eating habits—retaining common sense without over-stressing and adding a sprinkling of self-discipline—may help shift the current system to conceive a better vision of modernity. Education and entrepreneurship are critical factors. After moving from Scotland to Spain, I was impacted greatly by actually seeing the animal in the market when shopping for meat. In Britain, as a whole, meat is very neatly packaged and even the wording in English doesn't always make it clear where it comes from. Instilling a greater awareness in our children of the wider aspects of food, and of the great effort that takes place to ensure it arrives on our plate, is a worthy pursuit. The food industry could be used as a magnificent lens for educating young people in so many different fields, from supply chain to engineering, ethics, health, and politics.

The design field has started to pay more attention to the industry, with design schools such as the Eindhoven school of design developing curricula that looks at the infrastructure around the food industry but not actually at the food itself. IDEO recently redesigned the mealtime experience for state schools in the San Francisco area, and other start-up companies have looked at providing better food provision for busy professionals in the realization that our food affects performance. These are positive signs of the right type of modernity, combining lessons from the past with limits of the future. Yet we may easily be seduced by the perceived "busy-ness" of modern life and an ill-conceived view of what we need to make our lives better. The rapid growth of *Just Eat* in Europe, which promotes the tagline *Don't cook!* as part of a home delivery service that increases the consumption of convenience foods for their customers, is but one example.

Indicative of the hunger for a quick fix is the pursuit of a "magic bullet" diet that ignores the fact that the magic bullet is already there. Marc Van Ameringen, the Executive Director of the Global Alliance for Improved Nutrition, reflected in August 2014 on the remaining 500 days until the end of the Millennium Development Goals (MGD).[11] He notes that nutrition didn't even feature in the first set of MDGs and that it is often sidelined because there will never be a quick fix—vaccine or formula—for hunger or obesity. Again, the manifestation of behavior at the individual level, which is looking for change overnight, is transferred to the societal level. He is further frustrated by a fractured system: private companies are doing everything possible to prevent regulation, and governments are reluctant to step up. Unilever's Paul Polman, heading a responsibility driven company that is also the world's biggest ice cream maker, concurs on the need for a holistic solution, saying that the issue of Big Sugar is "not about who shouts the loudest." So with urgent action required, it falls to us to try to affect some change. If we can change our view to the sustainable leader, where patience and consistent practice is built in, we may be able to affect transformation at these broader levels as well. Part of that mind-set is to challenge global truths and conventional wisdom. Heinz von Fuerster placed emphasis on having choice and available alternatives: "Act always so as to increase the number of choices" was an ethical imperative of his. If we act, by changing and experimenting with our food habits, I think we will open up a number of choices necessary for our future world. And closer to the basic needs of that greatest of cybernetic systems: the human being.

14

TRAIN

All that I am, I am because of my mind.

—Paavo Nurmi

It was a dark, cold November evening, and the slightly built Czech runner could be seen doing endless rounds of the track. He would pick up a stone on one side, run one lap fast, drop it off, rest for 30 seconds, and then do the same thing again. And again. Coaches would laugh at what they perceived as mindless repetition. But there was method in the madness. The year was 1952 and the runner's name was Emil Zatopek. He would go on to win the 5,000 meters, 10,000 meters, and the marathon at the 1954 Helsinki Olympics, the home of his hero Paavo Nurmi—a feat which has never been repeated.

Zatopek's innovation of systematic interval training would transform track training, and eventually extend to other sports. If not quite as visual, it was certainly as transformational as U.S. high jumper Dick Fosbury and his flop during the 1968 Mexico Olympics. More than 60 years later, similar interval training concepts are used for people in their 80s as well as those recovering from heart attacks. Training is not just for professional sports, and there is much that we can learn on both a practical and conceptual level from how athletes train, for business health, well-being, and performance.

The final part of the SEP model is TRAIN, and here we cover two main areas. First is the physical fitness practices that can be implemented by a busy professional, finding efficiency and effectiveness in the scarce time available, and second, what we can learn by looking at the art, or discipline, of training. We have discussed several cases so far where physical training practice is shown to be a key part of peoples' lives who are not professional athletes, but who focus primarily on their mental abilities, from chess grandmasters such as Carlesen and Kasparov to great fiction writers like Murakami. Interval training is one practical takeaway for the business athlete, and we return to that in detail shortly. But let us look at how training—physical exercise for health—is usually conceived in the world of business.

> I would love to have 90 minutes to train, but generally I have to sacrifice some sleep—if I want to work out, I have to do it before breakfast. I usually train for around 45 minutes, 6 days a week. One day, I'll do weights, the next cardiovascular.

This quote came from Barack Obama speaking just after his election to office;[1] he talked about the importance of taking care of his physical condition as a means of coping with the marathon demand of an election campaign. There are two points worthy of highlight here: the first is in reply to many peoples' claim that they don't have enough time to exercise—if the President of the United States can find time, perhaps we all can! Okay, perhaps that's a little unfair given the large support network he enjoys (as an aside, build your own, as we discuss in Chapter 16, "Leading Change in the Triple Lens of Sustainability"), but the second point is that through the SEP program, we can learn a better strategy than that of the president of the United States. The key function is time. I hope from the preceding four elements of the SEP model that you are aware of small but highly impactful practices that can be completed in small pockets of time: for example, 30 seconds for breathing, 1 minute for being mindful, 3 minutes for stretching, 15 minutes for a post-lunch walk. All of these may be integrated by the professional and business athlete alike and are the true fundamentals of *Sustaining Executive Performance* in the workplace.

Time constraints were examined recently by management professor Russell Clayton and colleagues.[2] They found that dedicating time to exercise, which may be viewed as a luxury time item for busy professionals, is more valuable for those people with greater demands on their time. The reasoning is multiple—the structure and planning of training may be transferred with positive effect, improving self-efficacy, to other parts of a person's life, not to mention the more practical and readily acknowledged benefits of exercise, such as stress reduction—as long as exercise doesn't translate into *another* thing to do, and therefore become an additional source of stress.

After reflecting on legitimizing the practice of physical training into a time-constrained life, the next question often revolves around what type of exercise to do. For me, there are two main elements in TRAIN, which when combined with the mobility imperative of Chapter 6, "MOVE," give us the required 1-2-3 approach to physical health and well-being for the business athlete. First, we consider aerobic intensity—whatever gets the blood moving and the heart pumping faster—and second, core strength. These two elements mirror the fundamental approach taken by all athletes in their own training programs.

Beyond the type of training, another key factor pertains to finding an activity that you enjoy, and something that is feasible and/or accessible. We encourage running in SEP programs because it is something that the busy traveling professional can integrate easily, yet we understand that running can be torture for some! Perhaps the exercise can connect with your passion, or be shared with a family member. The key is that it doesn't become another source of stress or "work to do." With luck, you won't even be conscious that you are exercising—for instance, as in enjoying a dance class. Beware of *slogging*—where exercise becomes just another onerous task, sweaty, time consuming, and inefficient, where feelings of guilt arise because time is being taken away from the work-place or home.

Safety is another key factor. Many of the people we work with have been keen sportsmen and sportswomen in their 20s and 30s, yet with increasing demands placed on their time at both work and home, a gradual withdrawal from structured training and participation in sports usually takes place. Yet the memory of those days vividly remains. Combine that with renewed motivation, and this often results in injury. People tend to forget the hours of practice enjoyed in previous years and that the body becomes more susceptible to injury as it ages. So take care, even if, and probably more so, you have experience. Next we'll look at the two physical TRAIN elements of aerobic intensity and core strength.

Look for Aerobic Intensity

We have already considered heart rate in Chapter 8, "RECOVER"—specifically, the resting heart rate as a measure of recovery. Maximum heart rate is another factor we can consider, which allows us to make decisions based on heart zone and intensity. Cardiovascular-based work has been shown to have the greatest benefit for brain performance (see Chapter 1, Reference 9). A lower resting heart rate generally means a higher level of fitness, and getting a resting pulse of under 60 ought to be an aim for the business athlete. Yet how our heart reacts to activity is also a measure of fitness. In my most recent treadmill stress test at FC Barcelona, the doctor looked for a healthy acceleration of my heart as I ran faster, as well as a rapid decrease after I stopped. A common measure I use in my own training to gauge fitness is either measure my heart rate 60 seconds after the end of a hard training session, or note the time it takes for my heart rate to dip under 100 beats/minute.

The generic formula for maximum heart rate is 220 beats per minute minus your age. Some people may be higher, others may be lower, but this is a helpful starting point. From here, we may consider zones as shown in Table 14.1. The key zones for us to consider are weight management (60–70% of our maximum), aerobic (70–80%), and anaerobic (80–90%). The use of a heart rate monitor will allow you to accurately gauge both your real maximum (often on the penultimate effort of a hard interval session) and your heart zones, yet you can very easily gauge your zones through considering perceived exertion.

The principal factor in perceived exertion is whether you are able to maintain a conversation. On an "easy run" field session during SEP programs, we ask people to run at a pace where they are able to maintain a conversation. If you are able to talk comfortably, you are around a maximum of 60%, a relatively low level of intensity and in weight management zone. If you exercise at an intensity where you cannot easily talk, you are most likely in aerobic zone. Anaerobic is harder still, with breathing itself often very difficult.

So why is it called weight management? And what type of exercise should you do during the week? There are two main sources of energy in the body, fat and glycogen, and only a limited amount of the latter is stored in the muscles and the liver. Fat has the chemical structure C16

H32 O2. Glycogen is a sugar, and sugar has the chemical structure C6 H12 O6. Consider now what is required when we increase the intensity of exercise and what we "gulp" for as we move from conversation mode to something a little harder! Looking for more O2? Your body knows when to make the switch and will look for the oxygen-rich glycogen instead of fat.

Table 14.1   Heart Zones and Perceived Exertion

Heart Rate/ Maximum	Zone	Perceived Exertion
50–60%	Moderate	Relaxed, easy. Rhythmic breathing.
60–70%	Weight management	Comfortable. Slightly deeper breathing, conversation possible.
70–80%	Aerobic	Moderate pace, more difficult to hold conversation.
80–90%	Anaerobic	Fast and a bit uncomfortable. Breathing forceful.
90–100%	Maximum	Unsustainable for a long period, labored breathing.

So what are the takeaways for this? On a simple awareness level, when we train and we can talk, we are in weight management zone and our body is using primarily fat as energy. When we can't talk, we are in aerobic zone, and those glycogen stores are being depleted. However, this doesn't simply mean we always train in a low-intensity mode to lose weight. Many have tried this over the years, believing the weight-management heart zone to be the cure for losing weight, and have not been successful. When the body burns fat, it simply makes more to replace it. If we deplete our glycogen stores, the body will replenish them from the fat stores in our body. It's not a simple process but enough to say that training during a week should include both low intensity exercise in the weight-management zone, and higher intensity exercise in the aerobic zone. This will maintain heart health, an efficient cycle of metabolizing fat and therefore controlling weight.

The Paleo community has criticized the approach to heart health where the maximum time possible is spent with an elevated heart rate, labeling such an approach "chronic cardio" instead of following a regime based on more strength-based, short bursts of activity. If our ancestors moved up to 12 miles per day, as we noted in Chapter 6, it is reasonable to assume that many of those miles would be completed at a slow pace with short bursts of speed required now and then to either catch prey or escape that saber-toothed tiger! Yet I don't believe we should pay too much attention to recent hysteria surrounding the need to minimize time with one's heart rate elevated, with worries around enlargement of the heart one of the reasons for concern. Better to be a marathon runner than a couch potato, although it seems such hysteria is making the case for the latter! I have followed a reasonably intense training program since the age of 13 (almost 25 years). My heart is bigger as a result—the heart is a muscle, after all—and it is strong and efficient. I get a heart check on an annual basis, a simple check that will allow a person peace of mind before continuing with normal activity, or, as I hope, incorporating a more structured training program.

Older health guidelines focused on the time spent in higher intensity zones (for example, at least 20 minutes with the heart elevated to 70% of its maximum at least three times per week) yet newer advice, based on Metabolic Equivalent of Tasks, or METs, looks at the equivalent effort through higher intensity practices such as interval training. A MET is the amount of energy a person uses at rest. Two METs are 2 times the energy used, four METs are 4 times, and so on. Recent U.S. guidelines advocate a minimum of 500 MET minutes/week. This doesn't mean 500 minutes of exercise. A high MET activity, such as fast running (greater than 15 km/h or 9 mph) is a 15 MET activity, which means just over a half-hour per week would achieve the minimum. Walking is in the range 3–5, which would require 2.5 hours.

High Intensity Interval Training (HIIT) has been a growing area of research in the past few years and applies just as much to previously sedentary groups as well as older demographics. If we're considering the "talking zone" of perceived effort, which equates to the weight management zone for easy exercise, here we consider those higher heart zones, aerobic and anaerobic, where breathing as well as talking is difficult. A. G. Lafley talked of interval training for the workplace in his daily routine, and interval training is another powerful example of the importance of rhythms and waves in our lives, as we have discussed earlier in the book. Zatopek would complete monstrous interval sessions, often 40 × 400 meter repeats twice per day during one week. Yet recent research has shown that intervals of high intensity during just six seconds has a beneficial effect for elderly people.[3] This is another key factor. Many of us are often frightened of attaining these high levels of intensity, believing it to be a heart attack waiting to happen, yet we are more likely to suffer a heart attack sitting on the couch on a Sunday watching the TV (and sadly I have been aware of such cases in the world of business where email has been added to the mix).

A BBC Horizon documentary from 2011 on the myths of exercise looked at HIIT in detail. One of the memorable clips included the documentary narrator, Dr. Michael Mosley, trying a HIIT session on a stationary bicycle under the watchful eye of Professor Jamie Timmons. His work looks at the benefits of this high-intensity workout for sedentary groups, finding benefits in only 4 weeks specifically related to improved insulin sensitivity.[4] In other words, the pancreas releases less insulin, which in turn minimizes risk of metabolic syndrome, stroke, and Type 2 diabetes. Given the sedentary and sugar dangers already noted in previous SEP chapters, this is a key advantage for the business athlete. In the interval session, Dr. Mosley completes three bike sprints of 20 seconds at maximum effort. One minute of high-intensity exercise is repeated three times per week. Time efficiency is therefore one of the main benefits for a busy professional. Warming up and cooling down is necessary, yet even when doing both, an effective session can fit into a 15-minute time window. The intensity of the exercise is also highly beneficial, in my view, for relieving stress. After a frustrating day in the office you can conduct such a session and often feel mentally clear afterward. I normally do such a session in the evening—not so late that it would overstimulate my body close to bedtime, making it difficult to fall asleep, but leaving two or three hours for my body to relax again, and then take advantage of the tiredness that ensues from such a hard session to get a deep sleep as well as fall asleep fast. Circadian rhythm research generally points to the greater benefit of exercise, for both performance and health, in the afternoon and early evening. The graph in Figure 14.1 shows my heart rate during such a session close to my home in Barcelona.

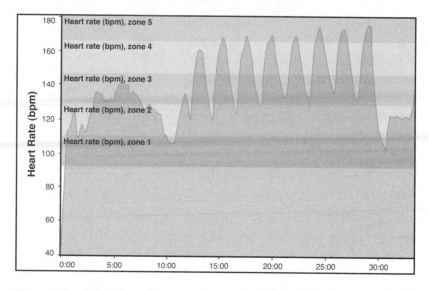

Figure 14.1 Heart rate during own interval session (hill repeats)

There are eight heart rate peaks showing the eight hill repeats I ran as part of the session. I warmed up during the 10 minutes or so it took me to run from my home to the park, and then sprinted to the top of the hill, recovering between each hill repeat by jogging back down. It was a very hard session, the core of which lasted only 15 minutes, but it was of great benefit to my heart. I was in different zones throughout the time, aiding weight management and aerobic health as well as mental recovery. You will notice my heart rate entering anaerobic territory (90% of my maximum, which is around 185 beats per minute) during my climb up the hill before lowering to about 130 beats on the jog back down.

The sprint up took around 45 seconds and the jog down around 1:20. The BBC documentary included two minutes of easy cycling between those 20-second sprints. Professor Martin Gibala and colleagues at McMaster University in Canada, a reference in HIIT training, settle on one minute as the optimum high-intensity period. Following such a protocol could give the following 15-minute interval session:

- 4 minute warm-up

- 3×1 minute high intensity, 2 minute recovery

- 4 minute cool down

The "high intensity" may be conducted on a hill, on a bicycle, or by running fast and slow on a level piece of ground. Shortening the recovery time between intervals or increasing the number of intervals will make the session harder. You can use the same interval principle to progress to continuous running through a walk-run program:

- Week 1: Run 1 minute, walk 90 seconds. Repeat 8 times, 3× per week.

- Week 2: Run 2 minutes, walk 1 minute. Repeat 7 times, 3× per week.

- Week 3: Run 3 minutes, walk 1 minute. Repeat 6 times, 3× per week.

- Week 4: Run 5 minutes, walk 2 minutes. Repeat 4 times, 3× per week.

- Week 5: Run 8 minutes, walk 2 minutes. Repeat 3 times, 3× per week.

- Week 6: Run 12 minutes, walk 1 minute. Repeat 3 times, 3× per week.

The key is high intensity, beyond your comfort zone, followed by recovery, and repeat—at least 3 or 4 times. Repeating on an interval basis increases the resistance on the high intensity part, which makes it progressively easier over time.

So how can you fit intervals into your week? What about during your business travels? When booking a hotel, I look for a multistory building of at least seven stories. Even if I have only 10 minutes available, I will complete an interval session in the stairwell of the hotel (which is of course deserted because everyone is waiting on the elevators and checking their smartphones) sprinting to the top before jogging back down. I will easily enter anaerobic territory on such a session, which also significantly increases core strength, given the need to bound the stairs as well as mental concentration and coordination to ensure stairs are ascended and descended safely. Such a session may be completed at a lower intensity or take into account a lower level of fitness by walking up and walking down. The heart rate will exhibit the same high and low rhythms as for any interval session.

Develop Your Core

The second physical element of TRAIN is core strength development—the abdominal area of the body that is a main area of focus for professional athletes and others noted so far, including Garry Kasparov and Mick Jagger, who worked on their core strength to aid their thinking and singing performance. Strengthening is required to build the strong base on which a consistent training regime can rest, to derive benefit over the long term and is the basis of personal resilience for a demanding career. The core keeps everything else in check on a physical level—top half and bottom half of the body—as well as your emotions, and it keeps decision making strong during a long day. Improved core strength is what will get you through the 12, 14, or 16-hour day necessity now and again with a key client or project.

It is not necessary to use weights at the gym to do this, because using your own body weight is often the most effective means of such training. Practitioners of yoga and Pilates will be familiar with such an approach. Short routines, built in to the day, can quickly and efficiently build strength. As well as focusing on improving abdominal strength, a stronger back is an additional benefit of core work; this is an area of the body especially susceptible to injury in the professional business domain given a simple lack of use. Excessive sitting progressively makes the back weaker. Standing for longer periods, as advocated in Chapter 6, will improve core strength on its own as well as provide a focus on maintaining good posture when sitting, by engaging the core and pulling in the belly button. Both yoga and Pilates have been revisited in the context of the office domain in recent years with new light versions of such practice conceived for short periods, even while sitting. Use of an elastic band, like Dynaband, is a further popular means of improving strength in the seated office environment. Consider professional credibility, as we have already noted in Chapter 6. If such routines are acceptable within your own company culture, then fine, but it is often just as easy to find a private space to do a quick 10-minute mat-based core session with your business dress on. Finishing with some of the recovery methods we have noted in Chapter 8, such as breathing and mindfulness, can give a powerful and quick boost within a demanding day.

Simple exercises, including a squat and plank, shown in Figure 14.2, need only take 30–60 seconds on a daily basis, yet if integrated within the daily routine will make a significant impact on core strength within a four-week period. A full range of core strength exercises are available on the book's website (mysep.net).

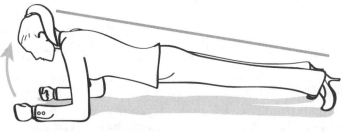

SEP: plank

Figure 14.2 The plank

A plank is easy in terms of technique, yet surprisingly hard to maintain good form for even a few seconds. Approaching a plank in the right way is important in order not to cause injury. A common mistake is moving directly into the plank position from standing. The following steps will ensure safety and progression:

1. Drop to one knee, and then the other, before falling forward to rest fully on your stomach.

2. Lift your head and upper body gently, without straining your back. Bend your elbows and prepare to sustain your weight on your forearms, as shown in the figure. Tuck in your toes at the back.

3. Lift your body from the floor, aiming to achieve a straight line from shoulder to heel. Keep your head and neck relaxed.

4. It is important not to have your backside too high or too low. Using a mirror to ensure a good straight line is advisable if you are doing it for the first time.

5. Hold for 10 seconds, then lower your body (middle section only, maintain form of your forearms and toes) to the floor and rest for 5 seconds.

6. Repeat three times.

I do this each morning and it helps me to wake up. As well as engaging the physical core, such an exercise engages the brain to make you more alert. You could therefore try it during the nap zone to achieve the same effect—something quick, effective, and where changing clothes is not necessary. Be as discreet as you like.

Planks are the second main consideration I have during my business travels. As well as stairwell intervals, I try to ensure that the room is at least big enough (and clean enough) to do plank work. U.S. readers may read this with incredulity, but you may be surprised at the size of some European hotel rooms! I've also found personally that push-ups are a fantastic method for making me tired just before bedtime and ensuring that I get a good night's sleep, and it's something I also try to do before air travel to maximize my chances of sleeping on the plane The third and final consideration I have for business travel is a suspension trainer, like a TRX. This is composed of two durable nylon straps that fit easily in a small bag for packing and that can be hung on the inside of a door to do a variety of body weight exercises. Just remember to lock the door and put on the do not disturb sign! In sum, three simple hacks that ensure health and fitness on the road.

Any body weight work such as planks, push-ups, and squats will improve your lean muscle mass. You may not see your six pack if it is hidden underneath some stomach fat, but you will still feel the benefit of a stronger core. By increasing the amount of lean muscle in your body you will also increase your base metabolic rate and therefore burn more calories at rest. So do you want to lose more weight sleeping or just watching TV? Do more planks! Or better still, do some planks while watching TV!

Aerobic intensity and core strength are the two practical areas of focus for effective and efficient executive training, which combine with the mobility imperative for business health, well-being, and performance. There are also three factors I believe we can learn on a conceptual level from the *art* of training.

The Art of Training I: Balancing ON and OFF

As we have discussed so far in the book, stress is good for us. Rhythms or waves allow us to maintain balance, and athletes are fantastic at balancing this ON and OFF. We have already noted briefly the importance of safety for a busy professional, even for those of you (and especially so) with a background in sports. Building progressively through a structured training program is therefore necessary to follow a safe and sustainable approach to physical fitness. This is no different from elite athletes who will build progressively to a goal in training that represents the upper limit of their abilities before allowing their bodies to recover. The key principle here is that of *periodization*: a three-phase approach where training load is built progressively over a period of time before maintaining that load and then allowing the body to recover, through a *taper*. A common training period for these three phases or cycle time is 6 weeks, but athletes will consider balancing this ON and OFF on a daily, weekly, seasonal, and even 4 yearly (Olympic) term.

So what is your own principal cycle time? This is a necessary reflection in order to design the requisite recovery mechanisms. Perhaps it is the business quarter. I've worked with managers in Oracle to develop their resilience rituals around a grueling Q4. Because it's a sales-driven organization, the fourth business quarter in Oracle, from March to May, is a challenging period that requires the right approach and corresponding action before, during, and after. Cycle time may also be longer than a business quarter. Consider, for example, the successful hotel proprietor in a tourist hotspot, "making hay while the sun shines" so to speak. The Esposito brothers in Capri manage a top boutique hotel, La Minerva, working 14-hour days, 7 days a week from May to October. Often, it is only the dream of vacation in November that sustains them during the nonstop high season, with no differentiation between days, a Sunday being the same as a Wednesday or Friday. Yet coping with the rigors of the high season is often not the principal challenge. How does one cope with switching off after "spinning wheels" at such a high speed for six months without a break? The winter months in Capri can be a desolate place, which has resulted in many younger people leaving the island to find their fortunes elsewhere. Different people require different coping mechanisms for such long on and off cycles, and I hope you can find your own secrets from within the possible SEP actions.

The Art of Training II: The Power of Positive Practice

So where does high performance come from? I think it is easy to look at modern Olympic Champions, following in the footsteps of people like Emil Zatopek and Paavo Nurmi, and think they are simply super-human—that they possess a talent that we don't. Talent is of course important, yet these superhuman feats are not as inaccessible as we may believe. We overlook the value of practice and don't always fully appreciate the countless hours of training that produce such performances and deliver those gold medals. In studies of expert performance in many fields, including music, tennis, and chess, researchers have found few signs of precocious achievement before the individuals started intensive training.[5]

The role of practice has been highlighted in recent years by Malcolm Gladwell[6] (himself a sub-5-minute mile runner at age 51), who states that 10,000 hours are required for world-class performance. The practice of many modern-day sports stars, including Tiger Woods, Michael Schumacher, and Lewis Hamilton, can be traced back many years, evidenced by photos of them practicing at a very early age. I hope your takeaway is not to put your children in a high-pressure sports academy to yield an Olympic or World Champion in 20 years' time! Rather, recognize the importance of practice. Patience is required, yet successfully reengineering habits and achieving consistent practice—preferably daily—can lead to transformation. Another example comes from the tennis player Rafael Nadal. In a Nike commercial from 2012, Nadal and his coach, his Uncle Toni, discussed his change from playing with two hands to becoming a left-handed player—a change that required many hours of practice to get right from an early age. The interviewer then asks Nadal if he can do anything else with his left hand, and he is shown having great difficulty with the most simple of tasks! Think about what Nadal can do with his left hand in tennis, destroying some of the greatest players the game has ever seen, and yet he can't write his name, or brush his teeth, or hit a dart board from a couple of feet away with that left hand. He hasn't practiced those things.

And yet practice on its own is not enough. John Jerome found that the "the only identifiable across-the-board advantage that good athletes seem to have over the rest of us is the quality of their attention. They pay attention to the task in hand a little better than you and I do."[7] Here I want to highlight the difference between practice and mindful practice. Paying attention and being mindful have been covered several times now, principally within Chapter 10, "FOCUS." Doing something over and over, without paying much attention to the practice, will not yield the improvement necessary, or at least the improvement that is possible. Let us look at an example that unites us all, a practice that we have been doing most of our lives, that of walking. In terms of hours of practice, most of us will have attained more than 10,000 hours. So applying a strict definition of the rule, should we all be world-class walkers? Let me ask you a couple of questions on walking. Answers are shown at the bottom of the page.[*]

1. Which part of the foot touches the ground first?

2. When the right foot is flat, what is the left foot doing?

3. When the left heel touches the ground, where is the right arm?

Did you get the answers? Perhaps so, but I don't think they come quickly. This is the difference between practice and mindful practice. If you ask Olympic walkers, they will know very well about foot contact, because if they don't do it correctly in a competition they will be cautioned and then disqualified. If you ask someone who is perhaps recovering from an accident and learning to walk again, the person will be acutely aware of the position of the arm in relation to the body, and if you ask someone with a running injury like plantar fasciitis (myself, during a large part of 2014), he will know exactly which part of the foot touches the ground first. Being mindful of practice, through tracking, measuring progress, and reflecting, as we have discussed as elements of the new self-management, is therefore the key in linking practice to progress. Forget about world-class performance and the 10,000 hour rule; build in daily small habits to transform yourself.

---

[*] 1. Heel. 2. Toes are touching (although it is possible that the foot is in the air, the greater probability is that the toes are touching). 3. In front of the body.

The Art of Training III: Finding Flow

I learned to cycle in Spain. The narrow, undulating roads of the Basque Country toughened me up, and my Girona companions added the necessary finesse. Between both places, I found *flow*. I didn't know it at the time, but flow is the main reason that I, and my many sports companions over the years, have spent so many hours dedicated to training and racing for a large part of our lives. So what is flow? As an introduction, I'll share the opening to an article on bicycle design that I penned in 2005 for the industrial design super site, Core77, subsequently republished by *Business Week*.[8]

¡¡¡¡KKKRRRAAAAACCCCKKK!!!!—that familiar push of the gears to the 53-12. I jumped out of the saddle and blasted away from the pack. One or two of the others entered the first of their Ks as I finished mine, but that was all I needed. For 8 seconds it was head down and a heavy pull on the legs as my cadence increased from around 60 to 120 revolutions per minute. I threw a quick glance under my right armpit—they still didn't have my wheel and I noticed the grimaces on their faces as they experienced the pull towards that high tempo. It was so effortless and I felt that I had gears left—I looked down at the sprocket but sure enough, the chain was sitting on the lowest level. It's then you hear the sound—the traffic, the groans, the wind—all disappear, and notice only a faint whirring, like the wing-flap of a humming bird may sound. And you do nothing; you're producing 500W of power, spinning your legs twice per second, traveling at over 35mph...but you do nothing, apart from listen to that sound ($2000 dollars of Italian-made carbon and steel singing a sweet song, operating at 98,6% efficiency). But it doesn't last, 'cause as soon as you hear it, you know there's only a few seconds left before the world comes crashing in, and your legs start falling from that high stroke and begin to protest the power they're being asked to produce. But the line is there, and so close. You feel the presence of other riders on all sides, and then you see front wheels, and then a head...that front wheel inching ever closer. You strain, and lunge—that sound a distant memory, and the line is yours. Hey, it was only a Thursday night ride with the pack in Girona, and the line was the sign for the town limit, but that feeling is what it's all about.

For me, that "feeling" is flow. Termed by the Hungarian psychologist Mihaly Csikszentmihalyi, *flow* is the state of complete immersion in an activity, where people are fully engaged and fulfilled. Flow, therefore, concerns high performance, and although there is much that we can learn from the sporting world, it is not their exclusive domain with other fields, including art and music being the subject of Csikszentmihalyi's research into the high performance state. Flow is characterized by both the skill level used and the challenge level faced being high. Those engaged in flow are therefore *stretched*, and using all their abilities to meet the challenge at hand. Flow may come from practice, yet it is also beyond practice—in a demonstration of the thing we were perhaps born to do, our purpose. We can watch the 800-meter runner David Rudisha, especially his performance in the final of the 2012 London Olympics, to witness what flow looks like.

Flow can also take us away from the physical self with Csikszentmihalyi finding that when such total immersion takes place, time, food, and ego all disappear. I've experienced a very simple example of this. I once had a severe running-related blister that led me to limp around for more than a week. I love teaching and am often very mobile. The only time I did not feel that blister—and I was completely oblivious to it—was during my classes. The minute I stopped, I felt it again. I also watched Rafa Nadal with what I assume was a similar experience during a match in 2013. He developed an enormous blister on his hand, but you wouldn't believe it given the performance level he maintained during each game. Only in the breaks did you see him grimace while his support staff tried to dress the wound. Nadal seemed to be turning his flow on and off.

So how may such characteristics be more present within the workplace? On a simple planning level, Lafley's workflow was discussed in Chapter 8, and Steven Kotler has looked at how to foster flow in the workplace through different triggers, including focused attention, shared risk, and shared, clear goals.[9] Other themes we have covered so far in *Sustaining Executive Performance*, including responsibility for one's own contribution, experimenting outside the comfort zone, and gaining feedback on action through measurement, all contribute to this high-performance state.

I also believe that we may uncover aspects of flow through reengaging with our physical selves—providing the necessary energy and control for flow to function. I have seen people transformed when getting on a bicycle or when changing into their sports clothes; the swagger that is missing in other parts of their life, including business, suddenly comes to the fore. And I have seen the opposite—the most powerful business-people who can hold a room with power and poise often seem to lose their cloak of invincibility when they put on their sports clothes. Some have that natural confidence in both areas, though it is rare. A very simple reason for that confidence disappearing is that it is not the norm, essentially constituting alien practice. And if we return to the power of positive practice, practice may lead to progress and then performance from which passion may emerge. These four Ps are discussed further in Chapter 16. Returning again to the design field, David Kelley's recent work on creative confidence[10] highlights similar points, with Kelley recounting his experience in design thinking workshops where top-level business executives, so familiar with the rational processes on which their success is based, suddenly coming unstuck with the ambiguity of the design process. Yet experiencing that discomfort and ambiguity is a necessary part of being a design thinker. In the same way, connecting with our physical selves will lead to building such body confidence or intelligence, and as we see in sporting performance, help contribute to flow.

Top Ten Takeaways: TRAIN

1. Legitimize physical training as a key part of a professional life that has benefits beyond the physical. Make time for it.

2. Do something you enjoy. Experiment. Involve a family member. Don't make it another thing on your to-do list.

3. Consider periodization and professional advice, more so if you have physical training or sports experience from an earlier stage in your life.

4. Look for aerobic intensity in general. Welcome periods in your week where you have the experience of having difficulty holding a conversation or breathing.

5. Try interval training. It's excellent for health, fitness, mental clarity, relieving pressure, and time efficiency.

6. Consider a physical training strategy for business travel that sets you apart from the "going to the hotel gym" crowd.

7. Develop your core strength. Stand more. Try body weight exercises like squats and planks.

8. Find out your own principal *cycle time* and design rituals that support it.

9. Recognize the power of positive practice that can lead to performance and personal change in a relatively short time. Forget about "world-class" performance and 10,000 hours.

10. Cultivate better body confidence or intelligence that will contribute to flow.

Emil Zatopek would run around as a child shouting "I am Nurmi, I am Nurmi!" Although he would surpass the times of the great Finnish runner, he wouldn't achieve his level of acclaim. Paavo Nurmi was the first global sports superstar, before Ali and Pelé. Touring the United States in 1925, running in front of thousands at Madison Square Garden and granted a private audience with President Coolidge, Nurmi encapsulated both the practical and conceptual, the physical and mental best practices of TRAIN. A skilled mathematician, he was one of the first to take a highly analytical approach to his running, even racing with a stopwatch in hand. The complete quote with which we began this chapter is: *"Mind is everything. Muscle—pieces of rubber. All that I am, I am because of my mind."* He would apply that mind to various successful business ventures and would become one of the richest men in Finland. After a long spell out of the limelight, he lit the Olympic flame at the 1952 Helsinki Olympics in which Zatopek would create history. They say that people openly wept when they saw him.

15

On Learning and Development for Organizational Transformation

You're gonna need a bigger boat.

—Chief Brody *(Jaws)*

"Ha, ha, no chance!" The year was 2006, and I was sitting with British Cycling President Brian Cookson in Girona's Plaza Independencia. Sipping on an ice-cold, and well-deserved, clara after a fine four hours cycling around the smooth roads of Baix Empordà, I listened for his reply: "Well, that's quite a common reaction, but we're going to do it." Brian had just shared the main strategic goal for British Cycling—simple and startling: a British winner of the Tour de France within five years. Something that no one had really gotten near in over a century of the famous annual cycling race. Tom Simpson in 1967 and Robert Millar in 1983 had been the closest in all that time: Simpson collapsing and dying on Mont Ventoux toward the end of the Tour in '67 and Millar making the podium 16 years later by winning the King of the Mountains jersey and fourth overall, yet never in serious contention for the Maillot Jaune. Fast forward to 2014 in the post-Armstrong drug scandal era. Armstrong was living in Girona when Brian made the trip over to see me, and the fact that a Brit didn't win the Tour de France this year is the most startling fact. Team SKY, as close to a national team as one may get in non-Olympic road racing, has suffered from an embarrassment of riches in recent years and have not been able to accommodate the two previous winners of the Tour in the same team, Bradley Wiggins and Chris Froome. The world's best sprinter, Mark Cavendish, also couldn't count on a team being built to support him and has moved on to pastures new.

alent attraction and retention are seen as some of the most pressing needs by leaders in companies today. Much has been made in recent years of a strategy to attract the very best, recognizing that "A" players tend to attract other "A" players who can transform the enterprise. Corporate social responsibility, or more broadly, purpose-driven organizations, has also been shown to attract a new generation of workers who are looking for something more in which to dedicate their lives, above and beyond the simple means to lead that life. The previous chapter looked at the SEP element of TRAIN for both practical (physical) and conceptual (mind-set) takeaways for the individual—the sustainable leader. Yet how may an organization implement a company-wide training system to develop their talent? Improving both skills and engagement is necessary to transform the organization, and, as we noted from Unilever CEO Paul Polman in Chapter 2, "The New Lanark Mills," to transform an organization from good to great.

Engagement in particular is something that may be improved in many companies—where better alignment with the practice and mind-set of the sustainable leader, by paying more attention to the SEP elements, may help transform an "autopilot" approach to a person's daily tasks and responsibilities to a more reflective, long-term approach to that person's craft. Talent attraction and retention is critical, yet much value may be gained by better talent management in the broader sense, developing the latent talent of an organization and recognizing the worth and contribution of each and every individual. Brian Cookson and British Cycling recognized the need to fully develop their latent talent and put in place a strategy that not only proclaimed, and later achieved, a bold stretch goal, but put in place a *system* to ensure continuous success and longevity. As with innovation, it is not enough to merely create value— capturing that value is also necessary.

Sporting performance has shown a more professional, business-based approach in recent years, and also offers a mirror back to the business world in the form of powerful reminders for that performance to be sustained. Keen observers of athletics, for example, will have noticed the common usage of the word "execution" from even the very young (yet highly trained) athletes in their post-race interviews. This lays bare not only the general strategic approach to their sport, but also recognizes that however critical their training, putting all the pieces together and performing on the day is the second piece of the strategic challenge. Tennis champions in recent years, with the game providing an ever-increasing physical challenge that tours the globe for the best part of 12 months, now comment frequently on the importance of their team and the larger support network that plays so crucial a part in their training, recovery, and resultant competition victory. Football in particular has been put under the business and leadership microscope in recent times with the retirement of Alex Ferguson, the Scottish manager of perennial English Champions Manchester United. As we commented in Chapter 9, "On the Criticality of Resilience for Our Future World," Ferguson was excellent at changing ahead of the survival imperative, which allowed him to simultaneously deconstruct and construct winning teams for more than 20 years. His leadership approach has been analyzed in interviews by *Harvard Business Review,* in which he highlighted the importance of building a strong youth system that may serve as the basis for sustainable success. This model, and others, have been examined by Professor Laurence Capron at INSEAD Business School, who develops the defining features of Build, Borrow, or Buy strategies employed in German football.[1] The youth system approach so highly valued by Ferguson is the Build model, which may be reflected on the company level as the development of internal resources through training and internal innovation. Borrowing, an increasing feature of the football transfer market in recent years through loan deals, may be likened to getting access to resources for a certain period of time through contractual relationships and alliances. Finally, to Buy, the headline-grabbing side of football business, is the acquisition of new resource and talent so effectively used by companies, including Cisco, over the years. The authors state that firms that carefully select and balance these three modes of growth outperform those that stick to one single mode, or grow opportunistically.

So sport offers a rich lens for thinking about transformation when focusing on the role of talent development. And a well-known cycling case offers us further clues as to how we may approach it. My life in Girona brought me into close contact with the professional cycling world, and I have long reflected on many aspects of cycling and how this connects to wider notions of business. Even on the simple tactical level and considering the practice of drafting, there is insight to be gained. Novice cyclists will often ride at the front of the group, believing power and speed on its own to be enough to win the race. Yet the aerodynamic advantage provided by the peloton is substantial, and knowing when to conserve one's energy, in order to attack at the right time, is the most important factor. Working as a team and taking the headwind only at certain times, even if that is with one's adversaries, is critical to build advantage. Constructing alliances depends on the stage of the race and is another factor that shows the complexities of cycle racing. The simple matter of being engaged at the right time was reflected in a recently designed *nudge* poster, as shown in Figure 15.1. This may apply to delegation and the dangers of micromanagement on a general level as well as looking more specifically at the creative process. The best new product development processes are characterized by senior managers being involved at the right time and knowing when to get out of the way, to give designers and engineers the necessary freedom to innovate.

The transformation of British Track Cycling, in moving from a position of long-term mediocrity to unprecedented success, offers us further insight. Track Cycling is a more popular sport than Road Cycling in many countries, with the explosive speeds and heavy reliance on tactics attracting thousands of people to velodromes, particularly in countries like Belgium and also Japan, where the famed "Kieran" event was conceived and attracts professional betting on a massive scale. Unlike the better known Road Cycling mode, which has its annual mecca to the Tour de France, the benchmark level of success is the Olympic Games with nations doing battle for scarce gold medals every four years, often decided by fractions of a second.

Great Britain had traditionally been a mediocre performer in Track Cycling at the Games, though headlines were made in 1992 when Chris Boardman won their first Gold Medal in 100 years at the Barcelona Olympics, using a bike that was engineered in collaboration with Lotus. Boardman and such high-tech collaboration would go on to make a key contribution in the coming years. Yet this was not quite the starting gun for continued success. Countries such as France and Australia would continue to dominate in Atlanta in 1996 and in Sydney in 2000.

Figure 15.1 Cyclists nudge by The LAB (Leadership Academy of Barcelona)

Yet in those Sydney Games, Great Britain won its second gold in those hundred odd years and things were starting to gain momentum behind the scenes. In Athens in 2004, two gold medals were procured, one of them from "flying Scot" Chris Hoy in a breathtaking performance in the "kilo" (an against the clock time-trial where riders complete four laps of the velodrome, 1,000 meters, as fast as possible). Starting in descending order to the number-one seeded rider, the final six had all broken the Olympic Games record until there was one man left. Hoy, the World Champion, and under incredible pressure, also broke the record and took the gold. I remember watching that performance clearly, my heart pounding in my chest, shouting at the television at a man I had met in person five years earlier in Edinburgh at the trophy presentation of the Edinburgh Triathlon. A very driven, humble man with an incredible work ethic, Hoy had sacrificed many things to get to this stage, living in Manchester close to the national velodrome in order to get those hours of practice in, and now he was Olympic Champion. The *Telegraph* newspaper in the UK described his performance as the "best by a British man in a generation."

The blue touch paper had been lit, and Great Britain would go on to dominate the Beijing games by winning eight gold medals. (Hoy won three of those and was the first British man in more than 100 years to win triple gold.) The nearest challenger, France, won only two. That success was sustained in the London games with another eight. Sixteen gold medals in two Olympic Games, where only one had been won in more than 100 years. Unprecedented success by any country in Olympic track cycling history (see Table 15.1).

Table 15.1   Great Britain Olympic Gold Progression

Olympic Games	Team GB Gold	Most Won/Nearest Challenger
2000 (Sydney)	1	France (5)
2004 (Athens)	2	Australia (6)
2008 (Beijing)	8	France (2)
2012 (London)	8	France/Australia (1)

So how did they do it? The cyclists, right? Champions like Hoy. Yet France and Australia and the rest of the nations also have these star athletes. What about technology? It is true that Great Britain worked with Formula 1 team McLaren to perfect its bicycle performance through wind-tunnel testing, as well as with clothing manufacturer Adidas to improve the aerodynamic nature of the cyclists clothing, yet many other countries would do the same. What I'd like to focus on is another man, Matt Parker, the Director of Marginal Gains. Essentially, Team GB recognized that if the difference between success and failure, between winning those gold medals and perhaps not even making the podium, came down to the width of a tire wheel, to the thousandth of a second, on such tiny fractions—that they should look for advantage also in those tiny fractions. And so began a maniacal focus on every conceivable possible advantage, no matter how small. The bicycle tires would be rubbed down with alcohol after each ride, in order to remove any particles of dust. Collaboration was exploited with Formula 1, but not in the traditional sense. The material that is used for the F1 car tires to keep them at the optimum temperature was used to make trousers for the riders, who would wear them between rounds in the velodrome—even if only for ten minutes. Riders were also instructed to take their own pillow with them when traveling abroad, to maximize their chances of a good night's sleep and prevent any possibilities of waking up with a neck injury. They also examined the bus timetable at the Beijing Olympics and believed there wasn't enough time to recover for their athletes by using the official Olympic transport from the velodrome to the athletes' village. The time was only about 20 minutes but enough in their view to make a difference. So they contracted their own bus company to ferry their own cyclists between both locations, the only country to do so.

But perhaps the best of all: *They taught their Olympic cyclists how to wash their hands.* They got them together and taught them how to wash their hands. They found out that no matter how thoroughly we think we wash our hands, we tend to neglect the area on the back of the thumb—where many pathogens can live that could result in a person catching a cold, a virus, and make those Olympic cyclists a couple thousandths of a second slower—the difference between success and failure. So did Team GB win 16 gold medals in two Olympic Games, having won only one in more than a hundred years—unprecedented domination in the history of Olympic Track Cycling—because they knew how to wash their hands better than countries like France and Australia? Maybe, maybe not. It was all part of an impressive focus on improving every single aspect of their operation, and they believed that all of them together would make the difference. Hence the driving strategy: *the cumulative effect of marginal gains.*

So what is the practical takeaway for you? That you wash your hands more thoroughly? Maybe it is. Especially if you have a high incidence of catching the common cold. A metalevel research study by the *Canadian Medical Association Journal* in January of 2014[2] brought together more than 20 years of research into the common cold. How to catch it less often, and when you do, how do you spend less time with it. The big conclusion? You guessed it, hand washing! If we take greater care on washing our hands, this has a much greater impact on the cold than any type of vitamin supplement or drug. Hospitals know this only too well, with an acute appreciation of the danger of disease and germs spread between wards by well-traveled and overworked nurses in particular. Yet can you ask nurses to wash their hands 50, 100 times a day? Even the recommended washing time of 20 seconds can feel like an eternity. Try it. So instead of disrupting the daily operation of the hospital in such a significant way, not to mention fight on a cultural level with behavior change, they made it easy by simply placing hand sanitizers on the back of each door, with the desired habit to have a quick spray and clean when entering and leaving each ward.

Hand washing has also been at the core of Unilever's sustainability strategy and particularly its Sustainable Living Plan. Building on the traditions of a company in which millions of children took part in a Clean Hands Health campaign in 1920s America, hand-washing classes have been offered in rural India since 2002. Unilever CEO Paul Polman extended this across the developing world with more hand-washing work offered in the past four years than in the previous 20. The 21-day course, using Unilever's Lifebuoy soap, has been shown by independent studies to reduce diarrhea cases by 25% and increases school attendance because children are sick less often.

In the case of the British Track Cycling transformation, where did the advantage really come from? Was it real or perceived? Does it matter? Isn't the most important aspect the mind-set of looking at every conceivable advantage? The confidence is delivered to the competitors in the cauldron of the Games and in riders from other nations believing they are less well-prepared. So whether it is real or perceived, psychological or material, the cumulative effect of marginal gains has many lessons for the sustainable executive performance of the modern-day professional. Barack Obama's marginal gain could be viewed as his approach to decision making, as we noted in Chapter 12, "FUEL," where minimizing the effects of decision fatigue by automating his approach to business dress and mealtime helps to keep him strong during a long, demanding day.

UPS also implemented a marginal gain to address its climate change and carbon emissions problems. As a courier company, minimizing its carbon footprint is a complex problem. How can it remain competitive and grow as a company, yet limit the damage it causes to the planet through its core activity? A very simple approach, and marginal gain, was identified: *UPS trucks don't turn left*. That's it. So why would such a simple change have such a massive impact? What happens when you have to turn left in a car? In most countries around the world—leaving out, for example, Great Britain—you wait. Either waiting on oncoming traffic to pass or a traffic light to turn green may result in a wait of just a few seconds, but UPS calculated that with all the left turns for all the trucks in all of the world, it was better to turn right ten times than turn left. Saving on driver and journey time, fuel costs, and minimizing carbon emissions were the multiple benefits from a simple change. The logic of small change in a scaled-up enterprise offers many opportunities to innovate, as well as cut costs in an age of austerity and scarce resources. I remember value reengineering projects at Unilever during my PhD, which looked at minimizing the wall thickness of product containers (water and shampoo bottles, for example) as a means of minimizing plastic material use. Manually collapsing water bottles and replacing the lid after drinking the contents was the focus of an awareness-raising campaign in Indonesia for Danone Water—whereby the transportation and recyclability of hundreds of thousands of bottles of water is vastly improved in the Asian Pacific Archipelago through a simple habit.

So the practical change and accompanying mind-set by *sweating the small stuff* can help to transform an organization. This doesn't mean collapsing the organization by looking to improve a thousand small initiatives at once, but by taking a more analytical and mindful view of action that is also tracked by the right metrics, and most importantly championed by the individual—the sustainable leader. A more analytical and mindful view of action was at the core of the British Cycling strategy, and was supported through several other key features:

- **Align the entire organization around an "impossible" goal:** The stretch goal of winning the Tour de France helped to focus thinking and provide a compass for all daily action, at all levels of the organization. Everyone was clear on the simple, yet bold, goal that lay ahead. Although technically a different sport, such boldness and ambition was transmitted to a track cycling team that was composed of several Tour riders, including Wiggins and Cavendish. Similarly bold targets were set for the Olympic track team, and a broad range of metrics were consulted on a regular basis to measure progress toward it.

- **Capture the energy to build a system:** British Cycling also recognized that one of the key long-term challenges was not the lack of talent or commitment by cyclists already in the system, but how to feed that system going forward. To this end, the British publics long-held apathy to the sport of cycling would compromise the grassroots system so important to ensuring a conveyer belt of talent. A media strategy and accompanying grassroots development program therefore helped to turn cycling into a respected sport and leisure activity on the street, with the transformation of cities such as London in a few short years nothing short of remarkable.

- **Nurture your flag bearer:** Chris Hoy was the flag bearer of the whole squad. Acting as inspiration for both the team and the public in general, he was carefully nurtured over a number of years as the champion who could help sustain the energy required in the system.

- **Look for inspiration outside your industry:** The Secret Squirrel club, led by former Olympic gold medalist and Tour de France stage winner Chris Boardman, was the Research and Development arm of the organization. Their focus was looking for inspiration, technology, and collaboration outside the cycling world, such as with Formula 1 team McLaren.

So, in the rough seas of a twenty-first century hyper-competitive business landscape, what type of boat do you need to build? Bigger? More agile? Faster? Sporting performance, and the British Cycling case, offers us some clues. I caught up again with Brian Cookson, recently installed as the President of the Union Cycliste Internationale (UCI), the world governing body for cycling, for the first time since that Girona *clara*. With world cycling in great need of transformation, he is in a good place to reflect on the success of British Cycling as he restarts the transformation journey. He believes in the power of leadership to ensure sustainable success and that leadership should include, "a sufficiently bold strategy, challenging but achievable, right at the start." Of course, this is not just about one person, and so building a strong, diverse team and supplying those people with the right resources is also key—and just as important is getting out of their way to let them get on with the job. Yet Cookson believes that leadership is also required once in the heat of battle and highlights the bravery necessary "to withstand the inevitable mid-term criticisms and attempts to distract and divert away from the strategy." Understanding the difference between governance and management is also important, two distinct behaviors that can easily be confused when the pressure is on. And finally, a healthy awareness of progress and when an intervention is required: "if the planets are not quite coming into alignment, then a push and a shove here and there can make all the difference."

The overriding focus in all of Cookson's reflection is the need to move beyond a one-off success to building a repeatable and sustainable process. So to our focus in this book. Let us now turn our attention to the last lap, Chapter 16, "Leading Change in the Triple Lens of Sustainability."

16

Leading Change in the Triple Lens of Sustainability

If we wish to help humans to become more fully human, we must realize not only that they try to realize themselves, but that they are also reluctant or afraid or unable to do so. Only by fully appreciating this dialectic between sickness and health can we help to tip the balance in favour of health.

—Abraham Maslow

"I usually get around 6–6.5 hours sleep, get into the office about 8 a.m., and spend 30 minutes reading. History and technology fascinate me, and I try to find interesting articles not directly related to my job. I then program my tweets for the rest of the day. Running every day gives me the energy to keep going as well as the space to think about the big decisions." José María Álvarez-Pallete was describing to me his typical day. Reporting to Executive Chairman Cesar Alierta, José María leads more than 130,000 employees worldwide as Chief Operating Officer of Telefónica, the Madrid-headquartered telecommunications group. "I work around 13–14 hours per day, and when I get home, I shower, relax, and later read again before going to sleep." He has a slim runner's build, dark wavy hair, and brown eyes that light up when discussing the challenges the company faces. No doubt there are a few dark circles under those eyes, but he looks younger than his 50 years. He describes his job as "making things happen." It's a demanding role—he says he'd like a little more sleep, a little more vacation (which he had to cancel for the second year in a row), and a little more quality time to get things in order. But he clearly relishes the challenge of mobilizing a massive company in a complicated market where the future for global telcos is uncertain. José María

applies his values in different areas of his life. It's not necessarily about switching off, but switching focus for recovery. Whether it is his running or family, he employs his skills and stays true to his nature in the work domain, and outside it. All of this has combined to make things happen in a company that operates across the Triple Lens. José María has been the architect of two notable initiatives. The Fundación Telefónica Proniño program in Latin America, founded when he was CEO of Latin America in the years 2004–2010 (when he maintained the family base in Madrid and had to "sleep well on a plane" to experience the deep recovery necessary to fulfill his role), has lifted almost half a million children out of child labor across Latin America, where the level of job satisfaction is one of the highest in the world in any industry. A second initiative, the Wayra start-up accelerator, has supported hundreds of start-ups in the past 5 years and has become the largest accelerator in the world with centers worldwide, including London, Barcelona, and Sao Paolo. Wayra is part of Open Future, Telefónica's program to partner with start-ups and entrepreneurs, from idea to market. It provides technical platforms, crowdworking spaces, investment, and access to the market.

Decisions are made quickly, driven by a concern that they may potentially cycle around again and cause delay. He notes that "The balance between execution, agility, and a good, logical reflection is important" but that he prefers to act quickly and then adapt (essentially a design-based iterative approach) rather than delay: "Because delaying things has a multiplying effect on the organization. When things get to your desk, they normally have gone through a lot of processes, and a lot of committees, and a lot of discussions."

He pays attention to the small things—reading every day and tweeting an average of 12 articles he finds interesting, running and planning races, and making frequent visits to the Corporate University north of Barcelona to teach. It's not part of his job description as COO, but these are things he feels he needs to do to "make things happen." He isn't afraid to act and change things if "the structure" isn't working: "If something is wrong, you need to reset the structure. For me, resetting the structure means that when I'm not feeling OK professionally, I tend to share it with my boss, with my colleagues. Even if it is hard, because I would rather have a hard decision, even if that affects me, than keep things eroding away." Other key themes that surfaced in the interview include the following:

- **Balance:** Although he concedes there is no line between work and life—"you are the same person in both places, it's not the case that the head is for work and the heart for home"—he pays keen attention to his family as the most important thing in his life. Flexing is necessary on both sides, depending on the context, but Saturday and Sunday is always reserved, a priori, for full, quality family time. His focus is on "building a personal project" at home in the same way that he builds projects at work.

- **Energy through motivation:** He gains great motivation from seeing his building plans progress, at home and work. His excitement comes from the responsibility placed on him as well as the freedom to act, something he thinks is true of all employees at the company. Maybe he's not always successful, but his actions get things moving as part of a grander mission.

- **No long-term planning:** He maintains that his career hasn't been planned to date and that he has no definite plans for the future. His focus is on enjoying what he is doing as well as the daily tasks that constitute his life. Reading and running are two examples that are greatly missed, even if for one day.

- **Being grateful:** One of the most common words or sentiments in the interview was his gratitude. He is genuinely thankful for his job, and for his previous work experiences. He has learned from all of his experiences and is grateful for the opportunity to do so.

Enjoying life in the moment, paying attention to the small, daily rituals, building a personal project outside work. José María is leading change in his world. So how will you lead change in yours? This begins by leading yourself. *What* will you change? *How* will you change?

I hope to have offered a range of action elements in the five elements of the SEP model that will help you pay more attention to your own basic human needs within the professional domain. This is the starting point for a journey that leads to being a sustainable leader. By appreciating the link between our own simple actions and habits, and the impact these

---

may have at the organizational and societal levels, we may positively affect the resilience, innovation, and leadership necessary at all three levels of the Triple Lens (see Table 16.1).

Table 16.1 Mapping Parts 2 and 3 to the Triple Lens

	Individual		Organizational		Societal
MOVE	Ch.6	→		←	Ch.7
RECOVER	Ch.8	→		←	Ch.9
FOCUS	Ch.10	→	Ch.11	→	
FUEL	Ch.12	→		←	Ch.13
TRAIN	Ch.14	→	Ch.15	→	

The five chapters of Part 2 offer various options for simple change and show the extension to the organizational setting. How will you diffuse positive practice in the workplace? What will you *hack*? Maybe you'll change the physical layout and design of the office. Maybe you'll think a little deeper about hotel selection in business travel, your menu choices during a business dinner, or take a different daily commute and listen to a podcast, or take your home pillow with you on a plane. Marginal gains, but with a Triple Lens view, to practice the principles of sustainable leadership (see Figure 16.1).

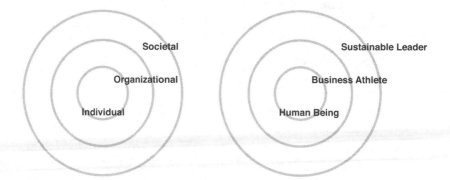

Figure 16.1 The Triple Lens of Sustainability and the sustainable leader journey

These principles allow a long-term and holistic view that makes sustainability work at the macro level. It also aligns with innovation—a process of practicing and embracing a new way of doing things to add value. Part 3 intended to show the extensions of individual elements in terms of the manifestation of individual choices on a societal level as well as the mind-set that can be applied to the organization. Leadership can be viewed as having the vision to see the overall system, understand how things interact, and identify the constituent parts that require change to improve the overall system.

I think we often confuse *friction* for work—this gives us the "suffering" that tricks us into thinking we are making progress: killing 100 emails, working long days chained to the desk, taking that conference call on the weekend. But *flow* is the state of high performance. Challenge and some degree of stretch should be present ideally, yet also happiness—in the clarity of thought, richer relationships, great conversations, and deep connection with our physical and mental selves.

Implementing change is not easy, even at the simple level. We don't change often—at least positively and consciously. I don't find these things easy. I don't preach to you from the pulpit of having "the secret." I have the same temptations and difficulties as anyone else. I smoked for several years and still miss it to a degree. In terms of alcohol, I'm Scottish, need I say more? Mobility is the starting point for personal-level change, but sometimes I just want to fall on the sofa. Sometimes I'm too tired to go for a walk or run, but do know the benefit of recharging this will give me. I love junk food now and again. I gave a talk on nutrition to a large company last year, found myself in the airport tired and hungry on the way home, and went for a Big Mac. This doesn't make me less credible, just human! I don't eat Big Macs every day, and I went for a Chinese Walk around the airport after eating it. I often take a small pack of dried fruit and nuts with me while traveling. On this occasion I didn't, but I didn't punish myself for not having it. Blood sugar can have a massive effect on our decisions, our energy throughout a long day, and our weight, but I had to kick an addiction to Lindt chocolate bars last winter! What I'm trying to highlight is that we shouldn't take an inflexible, humorless approach to personal change and sustainability. There is no dogma in the context of personal change and performance. Try new things, step outside the lines, and find what works for you. The approach works—I've seen it hundreds of times over the years. The key is action and then reflecting on the corresponding reaction. The cause and effect. Find your own secrets.

Sometimes I find my own, others remain elusive. The same goes for the executives I coach. I've found it difficult to disconnect on the weekends in recent years given my drive toward building a company and writing a book. I have been successful in implementing action such as the Chinese Walk, which, when combined with eating an evening meal late at night, allowed me to regain race weight and run fast again. My big commitment as I am in the process of finishing this book is to read more. Since finishing my PhD, I read very little, having experienced the pressure of reading so much, let's say, "less than entertaining prose" in such a short space of time during the research. And the joy of reading has been unveiled to me again as I have proceeded through this book project.

Looking back on my life, I appreciate the value of some of the small practices. For example, athletics training from an early age, taking public transportation to attend sessions in the neighboring town on a regular basis, knocking out interval repeats, and being held accountable by my peers and coach. These experiences and others have given me the discipline and resilience that I have counted on all my life. But neither does this mean that I have the answers. My blindness to my compromised recovery after a running injury by persisting with a standing desk resulted in extending that injury by an unnecessary two months. I'm still trying to experiment and tweak elements of my daily, weekly, and quarterly life that gives me the best performance and happiness in all aspects of it.

Flexing is important. During the main writing period of this book, at home in Scotland during August 2014, I began the month with a highly structured routine in which I tried to automate my willpower. Calling it my "Murakami method," I would rise at 5:30 each morning and write as much as I could until 10:00, followed by a long trail run along the River Clyde (downstream from Owen's Mills) until 11:00. I'd try to fit in a nap at some point and lead as normal a life as possible during the rest of the day, enjoying an aperitif at night with friends and family. I did this for eight straight days but became exhausted. The nonwriting part of my day took too much out of me, my napping was inefficient, and I wasn't recovering from the heavy load each morning. Three days of little progress followed. I simply needed the recovery, after which I resumed a different, flexible approach, rising a little later, at 6:30, cutting down on alcohol, and ensuring I got the right amount of sleep. I also changed some of my writing spaces and would switch between one family member house where I would read and review each morning before moving to another where I would write. I am a strong believer that spaces have *memory* with regard to the activities we do there. Each of these spaces had only the memory of the tasks I needed to do—no email, Facebook, Twitter, or any of the other many distractions that would have slowed my progress. Looking back, I had a fantastically productive month. I had designed a routine, changed it, tried new things, but stayed true to the basics I know work for me (and for many people)—quality sleep, physical mobility, and some time off and reward for a good job done. Hard work, but quality work. No *grinding* and paying attention to designing out needless friction. I also became convinced of my best creative output coming in the mornings, a time that I have typically spent on absorbing information. I am a moderately strong Lark and so have committed to keep trying to create in the mornings and consume later in the day.

Richer insights into the change process have been developed in recent years. Charles Duhigg looked at change through the habit loop in his 2012 book, *How Habits Work* (see Chapter 4, Reference 1). He showed how habits can be broken into three constituent parts: a cue, a habit, and then a reward. The *New York Times* journalist offered this three-step cycle as a means of implementing positive change as well as diagnosing and breaking bad habits. B. J. Fogg, a Stanford-based educator, is another who has inspired change around the world, most recently with his Tiny Habits method. He places particular emphasis on triggers that serve as powerful reminders to implement new, tiny changes.

Both approaches have elements of good practice that we can follow. In my teaching, I've asked people to consider certain key factors to help lock in change after they have identified a range of options they might implement. On a granular level, this is the 4S model with the wider context offered by the 4Ps.

The 4S Model—Small, Specific, Supported, Shared

Small

The law of marginal gains shows us that small changes can have massive impacts. By creating a habit, the periodic (normally daily) practice will have a cumulative effect. And by making it small, we have the best chance of making it a habit. Research has shown that the smaller the change, the quicker it gains "automaticity"—without conscious effort or mental load. Beware of grand ambition, which often derails our attempts at change because we can become despondent when the ambitious goals are not achieved. The small changes are the quick wins on which the grander goals are achieved.

Specific

Beware also of vagueness. Set a finish line. In the same way that we need to be specific in the workplace to understand what success is, so too with personal change. Rather than making an open commitment to always take the staircase, start with a commitment to always take the staircase for the remainder of the month. Achieving your objective will give you the motivation to keep going. Part of being specific is measuring. What is the right measure? Change it up. Rather than being disappointed looking at the bathroom scale each morning, try integrating more movement into a daily commute for two weeks and taking a tape measure around your waist.

Supported

Support your new action by placing it next to an existing one. We are all slaves to our existing habits. What do you do each day? Perhaps you have a consistent routine related to your morning: personal hygiene or preparing kids for school. Do a plank after brushing your teeth each morning—or if you're really ambitious, do the plank *while* brushing your teeth! Seriously though, triggers can be immensely powerful. B. J. Fogg talks of his "flushing the toilet" trigger, after which he would complete a couple of push-ups. That is a much easier way of getting 30 to 40 push-ups on a daily basis than doing them all at once.

Shared

Share your change with your family, with your friends, or with your boss. If you plan to go offline after a certain time each day, you'll need to manage expectations on a professional level. If you have a habit of collapsing on the sofa when you arrive home from work, tell your family so that they are waiting for you to go for a walk when you arrive home, after which you can fall on the sofa. Sharing your change makes you accountable. And we all need accountability from time to time. I didn't explicitly share my Chinese Walk commitment, but accountability made it work. Animals are amazing at picking up habits. After my initial enthusiasm for walking after my evening meal wore off, my faithful companion Harry the sheepdog ensured that I kept going. Now, as soon as I put my knife and fork down, Harry waits at the door and barks if I don't get moving!

4Ps: Passion, Practice, Performance, Progress

Passion

Some of the executives I have worked with have invested less and less in the things they love as they advance through their careers. More demands are placed on their time, whether it's family or work commitments, and they feel guilty and selfish when indulging in their passions. Yet reconnecting with your passions is perhaps the most unselfish thing you can do. Others, both at home and in the workplace, will get the best out of you. Sharing your passions with a family member or work colleague may further increase such a benefit. Uncovering such passions in your team will also increase engagement and performance as a whole. As we have traced so far, work is no longer about the quantity of time, rather the quality, engagement, and getting the best out of everyone in the enterprise. Unleashing such passions with the resultant improvement in happiness is a formal business strategy of some enterprises.

Practice and Performance

But where does passion come from? I believe there is a real link to practice. We are often passionate about the things we are good at, and as we have discussed, performance often comes from practice. Much of the dialogue around passion has centered on people finding the thing that they love, but we often love what we are good at.

Progress

Progress also fuels continual practice. Olympic track cyclist Chris Hoy, although slowing in certain measures toward the end of his career, was still setting personal bests in other areas, such as his leg strength. So look for progress along any measure. This could include a complex data set as employed in British Cycling to such good effect, or it may simply be finding another notch on your belt when you get dressed in the morning. Tracking helps us see the progress, being more mindful of it, and acts as fuel for continuing the tracking, and the practice. This is the virtuous circle of training.

Locking-in Change

4S and 4P give us a starting point on how to change. A broader view leads us to the following factors, which allow us to close our discussion:

- **Don't do it alone:** As we noted earlier, sharing a commitment will help to lock-in change because you will be held accountable. This point concerns sharing the load of change. So look for allies. Perhaps you need to push back against a work culture that is characterized by excessive hours, lack of recovery, poor engagement, and burn out. Managing upward is difficult if you are the only dissenting voice, so build political alliances for certain aspects of change.

- **Build a support network:** Like a professional athlete, look to surround yourself with people who fulfill different roles. Support networks increase in scale, quality, and attention to detail as athletes rise through the ranks, yet the opposite happens in the corporate world. As a professional is promoted through an organization, fewer and fewer people surround them who give critical feedback on their performance. More people may surround them in order to carry out tasks, yet few will tell them how they are performing, which may result in either the executive burning out or being sacked! Call someone a coach or mentor if you like, but look for people to build this network. They may act as a sounding board, offer the wisdom of their experience, or simply provide a service such as a good recovery massage. These roles could be fulfilled by a spouse, family member, friend, professional, or even stranger. Sometimes people with distance from a situation can offer the best advice about it. Beware of preconceptions regarding the value someone can offer. Two of the greatest 800-meter athletes of all time, Sebastian Coe and David Rudisha, enjoyed the services of quite unconventional coaches. Coe, with his father—an engineer who had no formal coaching experience but an inquiring mind—and Rudisha, with Brother Colm—an Irish Catholic missionary who aims to educate the whole person, body and mind, in his missionary work in Kenya.

- **Practice change:** The power of positive practice is a key element of an athlete's armory, and it has been shown to be important in many fields where high performance is prized. Beyond the performance level attained by practicing some discipline, I think there is a deep value in simply practicing change. Change is difficult because we don't experience it enough. And so by trying to change aspects of your life—anything—you can get better at *the process of change*. Hacking applied at the small, marginal-gain level with the iterative cycle inherent within it may be applied to life's grander challenges as and when they occur—thereby improving one's resilience. As Peter Drucker notes in his work on self-management, "No one can expect to live very long without experiencing a serious setback in his or her life or work." The more we are accustomed to failing and falling, the easier it will be to get back up. So change one thing today. Do something for the first time.

- **Apply the best of yourself in nonwork:** Your life is not your work, so why should your work get the best of you? By applying your skills and talents and thinking in other areas of your life, you may experience deep recovery as well as develop those same competences that are reapplied back within the workplace setting. Abraham Maslow said that *"Capacities clamor to be used, and cease their clamor only when they are well used. Not only is it fun to use our capacities, but it is necessary for growth. The* *unused skill or capacity or organ can become a disease center or else atrophy or disappear, thus diminishing the person."*[1] I think that for such capacities to be "well-used," they need to be employed at all levels of the Triple Lens, not just focused on work matters.

This is the new self-management. Drucker made a call for the business professional, the twenty-first century "knowledge worker," to identify their strengths, their patterns of work, values, where they belong, and what they can contribute. The journey toward the sustainable leader as described in *Sustaining Executive Performance* may help a deeper analysis of these factors by including a closer view of the physical self and connection with society at large. As inferred by Maslow in the opening quote of this final chapter, we have a responsibility to ourselves and to others to tip the balance toward health. We live in a fascinating age. There are so many opportunities available to us that previous generations didn't enjoy. Yet there are also many complex challenges and parts of society crying out for improvement and better "health." We each have a responsibility to make a change and try to make a positive impact. But have fun doing it. Life is to be lived. I wish you the best.

References

Chapter 1

1. E. Bergvall, ed., "The Official Report of the Olympic Games of Stockholm 1912," Swedish Olympic Committee: Stockholm (1913).

2. Pierre de Coubertin, *Olympism: Selected Writings* (Lausanne: IOC Press, 2000).

3. Nigel Spivey, *The Ancient Olympics* (Oxford: Oxford University Press, 2004).

4. B. Hayes, "Plato's Body, and Mine," *The New York Times* (April 21, 2012). http://www.nytimes.com/2012/04/22/opinion/sunday/platos-body-and-mine.html.

5. A. H. Maslow, "*A Theory of Human Motivation*," *Psychological Review* 50, no. 4 (1943): 370–96.

6. C. P. Alderfer, "An Empirical Test of a New Theory of Human Needs," *Organizational Behavior and Human Performance* 4, no. 2 (1969): 142–175.

7. M. Richter, "Digital Devices Deprive Brain of Needed Downtime," *The New York Times* (August 24, 2010). http://www.nytimes.com/2010/08/25/technology/25brain.html.

8. B. Sparrow, J. Liu, and D. M. Wegner, "Google Effects on Memory: Cognitive Consequences of Having Information at Our Fingertips," *Science* vol. 333 no. 6043 (July 14, 2011): 776–778.

9. S. J. Colcombe and A. F. Kramer, "Fitness Effects on the Cognitive Function of Older Adults: A Meta-analytic Study," *Psychological Science* vol. 14, (2003): 125–130.

10. F. Harburg, "Mental Muscle Power," Chief Learning Officer (April 2009). http://www.clomedia.com/articles/mental_ muscle_power.

11. K. I. Erickson, M. W. Voss, et al., "Exercise Training Increases Size of Hippocampus and Improves Memory," *Proc Natl Acad Sci USA.* vol. 108, no. 7 (2011): 3017–22.

12. J. Fields, *Uncertainty: Turning Fear and Doubt into Fuel for Brilliance* (New York: Portfolio Hardcover, 2011).

13. M. T. Gailliot, R. F. Baumeister, J. Brandon, C. Schmeichel, N. DeWall, J. K. Maner, E. A. Plant, D. M. Tice, and L. E. Brewer, "Self-Control Relies on Glucose as a Limited Energy Source: Willpower Is More Than a Metaphor," *Journal of Personality and Social Psychology* vol. 92, no. 2 (2007): 325–336.

14. S. Danziger, J. Levav, and L. Avnaim-Pesso, "Extraneous Factors in Judicial Decisions," *PNAS (Proceedings of the National Academy of Sciences of the United States of America)* vol. 108, no. 17 (April 26, 2011): 6889–6892.

15. C. Sullivan, "Why Don't Rock Stars Trash Hotel Rooms Anymore?" *The Guardian* (June 3, 2010). http://www.theguardian.com/music/2010/jun/03/rock-stars-hotels-caroline-sullivan.

16. Richard Stanton, *The Forgotten Olympic Art Competitions: The Story of the Olympic Art Competitions of the 20th Century* (Victoria: Trafford Publishing, 2000).

Chapter 2

1. I. Donnachie and G. Hewitt, *Historic New Lanark: The Dale and Owen Industrial Community Since 1785* (Edinburgh: Edinburgh University Press, 1993).

2. R. G. Garnett, *Co-operation and the Owenite Socialist Communities in Britain 1825-1845* (Manchester: Manchester University Press, 1972).

3. S. P. MacGregor and T. Carleton, eds., *Sustaining Innovation: Collaboration Models for a Complex World* (New York: Springer, 2011).

4. J. L. Bower and C. M. Christensen, "Disruptive Technologies: Catching the Wave," *Harvard Business Review* vol. 73, no. 1 (1995): 43–53.

5. M. Sawhney, R. C. Wolcott, and I. Arroniz, "The 12 Different Ways for Companies to Innovate," *MIT Sloan Management Review* vol. 47, no. 3 (2006): 75–81.

6. Ram Nidumolu, C. K. Prahalad, and M. R. Rangaswami, "Why Sustainability Is Now the Key Driver of Innovation," *Harvard Business Review* vol. 87, no. 9 (2009): 56–64.

7. D. Grayson and A. Hodges, *Corporate Social Opportunity! Seven Steps to Make Corporate Social Opportunity Work for Your Business* (Sheffield, UK: Greenleaf Publishing, 2004).

8. M. E. Porter and M. Kramer, "Creating Shared Value," *Harvard Business Review* vol. 89, no. 1 (2011): 62–77.

9. S. P. MacGregor and J. Fontrodona, "Exploring the Fit Between CSR and Innovation," *Indian Management Research Journal* vol. 2, no. 1 (2010): 38–51. (Originally IESE Working Paper no. 759, 2008.)

10. S. P. MacGregor and J. Fontrodona, "*Strategic CSR for SMEs: Paradox or Possibility?*" *Universia Business Review* 30, no. 2 (2011): 80–94.

11. K. Haanaes, M. Reeves, et al., "Sustainability Nears a Tipping Point," *MIT Sloan Management Review* vol. 53, no. 2 (January 2012): 69–74.

12. P. Polman, "Business, Society, and the Future of Capitalism," *McKinsey Quarterly* (May 2014). http://www.mckinsey.com/insights/sustainability/business_society_ and_the_future_ of_capitalism.

13. M. Korn, "Why Some MBAs Are Reading Plato," *Wall Street Journal* (April 30, 2014). http://online.wsj.com/news/articles/SB1000142405270230394810457953336 10289092866.

14. C. Gross-Loh, "Why Are Hundreds of Harvard Students Studying Ancient Chinese Philosophy?" *The Atlantic* (October 8, 2013). http://www.theatlantic.com/ education/archive/2013/10/why-are-hundreds-of-harvard-students-studying- ancient-chinese-philosophy/280356/.

15. P. Drucker, *The Age of Discontinuity; Guidelines to Our Changing Society* (New York: Harper and Row, 1969).

16. M. Kouchaki and I. H. Smith, "The Morning Morality Effect: The Influence of Time of Day on Unethical Behaviour," *Psychological Science* vol. 25, no. 1 (January 2014): 95–102.

Chapter 3

1. S. Pugh, *Total Design: Integrated Methods for Successful Product Engineering* (Upper Saddle River, NJ: Addison Wesley, 1990).

2. J. C. Jones, *Design Methods: Seeds of Human Futures* (Hoboken, NJ: John Wiley & Sons, 1970).

3. T. Brown, "Design Thinking," *Harvard Business Review* (June 2008): 84–92.

4. G. Zaltman, *How Customers Think: Essential Insights into the Mind of the Market* (Boston: HBS Publishing, 2003).

5. S. Thomke, A. Nimgade. "IDEO Product Development," *Harvard Business School* case 9-600-143 (2007).

6. G. Kembel, "The Classroom in 2020," *Forbes* (April 8, 2010). http://www.forbes. com/2010/04/08/stanford-design-2020-technology-data-companies-10-education. html.

7. R. Martin, *The Design of Business: Why Design Thinking Is the Next Competitive Advantage* (Boston: HBR Press, 2009).

8. C. Larson, "Light-Bulb Moments for a Nonprofit," *The New York Times* (January 11, 2014). http://www.nytimes.com/2014/01/12/business/international/light-bulb- moments-for-a-nonprofit.html.

Chapter 4

1. C. Duhigg, *The Power of Habit: Why We Do What We Do in Life and Business* (New York: Random House, 2012).

2. M. Currey, *Daily Rituals: How Artists Work* (New York: Knopf, 2013).

3. E. Brockes, "Haruki Murakami: 'I Took a Gamble and Survived,'" *The Guardian* (October 14, 2011). http://www.theguardian.com/books/2011/oct/14/haruki-murakami-1q84.

4. Twyla Tharp, *The Creative Habit: Learn It and Use It for Life* (New York: Simon & Schuster, 2006).

5. M. L. Tushman and C. A. O'Reilly, *Winning Through Innovation: A Practical Guide to Leading Organizational Change and Renewal* (Boston, MA: Harvard Business School Press, 2002).

Chapter 5

1. J. A. Byrne and L. Gerdes, "The Man Who Invented Management," *Business Week* (November 27, 2005). http://www.businessweek.com/stories/2005-11-27/the-man-who-invented-management.

2. P. Drucker, "Managing Oneself," *Harvard Business Review* vol. 77, no. 2 (1999): 64–74.

3. C. Christensen, "How Will You Measure Your Life?" *Harvard Business Review* 88 (2010): 7–8, 46–51.

4. M. McGannon and J. McGannon, *The Business Leader's Health Manual* (Basingstroke, UK: Palgrave Macmillan, 2009).

Chapter 6

1. B. Berkowitz and P. Clark, "The Health Hazards of Sitting," *The Washington Post* (January 20, 2014). http://apps.washingtonpost.com/g/page/national/the-health-hazards-of-sitting/750/.

2. N. Merchant, "Sitting Is the Smoking of Our Generation," HBR Blog (January 14, 2013). https://hbr.org/2013/01/sitting-is-the-smoking-of-our-generation/.

3. L. F. Cherkas, J. L. Hunki, B. S. Kato, et al., "The Association Between Physical Activity in Leisure Time and Leukocyte Telomere Length," *Arch Intern Med.* 168 no. 2 (2008): 154–158.

4. G. N. Healy, C. E. Matthews, D. W. Dunstan, E. A. H. Winkler, and N. Owen, "Sedentary Time and Cardio-Metabolic Biomarkers in US Adults: NHANES 2003-06," *European Heart Journal* vol. 32, no. 5 (2010): 590–597.

5. L. L. Craft, T. W. Zderic, S. M. Gapstur, E. H. VanIterson, D. M Thomas, J. Siddique, M. T. Hamilton. "Evidence That Women Meeting Physical Activity Guidelines Do Not Sit Less: An Observational Inclinometry Study," *International Journal of Behavioral Nutrition and Physical Activity* 9 no.1 (2012): 122.

6. T. Jeal, *Livingstone: Revised and Expanded Edition* (New Haven, CT: Yale University Press, 2013).

7. H. van Praag, "Exercise and the Brain: Something to Chew On," *Trends in Neuroscience* vol. 32, no. 5 (2009): 283–290.

8. C. W. Cotman, N. C. Berchtold, and L. A. Christie, "Exercise builds brain health: key roles of growth factor cascades and inflammation," *Trends in Neuroscience* vol. 30, no. 9 (2007): 464–472.

9. J. E. Ahlskog, Y. E. Geda, N. R. Graff-Radford, and R. C. Petersen, "Physical Exercise as a Preventive or Disease-Modifying Treatment of Dementia and Brain Aging," *Mayo Clinic Proceedings* 86, no. 9 (September 2011): 876–884.

10. J. Nithianantharajah and A. J. Hannan, "The Neurobiology of Brain and Cognitive Reserve: Mental and Physical Activity as Modulators of Brain Disorders," *Progress in Neurobiology* 89 (2009): 369–382.

11. S. P. MacGregor, "Describing and Supporting the Distributed Workspace: Towards a Prescriptive Process for Design Teams," PhD Thesis, University of Strathclyde (2003).

12. Henry, M. and S. Greenhalgh, "The Reality of Virtual Teams," *Time-Compression Technologies* 7 (1999): 18–19.

13. R. Kraut, C. Egidio, and J. Galegher, *Patterns of Contact and Communication in Scientific Research Collaboration*, (London: Lawrence Erlbaum Associates, 1990).

14. B. Grubb, "Do as We Say, Not as We Do: Googlers Don't Telecommute," *The Sydney Morning Herald* (February 19, 2013). http://www.smh.com.au/it-pro/business-it/do-as-we-say-not-as-we-do-googlers-dont-telecommute-20130218-2eo8w.html.

15. O. Judson, "Stand Up While You Read This!" *The New York Times* (February 23, 2010). http://opinionator.blogs.nytimes.com/2010/02/23/stand-up-while-you-read-this/.

16. "Calorie burner: How much better is standing up than sitting?" *BBC News Magazine* (October 16, 2013). http://www.bbc.co.uk/news/magazine-24532996.

17. R. E. Silverman, "Where's the Boss? Trapped in a Meeting," *The Wall Street Journal* (February 14, 2012). http://online.wsj.com/news/articles/SB10001424052970204642604577215013504567548.

18. R. E. Silverman, "No More Angling for the Best Seat; More Meetings Are Stand-Up Jobs," *The Wall Street Journal* (February 2, 2012). http://online.wsj.com/news/articles/SB10001424052970204652904577193460472598378.

19. J. J. Ratey and E. Hagerman, *Spark! How Exercise Will Improve the Performance of Your Brain* (London: Quercus, 2008).

20. D. Pallotta, "Take a Walk, Sure, But Don't Call It a Break," HBR Blog (February 27, 2014). http://blogs.hbr.org/2014/02/take-a-walk-sure-but-dont-call-it-a-break/.

21. M. Oppezzo and D. L. Schwartz, "Give Your Ideas Some Legs: The Positive Effect of Walking on Creative Thinking," *Journal of Experimental Psychology: Learning, Memory, and Cognition* vol. 40, no. 4 (2014): 1142–1152.

22. Scott Doorley and Scott Witthoft, *Make Space: How to Set the Stage for Creative Collaboration* (Hoboken: Wiley, 2012).

23. A. P. Knight and M. Baer, "Get Up, Stand Up: The Effects of a Non-Sedentary Workspace on Information Elaboration and Group Performance," *Social Psychological and Personality Science*, vol. 5, no. 8 (November 2014): 910–917.

Chapter 7

1. W. Thom, *Pedestrianism; or an Account of the Performances of Celebrated Pedestrians During the Last and Present Century: With a Full Narrative of Captain Barclay's Public and Private Matches* (Aberdeen: D. Chalmers & Co, 1813).

2. D. Gillon, "The Life and Prodigious Feats of Scotland's First Great Sporting Champion," *The Glasgow Herald* (August 24, 2001). http://www.heraldscotland.com/sport/spl/aberdeen/barclay-defied-death-in-his-quest-for-fame-the-life-and-prodigious-feats-of-scotland-s-first-great-sporting-champion-reviewed-by-doug-gillon-1.175898.

3. The Economic Intelligence Unit, Global Liveability Ranking and Report, August 2013. http://www.eiu.com/liveability2013.

4. D. Safarik, A. Wood, M. Carver, and M. Gerometta, "CTBUH Year in Review: Tall Trends of 2013," Council on Tall Buildings and Urban Habitat, http://ctbuh.org/TallBuildings/HeightStatistics/AnnualBuildingReview/Trendsof2013/tabid/6105/language/en-US/Default.aspx.

5. I. Gazibara, J. Goodman, P. Madden, and R. Fausset, "Mega Cities on the Move, Forum for the Future," http://www.forumforthefuture.org/project/megacities-move/overview.

6. R. Yu, C. Murphy, and K. Tian, "Car Makers Renew Efforts to Woo First-Time Buyers in China," *The Wall Street Journal* (April 18, 2014). http://online.wsj.com/news/articles/SB10001424052702303887804579503151993326852.

7. J. M. Roney, "Bicycles Pedaling into the Spotlight," Earth Policy Institute Eco-Economy Indicators (May 12, 2008). http://www.earth-policy.org/indicators/C48.

8. T-wei Hu, M. Li, and S. Wei, "Household Durable Goods Ownership in Tianjin, China," *The China Quarterly* vol. 120 (December 1989): 787–799.

9. D. Bruno, "The De-Bikification of Beijing," Citylab, *The Atlantic* (April 9, 2012). http://www.citylab.com/commute/2012/04/de-bikification-beijing/1681/.

10. E. Flint, S. Cummins, and A. Sacker," Associations Between Active Commuting, Body Fat, and Body Mass Index: Population-Based, Cross-Sectional Study in the United Kingdom," *BMJ* 349 (2014): g4887.

11. F. K. Benfield, "How Transit, Walkability Help Make Cities More Affordable," *Huffington Post* (August 25, 2014). http://www.huffingtonpost.com/f-kaid-benfield/how-transit-walkability-h_b_5704997.html.

12. Office for National Statistics (UK), "Commuting and Personal Well-Being" (February 12, 2014). http://www.ons.gov.uk/ons/rel/wellbeing/measuring-national-well-being/commuting-and-personal-well-being--2014/art-commuting-and-personal-well-being.html.

13. B. Schiller, "Your Car-Centric City Is Why You're Fat," *Fast Company* (August 14, 2014). http://www.fastcoexist.com/3034289/why-youre-fat/your-car-centric-city-is-why-youre-fat.

14. G. Hack, *Business Performance in Walkable Shopping Areas* (Princeton, NJ: Active Living Research, a National Program of the Robert Wood Johnson Foundation, 2013).

15. "IPSOS polls North America" (July 15, 2014). http://www.ipsos-na.com/news-polls/pressrelease.aspx?id=6565.

16. P. Brown, "In a Successful Modern City, the Car Must No Longer Be King," *The Guardian* (July 7, 2014). http://www.theguardian.com/cities/2014/jul/07/ in-a-successful-modern-city-the-car-must-no-longer-be-king.

17. A. Davies, "People in Pedestrian-Friendly Cities Make More Money," *WIRED* (June 23, 2014). http://www.wired.com/2014/06/walkable-cities-income-education/.

18. D. Olick, "A City's 'Walkability' Drives Real Estate Values," CNBC (June 17, 2014). http://www.cnbc.com/id/101766206.

19. M. Andersen, "The Protected Bike Lane Ridership Bump, City by City," *People for Bikes* (June 3, 2014). http://www.peopleforbikes.org/blog/entry/everywhere-they-appear-protected-bike-lanes-seem-to-attract-riders.

20. E. Weiss, "Bike Share's Rough Ride," *The New York Times* (May 23, 2014). http://www.nytimes.com/2014/05/24/opinion/bike-shares-rough-ride.html.

21. B. McKenzie, "Modes Less Traveled—Bicycling and Walking to Work in the United States: 2008–2012," American Community Survey Reports, U.S. Census Bureau (May 2014). http://www.census.gov/prod/2014pubs/acs-25.pdf.

22. S. Goodyear, "Why the Streets of Copenhagen and Amsterdam Look So Different from Ours," Citylab, *The Atlantic* (April 25, 2012). http://www.citylab.com/commute/2012/04/why-streets-copenhagen-and-amsterdam-look-so-different-ours/1849/.

23. A. Peters, "In Sweden, Free Bikes to Commuters Who Promise to Drive Less," *Fast Company* (May 19, 2014). http://www.fastcoexist.com/3030704in-sweden-free-bikes-to-commuters-who-promise-to-drive-less.

24. N. Padukone, "The Unique Genius of Hong Kong's Public Transportation System," *The Atlantic* (September 10, 2013). http://www.theatlantic.com/china/archive/2013/09/the-unique-genius-of-hong-kongs-public-transportation-system/279528/.

25. S. Vedler, "Free Public Transit in Talinn Is a Hit with Riders but Yields Unexpected Results," Citiscope (January 27, 2014). http://citiscope.org/story/2014/free-public-transit-tallinn-hit-riders-yields-unexpected-results.

Chapter 8

1. J. Medina, *Brain Rules: 12 Principles for Surviving and Thriving at Work, Home, and School* (Edmonds, WA: Pear Press, 2009).

2. Lawrence Epstein and Steven Mardon, *The Harvard Medical School Guide to a Good Night's Sleep* (New York: McGraw-Hill, 2006).

3. J. Horne, *Sleepfaring: A Journey Through the Science of Sleep* (Oxford University Press: Oxford, 2007).

4. P. Martin, *Counting Sheep: The Science and Pleasures of Sleep and Dreams* (Thomas, New York: Dunne Books, 2004).

5. S. Hegarty, "The Myth of the Eight-Hour Sleep," *BBC News* magazine (February 22, 2012). http://www.bbc.com/news/magazine-16964783.

6. M. E. Ansfield, D. M. Wegner, and R. Bowser, "Ironic Effects of Sleep Urgency," *Behaviour Research and Therapy* vol. 34, no. 7 (1996): 523–531.

7. D. Dawson and K. Reid, "Fatigue, Alcohol and Performance Impairment," *Nature* (July 17, 1997): 388, 235.

8. J. Kirby, "Change the World and Get to Bed by 10:00," HBR Blog (May 13, 2013). http://blogs.hbr.org/hbr/hbreditors/2013/05/change_the_world_and_get_to_be.html.

9. "NASA Naps," http://science.nasa.gov/science-news/science-at-nasa/2005/03jun_naps/.

10. J. Loehr, T. Schwartz, "The Making of a Corporate Athlete." *Harvard Business Review* vol. 79, no. 1 (2001): 120–128.

11. C. Murphy, "Secrets of Greatness: How I Work," *Fortune Magazine* (March 2006). http://money.cnn.com/2006/03/02/news/newsmakers/howiwork_fortune_032006/.

12. J. Loehr and T. Schwartz, *The Power of Full Engagement: Managing Energy, Not Time, Is the Key to High Performance and Personal Renewal* (New York: Free Press, 2005).

Chapter 9

1. P. Patton, "A 3-Wheel Dream That Died at Takeoff," *The New York Times* (June 15, 2008). http://www.nytimes.com/2008/06/15/automobiles/collectibles/15BUCKY.html.

2. S. Sternthal, "Moscow's Stray Dogs," *FT Magazine* (January 16, 2010). http://www.ft.com/cms/s/0/628a8500-ff1c-11de-a677-00144feab49a.html.

3. A. Zolli and A.M. Healy, *Resilience: Why Things Bounce Back* (New York: Simon & Schuster, 2013).

4. A. Zolli, "Learning to Bounce Back," *The New York Times* (November 2, 2012). http://www.nytimes.com/2012/11/03/opinion/forget-sustainability-its-about-resilience.html.

5. C. M. Christensen, *The Innovator's Dilemma: When New Technologies Cause Great Firms to Fail* (Boston, MA: Harvard Business School Press, 1997).

6. W. J. Abernathy and J. M. Utterback, "Patterns of Industrial Innovation," *Technology Review* vol. 80 (June/July 1978): 40–47.

7. R. Foster, *Innovation: The Attacker's Advantage* (NY: Summit Books, 1986).

8. "Sustainable Lifestyles 2050," SPREAD scenarios, http://www.sustainable-every-day-project.net/spread/2012/10/10/thefourscenarios/.

9. Open Culture, "Philip K. Dick Previews Blade Runner: The Impact of the Film Is Going to Be Overwheming" (March 25, 2013). http://www.openculture.com/2013/03/philip_k_dick_previews_blade_runner.html.

Chapter 10

1. C. D. Fisher, "Boredom at Work: A Neglected Concept," *Human Relations* vol. 46, no. 3 (March 1993): 395–417.

2. J. D. Eastwood, A. Frischen, M. J. Fenske, and D. Smilek, "The Unengaged Mind: Defining Boredom in Terms of Attention," *Perspectives on Psychological Science* 7 (September 1, 2012): 482–495.

3. S. Mann and R. Cadman, "Does Being Bored Make Us More Creative?" *Creativity Research Journal* vol. 26, no. 2, (2014): 165–173.

4. S. P. MacGregor and T. Torres, eds., *Higher Creativity for Virtual Teams: Developing Platforms for Co-Creation* (Hershey, PA: IGI Group, 2007).

5. S. J. Kass, J. C. Wallace, and S. J. Vodanovich, "Boredom Proneness and Sleep Disorders as Predictors of Adult Attention Deficit Disorders," *Journal of Attention Disorders* vol. 7, no. 2 (November 2003): 83–91.

6. "Always Connected: How Smartphones and Social Keep Us Engaged," An IDC Research Report, sponsored by Facebook (2013).

7. Schumpter blog, "Slaves to the Smartphone," *The Economist* (March 10, 2012). http://www.economist.com/node/21549904.

8. L. Perlow, *Sleeping with the Smartphone: How to Break the 24/7 Habit and Change the Way You Work* (Boston: HBR Press, 2012).

9. L. Bock, "Google's Scientific Approach to Work-Life Balance (and Much More)," HBR Blog (March 27, 2014). http://blogs.hbr.org/2014/03/googles-scientific-approach-to-work-life-balance-and-much-more/.

10. N. Carr, *The Shallows: What the Internet Is Doing to Our Brains* (New York: WW Norton & Company, 2011).

11. D. Goleman, *Focus: The Hidden Driver of Excellence* (New York: Harper, 2013).

12. Q. R. Jett and J. M. George, "Work Interrupted: A Closer Look at the Role of Interruptions in Organizational Life," *Academy of Management Review* 28 (July 1, 2003): 494–507.

13. London Transport Cycling Safety Campaign, "Awareness Test," https://www.youtube.com/watch?v=Ahg6qcgoay4.

14. A. Mack and I. Rock, *Inattentional Blindness* (Cambridge, MA: MIT Press, 1998).

15. E. Ophir, C. Nass, and A. D. Wagner, "Cognitive Control in Media Multitaskers," *PNAS* vol. 106, no. 37 (September 2009): 15583–15587.

16. L. Bailyn, "Unlimited Vacation Time Is Better in Theory Than in Practice," *Quartz* (August 27, 2013). http://qz.com/118732/unlimited-vacation-time-is-better-in-theory-than-in-practice/.

17. M. Popova, "A Beautiful 1928 Letter to 16-Year-Old Jackson Pollock from His Dad," Brain Pickings. http://www.brainpickings.org/2012/02/02/jackson-pollock-father-letter/.

18. J. Tierney, "Do You Suffer from Decision Fatigue?" *The New York Times* (August 17, 2011). http://www.nytimes.com/2011/08/21/magazine/do-you-suffer-from-decision-fatigue.html.

19. T. M. S. Neal and E. M. Brank, "Could Mindfulness Improve Judicial Decision Making?" *Judicial Notebook* vol. 45, no. 3 (2014): 26.

20. R. F. Baumeister and J. Tierney, *Willpower: Rediscovering the Greatest Human Strength* (New York: Penguin, 2012).

21. M. Lewis, "Obama's Way," *Vanity Fair* (October 2012). http://www.vanityfair.com/politics/2012/10/michael-lewis-profile-barack-obama.

Chapter 11

1. Innosight Executive Briefing Winter 2012, "Creative Destruction Whips through Corporate America." http://www.innosight.com/innovation-resources/strategy-innovation/upload/creative-destruction-whips-through-corporate-america_final2012.pdf.

2. V. Govindarajan and C. Trimble, *Ten Rules for Strategic Innovators: From Idea to Execution* (Boston, MA: Harvard Business School Press, 2005).

3. J. L. Bower and C. M. Christensen, "Disruptive Technologies: Catching the Wave," *Harvard Business Review* (January–February 1995): 43–53.

4. W. Cockayne and S. P. MacGregor, *Innovation Metrics* (Chicago: PDMA Body of Knowledge, 2008).

5. A. Muller, L. Valikangas, and P. Merlyn, "Metrics for Innovation: Guidelines for Developing a Customized Suite of Innovation Metrics," *Strategy and Leadership* 33, no. 1 (2005): 37–45.

6. J. Vila and S. P. MacGregor, "Business Innovation: What It Brings, What It Takes," *IESE Alumni Magazine* (July–September 2007): 8–13.

7. L. Keeley, "Inspiring Innovation: Abandon the Crowd," *Harvard Business Review* 80, no. 8 (2002): 39–49.

8. G. A. Moore, *Dealing with Darwin: How Great Companies Innovate at Every Phase of Their Evolution* (New York: Portfolio Trade, 2008).

9. P. F. Drucker, "The Discipline of Innovation," *Harvard Business Review* 63, no. 3 (1985): 67–73.

10. M. Sawhney, R. C. Wolcott, and I. Arroniz, "The 12 Different Ways for Companies to Innovate," *MIT Sloan Management Review* 47 no. 3 (Spring 2006): 75–81.

11. G. Hamel, "The Why, What, and How of Management Innovation," *Harvard Business Review* 84, no. 6 (2006): 72–83.

12. J. McGregor, "GE: Reinventing Tech for the Emerging World," *Business Week* (April 16, 2008). http://www.businessweek.com/stories/2008-04-16/ge-reinventing-tech-for-the-emerging-world.

Chapter 12

1. Foundation Alicia workshops, http://www.alicia.cat/en/workshops/workshops.

2. B. Piqueras-Fiszman, J. Alcaide, E. Roura, and C. Spence, "Is It the Plate or Is It the Food? Assessing the Influence of the Color (Black or White) and Shape of the Plate on the Perception of the Food Placed on It," *Food Quality and Preference* vol. 24, no. 1 (April 2012): 205–208.

3. K. Van Ittersum and B. Wansink, "Plate Size and Color Suggestibility: The Delboeuf Illusion's Bias on Serving and Eating Behavior," *Journal of Consumer Research* vol. 39, no. 2 (August 2012): 215–228.

4. B. Wansink and K. Van Ittersum, "Portion Size Me: Plate-size Induced Consumption Norms and Win-Win Solutions for Reducing Food Intake and Waste," *Journal of Experimental Psychology: Applied* vol. 19, no. 4 (December 2013): 320–332.

5. M. McGannon and J. McGannon, *Fit for the Fast Track: The Survivor's Guide to Modern Business Life* (London: Pearson Education, 2001).

6. L. DiPietro, A. Gribok, M. S. Stevens, L. F. Hamm, and W. Rumpler, "Three 15-min Bouts of Moderate Postmeal Walking Significantly Improves 24-h Glycemic Control in Older People at Risk for Impaired Glucose Tolerance," *Diabetes Care* (June 11, 2013): 3262–3268.

7. M. Garaulet, P. Gómez-Abellán, J. J. Alburquerque-Béjar, Y-C Lee, J. M. Ordovás, and F. A. J. L. Scheer, "Timing of Food Intake Predicts Weight Loss Effectiveness," *International Journal of Obesity* 37 (April 2013): 604–611.

8. D. M. Arble, J. Bass, A. D. Laposky, M. H. Vitaterna, and F. W. Turek, "Circadian Timing of Food Intake Contributes to Weight Gain," *Obesity* (Silver Spring) 17, no. 11 (November 2009): 2100–2102.

9. William Robert Lunn, "Chocolate Milk as a Recovery Beverage Following Endurance Exercise: Impact on Human Skeletal Muscle Protein Kinetics, Intracellular Signaling Proteins, and Proteins of the Ubiquitin-Proteasome Pathway," *Doctoral Dissertations,* Paper AAI3420193 (2010).

10. J. Cloud, "The Myth About Exercise," *Time* (August 17, 2009). http://content.time.com/time/magazine/article/0,9171,1914974,00.html.

11. D. L. Katz and S. Meller, "Can We Say What Diet Is Best for Health?" *Annual Review of Public Health* vol. 35 (March 2014): 83–103.

12. M. Pollan, "Unhappy Meals," *The New York Times* (January 28, 2007). http://www.nytimes.com/2007/01/28/magazine/28nutritionism.t.html.

13. M. Pollan, *Food Rules: An Eater's Manual* (New York: Penguin, 2009).

14. J. C. Burani, J. Brand-Miller, and K. Foster-Powell, *The Glucose Revolution: The Authoritative Guide to the Glycemic Index* (Washington, DC: Marlowe & Company, 1999).

15. J. K. Kiecolt-Glaser, D. L. Habash, C. P. Fagundes, R. Andridge, J. Peng, W. B. Malarkey, and M. A. Belury, "Daily Stressors, Past Depression, and Metabolic Responses to High-Fat Meals: A Novel Path to Obesity," *Biological Psychiatry* (July 13, 2014). http://www.ncbi.nlm.nih.gov/pubmed/25034950 (e-pub ahead of print).

Chapter 13

1. "Obesity and Overweight, Fact Sheet No. 311," World Health Organization, updated August 2014. http://www.who.int/mediacentre/factsheets/fs311/en/.

2. J. Costa-Font, N. Mas, and P. Navarro, "Globesity: Is Globalization a Pathway to Obesity?" LSE Working Paper no. 31 (March 2013).

3. N. Teicholz, *The Big Fat Surprise: Why Butter, Meat and Cheese Belong in a Healthy Diet* (New York: Simon & Schuster, 2014).

4. D. Katz, "The Paleo Diet: Can We Really Eat Like Our Ancestors Did?" *Huffington Post* (July 6, 2011). http://www.huffingtonpost.com/david-katz-md/paleo-diet_b_889349.html.

5. "Global Food: Waste Not, Want Not," (London: Institution of Mechanical Engineers, January 2013).

6. J. Simpson, "We Ignore Expiry Dates, Say Supermarket Chiefs," *The Times* (May 24, 2014). http://www.thetimes.co.uk/tto/business/industries/retailing/article4099206.ece.

7. R. Sturm and R. An, "Obesity and Economic Environments," *CA: A Cancer Journal for Clinicians* vol. 64, no. 5 (September/October 2012): 337–350.

8. M. M. Mekonnen and A. Y. Hoekstra, "The Green, Blue and Grey Water Footprint of Farm Animals and Animal Products," UNESCO Institute for Water Education (December 2010). http://www.waterfootprint.org/Reports/Report-48-WaterFootprint-AnimalProducts-Vol1.pdf.

9. V. Mock, "Celebrity Chefs Tout Bug Cuisine," *The Wall Street Journal* (August 21, 2014). http://online.wsj.com/articles/celebrity-chefs-tout-bug-cuisine-1408674798.

10. M. Zaraska, "Lab-Grown Beef Taste Test: 'Almost' Like a Burger," *The Washington Post* (August 5, 2013). http://www.washingtonpost.com/national/health-science/lab-grown-beef-taste-test-almost-like-a-burger/2013/08/05/921a5996-fdf4-11e2-96a8-d3b921c0924a_story.html.

11. E. Anyangwe, "Nutrition: There's No Quick Fix for Hunger or Obesity," *The Guardian* (August 21, 2014). http://www.theguardian.com/global-development-professionals-network/2014/aug/21/mdgs-500-nutrition-gain.

Chapter 14

1. *Men's Health* (España), "Barack Obama: 9 lecciones del hombre más ocupado del mundo," (November 2008): 62–68.

2. R. Clayton, "How Regular Exercise Helps You Balance Work and Family," HBR Blog Network (January 3, 2014). http://blogs.hbr.org/2014/01/how-regular-exercise-helps-you-balance-work-and-family/.

3. J. Gallagher, "Six Seconds of Exercise 'Can Transform Health'," BBC News Health (July 26, 2014). http://www.bbc.com/news/health-28400968.

4. Catharine Paddock, "How to Get Fit with 3 Minutes of Exercise a Week: BBC Doc Tries HIT," http://www.medicalnewstoday.com/articles/242498.php.

5. K. A. Ericsson, R. T. Krampe, and C. Tesch-Romer, "The Role of Deliberate Practice in the Acquisition of Expert Performance," *Psychological Review* vol. 100, no. 3 (1993): 363–406.

6. M. Gladwell, *Outliers: The Story of Success* (New York: Back Bay Books, 2011).

7. J. Jerome, *The Sweet Spot in Time: The Search for Athletic Perfection* (Halcottsville, NY: Breakaway Books, 1999).

8. S. P. MacGregor, "Reinventing the Wheel: Pushing the Limits in High Performance Bike Design," Core77, 2006. http://www.core77.com/reactor/01.06_reinventing.asp.

9. S. Kotler, *The Rise of Superman: Decoding the Science of Ultimate Human Performance* (Seattle: New Harvest, 2014).

10. T. Kelley and D. Kelley, *Creative Confidence: Unleashing the Creative Potential Within Us All* (New York: Crown Business, 2013).

Chapter 15

1. L. Capron and W. Mitchell, *Build, Borrow, or Buy: Solving the Growth Dilemma* (Boston: HBR Press, 2012).

2. G. M. Allan and B. Arroll, "Prevention and Treatment of the Common Cold: Making Sense of the Evidence," *CMAJ* (January 27, 2014). http://www.cmaj.ca/content/early/2014/01/27/cmaj.121442.extract.

Chapter 16

1. A. Maslow, *Toward a Psychology of Being*, 3rd ed. (New Jersey: Wiley, 1999).

Index